LORENZO DE' MEDICI: SELECTED WRITINGS

PUBLICATIONS OF THE FOUNDATION FOR ITALIAN STUDIES
UNIVERSITY COLLEGE, DUBLIN

General Editor: John C. Barnes

Dante Comparisons: Comparative Studies of Dante and: Montale, Foscolo, Tasso, Chaucer, Petrarch, Propertius and Catullus, ed. E. Haywood and B. Jones

Dante Readings, ed. E. Haywood

Dante Soundings: Eight Literary and Historical Essays, ed. D. Nolan

J. Petrie, *Petrarch: The Augustan Poets, the Italian Tradition and the "Canzoniere"*

T. O'Neill, *Of Virgin Muses and of Love: A Study of Foscolo's "Dei Sepolcri"*

Italian Storytellers: Essays on Italian Narrative Literature, ed. E. Haywood and C. Ó Cuilleanáin

BELFIELD ITALIAN LIBRARY

Luigi Pirandello, *Il berretto a sonagli*, ed. J. C. Barnes

Lorenzo de' Medici

SELECTED WRITINGS

Edited

with an English verse translation of the
Rappresentazione di San Giovanni e Paolo

by

CORINNA SALVADORI

[handwritten dedication:]
Per il carissimo ed
ammiratissimo studioso
Cecil Clough con
tanta stima

Corinna Salvadori

BELFIELD ITALIAN LIBRARY

1992

Printed and bound by Billing and Sons Ltd, Worcester, England

Research for this book was partially financed by grants from the Arts and
    Social Sciences Benefactions Fund of Trinity College, Dublin.
Publication of this book was assisted by a grant from the Trinity College
    Dublin Association and Trust.

BELFIELD ITALIAN LIBRARY

Published by
The Foundation for Italian Studies
Department of Italian
University College
Dublin 4
Ireland

ISBN 1 870089 72 3 hard covers
ISBN 1 870089 71 5 paperback

Detail of Pediment and Entablature on the Entrance Front of the
Medici Villa at Poggio a Caiano
Courtesy Maria Salvadori (Ottica Spizzone, Florence) and Brendan
Dempsey (Photographic Centre, Trinity College, Dublin)

In memoriam mariti carissimi atque amantissimi

PREFACE

The purpose of this selection of poetry and prose by Lorenzo de' Medici is to represent the great variety of his literary output and to do justice to his high achievement. While the book is intended primarily for students of Italian literature, it should serve as a good anthology for anyone interested in the writings of one of the most important figures of the Renaissance. The selection includes Lorenzo's play, which is the best *sacra rappresentazione* of the Quattrocento; it is here translated into English octaves, and should prove useful to those interested in the development of drama. Faithfulness to the original has been the guiding principle for the translation. The extensive Notes and the Vocabulary are designed to help those whose familiarity with Italian is limited, although some knowledge of Dante, Petrarch and the broad outlines of Italian literature will help the reader to draw maximum benefit from these aids. The Introduction deals first, in a general way, with the corpus of Lorenzo's literary work and with problems of text and dating; it then analyses the selected writings in greater detail, in the hope of making as accessible and enjoyable as possible a type of writing that many students profess to find frightening—poetry.

All translations are by the editor, unless otherwise stated. Quotations from the Bible are from the Douay version, a translation from the Latin Vulgate, which Lorenzo would have used. All references to Petrarch are to the *Canzoniere*.

When works listed as Suggested Ancillary Reading are cited elsewhere in the book, abbreviated forms of reference are used.

Only the prose texts and the *Rappresentazione* are burdened with superscript numerals referring the reader to the Notes. The latter, however, also contain observations on every sonnet here presented and on virtually every octave of the poems in *ottava rima*. In the case of other kinds of poem a dagger (†) is used to indicate the presence of a pertinent observation in the Notes.

I am grateful to the various copyright-holders for their unanimous and gracious permission to reprint their editions of Lorenzo's texts. The provenance of each text in the present volume is stated at the beginning of the relevant section of the Notes.

The help of two scholars underlies the very existence of this book. One is Mario Martelli, the foremost authority on Lorenzo as a writer; his *Studi laurenziani* (1965) gave confidence to my youthful enthusiasm for Lorenzo, and his writings have informed and guided me on a most happy route. The other is Barbara Reynolds, from whom I have learnt much, not least how to write octaves; I acknowledge her help with gratitude, as she prevented the "folle volo" (the translation of Lorenzo's play) from ending in disaster.

It is with pleasure that I record my gratitude to John Barnes for accepting this volume into the Belfield Italian Library, for the professional rigour of his editing, for his aid with the translation of the play, and for the amiability with which all this was done. I wish to express formally my indebtedness to Barbara Wright for two decades of committed assistance to small departments and to their overworked heads. Moreover, this work would never have been completed without the help, always generously given, of the Italian Department's other *tre ruote del carro*, and of Shirley Caracciolo: all four relieved me of many a burden. I gratefully acknowledge also the help of Edward McParland, which included selecting and preparing the illustrations; of Christine Meek for her contribution to the section on Lorenzo as a political figure; of Cormac Ó Cuilleanáin for the final felicitous touches to the English octaves; and of colleagues and friends (these generally being synonymous) who assisted with the translation of the play or provided information on matters ranging from roses *not* by Ausonius to the fumaroles of Volterra. I extend my thanks also to Fiona O'Connor, who scrutinized the draft as a potential user; it was an enjoyable shared experience. What errors remain are strictly mine. Lidia and Eric Lonergan helped in unexpected ways and rightly pushed me into the turbulent currents of word-processing; Michael Doherty saved me from drowning, while Brian Morrissey also helped with the preparation of computer files. Gianna and Gianni Giannangeli gave me a home in Florence, very close to Lorenzo's own, and the help given by Mother Bernard Sheehan, IBVM was different but equally vital.

CONTENTS

INTRODUCTION

Quant' è bella giovinezza
che si fugge tuttavia:
chi vuol esser lieto, sia,
di doman non c'è certezza.

With these lines Lorenzo the Magnificent (1449–92) has been introduced as a poet to generations of Italian schoolchildren. They
constitute the refrain of the "Canzona di Bacco", a poem that is
offered in all anthologies, out of the context of the whole corpus of
Lorenzo's poetry, as the hedonistic *carpe diem* of an Epicurean
dabbler in verse. Some editors have gone so far as to present the
author as a scheming tyrant who indulged the populace in merrymaking so that their eyes would be deflected from his tyranny. Mis-
conceptions die hard, and Lorenzo's reputation has been much dis-
figured by successive strata of prejudice, good and bad, that modern
scholarship has been at pains to dissolve. Documentary evidence,
rigorously examined, has been the basis of Laurentian scholarship
in the last four decades, and has led to a reassessment of the *persona*
styled Lorenzo and described over some four centuries with rather
more conjecture than verifiable proof. This has perforce entailed a
close look at Lorenzo's creative writing, and what has emerged is
a realization that it was not a marginal part of this versatile man's
multifarious activity. The most revolutionary statement, inspired
not by zeal but by veracity, comes from Mario Martelli, the critic to
whom readers of Lorenzo are most indebted: "È convinzione
tradizionale che Lorenzo sia stato un uomo politico, il quale, a
tempo perso, si dilettò di poesia; [...] Lorenzo sarà, a nostro avviso
piuttosto da ritenere un poeta, che dalla poesia si allontanò talvolta
e contraggenio, perché chiamato, di quando in quando, da piú
pressanti necessità."[1] A guiding consideration when dismantling
the politician dabbling in poetry and erecting the poet dabbling in

politics is not so much his substantial productivity—some half-dozen *poemetti*, more than two hundred assorted short poems, a religio-philosophical work in *terza rima*, a verse play, two stories and a prose commentary—set against the brevity and intensity of his life, as his attitude towards this work, little of which he would have considered definitive at the time of his death. It was work in progress subject to revision and rewriting, needing "but world enough, and time".

In order to be better equipped for our reading of some of this literary work, we should cast a glance, albeit generic and therefore distorted, at some of Lorenzo's other activity and at the *ambiente mediceo*.

The designation *il Magnifico* did not denote noble lineage, but was accorded as a title of respect to anyone with political prominence. The fact that it has defined Lorenzo for half a millennium is indicative of the aura of magnificence that has invested his memory because of what was perceived as his achievement. (A similar case is that of Dante's *Commedia*, by many, but not by Dante, styled *Divina*.) He was the leading and most important citizen of Florence for two decades, from the death in 1469 of his father Piero, son of the great Cosimo (1389–1464), to his own premature death in 1492. Nonetheless the *palazzo* in Via Larga, despite the distinction in matters public or intellectual of those received there, and despite the quality and quantity of the works of art there displayed, was the city dwelling of a wealthy man, certainly not a court. Lorenzo prided himself on being a private citizen; he did not hold a regular office in government and his influence was mainly indirect. In internal politics he was in much less firm control than was maintained by outsiders at the time or by nineteenth-century tradition. In a sense he, like his father and grandfather, was at the centre of an oligarchic group, trying to balance competing interests and also to devise institutions (notably the Council of Seventy set up in 1480) that would ensure they could get their measures through.[2] Internally, his policy was not really different in direction from that of his immediate predecessors, though he carried developments further. It must be borne in mind that Florence was a republic, though when three generations of the one family had a strong hold on civic affairs one justifiably questions how much the republican principles valued by the Florentines were being protected. According to J. R. Hale, the Florentines accepted "that Cosimo manipulated the constitution [and] was a 'father' in the Mafia sense long before he was posthumously voted the 'Father of the *Patria*' in 1464 [...]. It was done decorously."[3]

Less decorous was Lorenzo's involvement, in 1472, in the incident at Volterra. What had started as a dispute over the control of alum evolved into one about power, and the city was sacked by the soldiers of the renowned *condottiere* Federico da Montefeltro—a glaringly infamous exploit in the career of this otherwise praiseworthy man.[4] It was then felt that Lorenzo had put personal interest before that of Florence, though historians are more likely to argue that "Florentine industry as a whole benefited from the war, and [it is] impossible to suggest that only the private interests of the Medici had been served."[5] Nonetheless, it was quite a serious mistake that can be excused only in part by his youth. His intervention in Romagna, which was papal territory, caused festering discontent to ooze and left a scar on Lorenzo that was not metaphorical. It sparked off the Pazzi conspiracy, an assassination attempt in 1478, in which he was wounded; a priest's lack of experience in the use of a dagger saved his life but he lost his beloved, handsome, younger brother, Giuliano, and he came too near to death himself not to be deeply changed by the experience. This helps us to understand if not to condone the cruelty of the revenge. The Pazzi conspiracy was not a parochial affair: Florence and the Medici were inextricably linked with the fortunes of the major states in the peninsula. Behind the Pazzi were the King of Naples, Pope Sixtus IV and the Duke of Urbino; not surprisingly, war followed. That relative peace was achieved in 1480 was in great part due to Lorenzo's diplomatic skill, and to his bold step in going to Naples at some personal risk to negotiate it. Florence enjoyed some prosperity in the last decade of Lorenzo's leadership, but political crises involving other states with possible repercussions for Florence followed in regular succession. His remaining years were thus filled with diplomatic activity seen by later generations as a major factor in the maintenance of a balance of power in the peninsula. Scholars have found merit in Filippo de' Nerli's figurative comment that Lorenzo was "l'ago della bilancia intra ' principi", but this must not entirely hide the fact that even then Lorenzo, just like anyone else, was prepared to risk disturbing the peace for minor territorial gains.[6] The precarious peace was to be definitively shattered not by the enemy within but by France, the former ally turned invader. Lorenzo was certainly more aware than other contemporary politicians that France posed a real threat, and the invasion in 1494, two years after his death, proved him right: it was to be the beginning of the Italian wars.

Less successful was Lorenzo the financier. The source of Medici wealth was primarily banking, but Lorenzo was as desultory a banker as he was a committed diplomat. Financial activity, in his view, had a primary political purpose: it bought allies. Historians still stand by Machiavelli's view that Lorenzo was "quanto alla mercanzia infelicissimo" and that this was mainly due to "il disordine de' suoi ministri" (*Istorie fiorentine*, VIII. 36). His administrators were ill-chosen, some incompetent, some dishonest.[7]

Lorenzo's prominence in Florence coincided with a period of renewed cultural splendour in that gifted city. Lorenzo commissioned much less, however, than his grandfather had; his patronage consisted more of ensuring that talent was recognized and that artists were given work by other business and banking members of the community. He had less money than Cosimo or Piero, but he was a keener collector of cameos, small works of art and valuable antiques, as is clear from the inventory of Medici property after their expulsion in 1494.[8] Lorenzo also spent money on precious manuscripts. There was a dearth of Greek ones in Cosimo's acclaimed collection, and agents were sent eastwards to rectify this; some eighty codices not previously known in western Europe were acquired.[9] He recognized the importance of printing, though early efforts in that sphere produced books quite inferior, aesthetically, to the splendid illuminated manuscripts that featured in the Medici collection. It was not he but his cousin, also named Lorenzo, who commissioned Botticelli's *Primavera* and *The Birth of Venus*. Other artists active in Florence at the time were Filippino Lippi, Verrocchio (under whom Leonardo trained until he left for Milan in 1482–83) and Ghirlandaio (with whom Michelangelo was serving his apprenticeship).

Rather more attention needs be paid, in the context of Lorenzo the writer, to the intellectuals in his inner circle. One was the humanist who held the chair of rhetoric and poetry in the Florentine *studio*, Cristoforo Landino (1424–98). His most famous work is the *Disputationes camaldulenses* (1474), which records imaginary debates between Lorenzo and Alberti on the active and contemplative lives, and between Alberti and Ficino on the supreme good. Famous also is his commentary on Dante's *Commedia* (1481); it was written at the instigation of Lorenzo, whose wish it was that it be in the vernacular rather than Latin. Lorenzo's vigorous defence of the *volgare* in the introduction to his *Comento* sprang from a deep-rooted belief in the power and range of his native tongue, which Dante, Petrarch and Boccaccio had ennobled by their writings—though a case needed to be made for it in the strongly humanist climate of the Quattrocento with its reverence for Latin. The two poets most closely associated with Lorenzo, Luigi Pulci (1432–84) and Angelo Poliziano (1454–94), filled the ambiguous position of friends and dependents. The former is famed for his largely humorous and somewhat bizarre chivalric poem *Morgante* (1478, 1483), and he was undoubtedly influential in the poetic apprenticeship of the young Lorenzo, as is reflected in the latter's jocular poetry. Poliziano, author of the exquisite *Stanze per la giostra del Magnifico Giuliano*, unfinished because of Giuliano's assassination in 1478, came onto the scene later, as secretary to Lorenzo in 1473, and in 1475 he was appointed tutor to Lorenzo's children. He became an erudite philologist, the greatest textual scholar of his age, and Lorenzo gave him the chair of Greek and Latin eloquence in the Florentine *studio*. That Lorenzo and Poliziano worked closely together is reflected in similarities of expression and theme to be found in their poetry. After 1474 Pulci, the deliberately non-intellectual writer of humorous verse, fitted ill in the *brigata medicea* and Poliziano took over as its leading poet.[10]

Marsilio Ficino (1433–99) was probably responsible for the ousting of Pulci. The most influential of the intellectuals who surrounded Lorenzo,[11] he had been employed by Cosimo to prepare a translation of Plato's dialogues into Latin. Very few of the Greek philosopher's works were known in the Middle Ages, though indirect knowledge of his ideas had come through such writers as Cicero, St Augustine and Boethius. Greek manuscripts of his works had come into Italy early in the Quattrocento, and Ficino's translation of all Plato's writings was the standard source of Platonism for several centuries. The gathering in Plato's *Symposium* was imitated by a group of intellectuals who came together in the Medici villa at Careggi; the meetings began in the 1460s and came to constitute an informal academy, more properly a circle of friends, patronized by Lorenzo and styled neo-Platonist. Ficino was the leading spirit in this gifted group. After completing his translation of Plato he translated another philosopher who for centuries had been known only indirectly: Plotinus, the chief exponent of Alexandrian neo-Platonism, which had flourished in the third century AD. By 1474 a marked change had occurred in Ficino's philosophical evolution, following a very severe illness and his entry into holy orders: he moved from an essentially pagan-based philosophy to a Christian one. Within some two years Ficino's ascendancy became dominant. His own philosophical writings, an attempt to synthesise Platonism and Christianity, were mainly concerned with two fundamental concepts: the hierarchy of being from the inanimate through the vegetative, the sensual and the rational to the angelic and the divine; and the immortality of the soul, its pre-existence and its independence of the body. He advocated contemplation as a process through which, with will and reason, man can free himself from matter and find God. His writings on the topic loosely termed "Platonic love" (because it took as its starting-point Plato's dictum that Love is Desire aroused by Beauty) became essential for an understanding of the imagery used in literature and painting in subsequent centuries. The influence of neo-Platonism on Lorenzo must not be underestimated; after 1473 he so espoused its creed that one critic writes of it becoming a "religione di stato" flourishing on soil well prepared by his father and grandfather.[12] Nonetheless, there was a change in the last two years of Lorenzo's life as the poetic Plato began to yield to Aristotle, whose works Poliziano started to teach in the academic year 1490–91.[13]

Mention should also be made of Lorenzo's patronage of the brilliant Giovanni Pico della Mirandola (1463–94), whose exceptional talent he quickly recognized, and whom he defended against ecclesiastical authority and political expediency. Pico was a polyglot who included Arabic, Hebrew and Chaldean among his languages and was famed for his prodigious memory; his spectacular eclecticism went beyond Plato and Christianity and, armed with the belief that all philosophies contain some truth, he attempted to draw together Averroes and Arabic thought, Jewish Cabbalism and Hermeticism, while showing Christianity to be a point of convergence. Thirteen of his nine hundred *Conclusiones* fell foul of the authorities, and his answer to accusations of possible heresy was an *Apologia*, dedicated to Lorenzo, which obliged Pico to take refuge in France to avoid arrest in Rome. The French monarch, wary of trouble with the Pope, imprisoned Pico, but Lorenzo's diplomatic efforts led to his release and to his finding a haven in Florence. His *Oration on the Dignity of Man* differed from other neo-Platonist writing in that it placed man outside the hierarchy of being and saw him as an entity with infinite potential for spiritual development.

Lorenzo's relationship with Savonarola (1452–98), the Ferrarese Dominican who first preached in Florence during 1482–85 and was invited by Lorenzo to return there in 1490, was very different from the one of antagonism turning to enmity that tradition has perpetuated. The friar did not enjoy immediate popular appeal in Florence: at first he was not liked and his sermons were badly attended. That he remained in the city at all, and that he rose in position to become prior of S. Marco, which was subject to Medici patronage, must have been due to Lorenzo's support. The influence of this fearless, emotional zealot is reflected in the final phase of Lorenzo's philosophical thinking—which sheds some of its neo-Platonist aspects—and of his poetry, as the classical substratum gives way to a Scriptural one. Savonarola shifted from Medici preacher to Medici accuser with the death of Lorenzo, and his ultimate fate—he was hanged and burned—was harsher than that of the man he may have brought nearer to God.[14]

The rhetorical devices used by Lorenzo in his poetry—his favouring of repetition and the phonic effects he achieves—show some of the characteristics of musical composition. Orvieto puts it pithily: "La musica costituiva un presupposto integrante la poesia."[15] It comes as no surprise to discover that Lorenzo was an accomplished musician, taught by Antonio Squarcialupi (1416–80), the cathedral organist, and the two worked together in setting various items to music. Lorenzo liked to hear his own verse sung to the accompaniment of the viol. It was he who on Squarcialupi's death enticed to Florence one of the greatest musicians of the time, some of whose works are extant: Heinrich Isaac (*c.* 1450–1517), known as Arrigo Tedesco though he was probably Flemish. He taught Lorenzo's sons and composed music for some of his poems as well as for his play. Music was very much part of Florentine public life, as was spectacle, and in his later years Lorenzo's sponsorship of tournaments and public festivities became a show of magnificence with the employment of distinguished artists to decorate what were perforce ephemera. A crux for some is his motivation: why did he do it? Was it to divert the Florentines' attention from the less palatable reality of Medici domination? Or, less deviously, was it to satisfy an interest that was part of his personality?

If Lorenzo was regarded as a connoisseur in matters pertaining to the visual arts, he was also something of a practitioner, having apparently even submitted a design for the façade of the *duomo*. A felicitious commission he awarded was to Giuliano da Sangallo for the remodelling of the villa Ambra on his estate at Poggio a Caiano, a village mid-way between Florence and Pistoia. That Lorenzo worked closely with the architect is certain, indeed it seems that the design for the villa was Lorenzo's own.[16] He spared no effort in the creation of what was to become his favourite country residence, and, although the countryside has changed beyond recognition, the fine villa, which incorporated several features of the architecture of antiquity, is extant and open to the public. The visitor attuned to Lorenzo will immediately spot that the gardens are planted extensively with laurel trees, the shrub to which the poet owes his name, as he tells us in *Stanze*, I. 6. The villa was created as a functional environment, and descriptions of life there indicate both princely magnificence and a sharp sense of husbandry.[17] The fields were extensively cultivated and fertile; water was brought by an aqueduct from the neighbouring mountains; there were three crops of hay each year and good manuring to avoid soil exhaustion. The estate was renowned for its cheese and also for the silk from its mulberry trees. Quails and other birds were so abundant that fowling could be enjoyed without difficulty, and the woods had pheasants and peacocks.[18] Lorenzo loved country life and saw his sojourns on his various estates in the Tuscan countryside as revitalizing retreats from an ever-stressful city life; he said so too often for us not to believe him. He took an active interest in his farms and in the welfare of those he employed, but he also enjoyed the sporting side of country life—fishing and hunting.

There is consensus that Lorenzo was a committed family man, devoted to his children, whose interests he protected relentlessly. He was determined that the cleverest of them, Giovanni, should become a cardinal, and he died in the happy knowledge that this ambition was fulfilled: the sixteen-year-old youth was formally proclaimed a cardinal in March 1492, two years after the promise had been extracted from Innocent VIII and some three weeks before Lorenzo's death. (The father's letter to the son at Rome, one of his last, ends our selection of his writings.) Not only did Giovanni subsequently become pope, as Leo X, but his cousin Giulio, natural son of Giuliano who had been accepted into the family on his father's assassination, was also to achieve the papal throne as Clement VII. Such exaltation may have been even beyond Lorenzo's dreams.

An easily forgotten feature of Lorenzo's daily life is that it was lived in severe pain from gout and arthritis; these plagued him continually and led to an early death. There was no inner tranquillity to counterbalance the physical suffering. The Pazzi conspiracy was followed by two further assassination attempts in 1481, and there were to be others. Personal losses caused him much grief; within weeks in 1488 he lost his twelve-year-old daughter Luisa and his wife Clarice. Historians have, at best, been indifferent to the latter, but we have no evidence of any unhappiness in Lorenzo's marriage to this young woman originally chosen for him as much for political reasons as for ones of good health (the gouty Medici needed an infusion of new blood). When she died he wrote Pope Innocent VIII a letter the sincerity of which we have no reason to doubt; it reveals how troubled he perceived his life as being:

Ma la morte della Clarice, mia carissima e dolcissima consorte, nuovamente successa me è stata ed è di tanto danno, pregiudicio e dolore per infinite cagioni, che ha vinto la mia pazienza ed obdurazione nelli affanni e persecuzioni della fortuna, la quale non pensavo che mi potessi portare cosa che mi facesse molto risentire. E questo, per essere privato di tanto dolce consuetudine e compagnia, certamente ha passati i termini e mi ha fatto e fa risentire tanto cordialmente che non truovo luogo. Pure come

non resto pregare nostro Signor Dio che mi dia pace, cosí ho ferma
speranza nella sua bontà infinita che porrà fine al dolore e non
manco a tante spesse visitazioni quali in simili amarezze me ha
fatte da qualche tempo in qua.[19]

For some time after her death he was incapable of working.

Lucrezia Donati and Simonetta Cattaneo, who are associated
with his love poetry, were no more fictional than Beatrice or Laura,
but equally the love they inspired was imaginatively fertile in as
much as it was physically unreal.

The most obvious and incontrovertible fact about Lorenzo's literary
output is that it is remarkably diverse. Were one to take its two
extremes, the bawdiest *canzoni a ballo* and the spiritual *De summo
bono*, one could aptly define it with Machiavelli's famous statement
about Lorenzo the man—that he was "due persone diverse, quasi
con impossibile congiunzione congiunte" (*Istorie fiorentine*, VIII. 36).
But what fits Lorenzo more aptly is a description that the Florentine
Secretary gives of himself and of Francesco Vettori as they appear
from their correspondence: "uomini gravi, tutti volti a cose grandi", with thoughts only of "honestà et grandezza", while over the
page they appear "leggieri, incostanti, lascivi, volti a cose vane".
This is not to be condemned, adds Machiavelli, but rather it is
praiseworthy, "perché noi imitiamo la natura che è varia".[20] Nature
is varied, be it human nature or the physical world we inhabit.
Lorenzo could render the latter with the keen eye of the observer,
and he has been justly hailed as a writer of "outdoor poetry" rather
than of pastoral;[21] equally he could express the contradictory quality of human nature, with its buoyancy and dejection, its longing
and rejecting in that Ficinian duality of body and soul, and in the
poignant awareness that our only certainty in life is death. Traditionally, literary histories accord pride of place to Poliziano in
discussions of Quattrocento lyric poetry, and this is justified on
grounds of consistent perfection; but while one admires the rarified
Poliziano with awe, one loves the inconsistent Lorenzo.

For a long time Lorenzo suffered a fate analogous to that of
another first-class poet, Michelangelo, and for much the same
reason. The two writers were classified respectively as politician
and artist, with the result that their poetry was marginalized, and

what attention was paid to it was focussed on what it could reveal of the author's "proper" activity. Approached with inflexible expectations, both poets were found disappointing. What Lorenzo said on power was that he wanted none of it (but was that true?); and because Michelangelo did not leave a *Pietà* in verse his poetry was found wanting. There have been more enlightened voices crying in the wilderness, but with much the same unsatisfactory results, and the net outcome has been a lack of accurate critical editions until recently, making critical analysis and assessment exceptionally difficult. Laurentian scholars have a particularly difficult task because of the large quantity of work that Lorenzo left in disarray and still under revision; furthermore, some of his works exist in several versions, and it can be well-nigh impossible to establish a chronological progression for the variants. The publication landmarks are few and easily listed: *Canzoniere* (styled *Poesie volgari*) and *Comento* in Venice in 1554 in what can properly be described as an *editio princeps*; *Rime sacre* in Florence in 1680; a much fuller selection entitled *Poesie*, in Bergamo in 1763; while a different selection appeared in Liverpool in 1795 edited by an enthusiastic and enlightened Englishman, William Roscoe.[22] The first complete collection of Lorenzo's work, promoted by Grand Duke Leopold II and edited by him and the Crusca academicians,[23] appeared in Florence in 1825 (Molini, four volumes). It was superseded by the complete *Opere* edited by A. Simioni (Bari, Laterza, two volumes, first edition 1913–14, second edition 1939), who did some pioneering work on manuscripts and incunabula but himself acknowledged the limitations of his edition. Simioni's text has constituted the basis of almost all subsequent editions, though since 1955 these have also taken account of the revisions made by Bigi.[24] Textual history was made in 1966 by the appearance of Mario Martelli's critical edition of the *Simposio*, and although no more critical editions followed for twenty years a busy *officina laurenziana* has issued several since the mid-1980s. A changing text means a changing base-line, a matter of no small concern for someone such as the present editor; critical editions of the *Canzoniere* and *Comento* appeared when the present edition was virtually completed—their author having been dead for a mere five hundred years!

Textual work has led to changes in titles that have been found to lack authorial sanction. Readers consulting critical works will avoid confusion if they bear in mind that the former *I beoni* is retitled *Simposio*, the *Altercazione* is now *De summo bono*, *La caccia col falcone* is *Uccellagione di starne*, the *Selve* are *Stanze*, and the *Rime* have become the *Canzoniere*, though this includes not only the former *Rime* but also the sonnets of the *Comento* and three other poems differently classified until 1991. The critical edition of *Ambra* gives it the accompanying title of *Descriptio hiemis* because it is not clear that the *poemetto* had a definite title; Lorenzo may have intended returning to it to make it part of a greater whole. It has emerged that two *poemetti* generally attributed to Lorenzo—*Nencia* and *Uccellagione di starne*—may not actually be his (and that the former may not even be a cohesive poem). This will convey some idea of the difficulties with which work on Lorenzo's texts is fraught. If the reader is surprised that the two works in question appear in the present selection, it may be answered that they are too fine not to be enjoyed and that while there is no evidence either for or against Lorenzo as author, tradition has merit until proof do us part. The appendix to *Nencia* will indicate just how much scholars are still in a labyrinth, with no Ariadne offering a thread.

Progress on the textual front is leading to progress in the equally labyrinthine task of establishing dates. Emilio Bigi undertook pioneering work involving the elimination of what was found to be creative guesswork so that evidence could emerge at least tentatively;[25] and subsequent scholars, for all their querying a number of his conclusions, are greatly indebted to him. It is safest to remain generic in matters of dating as there is little that we can date with absolute certainty apart from Lorenzo's play, which we know was performed in February 1491. Two important documents in this area are the *Raccolta aragonese* and Poliziano's *Nutricia*. The first is an anthology of poems in the Tuscan *volgare*, mainly by the *stilnovisti*, but including some of Lorenzo's own. It is prefaced by a letter in the name of Lorenzo but probably written by Poliziano, which contains a eulogy of the Tuscan *volgare*. All of this was sent in 1477 to the younger son of the king of Naples. *Nutricia*, written in 1486, are Latin verses in which Poliziano celebrates the magnificent history of poetry through the ages, finally mentioning works by Lorenzo. What does seem clear is that Lorenzo began writing seriously at a very early age. *Corinto* belongs to 1464–65, though the final section was added after 1486; the *Simposio* was begun between August 1466 and August 1467, though it is likely that Lorenzo had no definite plan for it and that he modified it in or after 1486 in a manner that changed its nature; 1469 seems to be a reasonable supposition as the date of the story "Ginevra". Some form of *Nencia* was in circulation by 1470, and 1473–76 is the likely period for the *Uccellagione*. We know that in September 1473 Ficino was speaking with enthusiasm of *De summo bono*, but this poem was much expanded and a whole new central part was written in 1486. Lorenzo had written some seventy poems when, around 1474–75, "il Magnifico dovette raccogliere i fogli sparsi contenenti gli autografi dei suoi componimenti, ordinarli secondo un preciso disegno [...] e consegnarli nelle mani dei suoi segretari, affinché li trascrivessero in un 'libro'; ed è probabilmente in questa fase del lavoro di ricopiatura che si depositarono [...] alcuni errori, già presenti dunque *ab origine* nel testo."[26] (From this it will also be clear how certain textual problems arose.) This was the first assembling of a *Canzoniere,* and the poet may have begun writing prose commentaries to some sonnets in 1480. In 1487 and probably also in 1490, he was still working on the two collections of poems, the *Canzoniere* and the *Comento,* giving some organic shape to both of them. There is nothing to indicate that he considered he had finished at the time of his death.

Lorenzo's output diminished in the couple of years that followed the death of his father Piero and the ensuing acceptance of a public role by the twenty-year-old poet. For some six years he wrote only occasional love poems together with accompanying commentary, and perhaps a few *canti carnascialeschi,* but he re-emerged with *Apollo e Pan* possibly in 1474, if Martelli is right, though Orvieto would date it earlier.[27] The effect of the Pazzi conspiracy of 1478 was much more devastating, and was to prove a rite of passage whereby the capable versifier became a great poet. Lorenzo's finest work, whether new or the metamorphosis of what he had conceived and written previously, was born of an awareness of his political and public activity in the context of life's fragility and transience and his experience of much physical illness. Sadness, in varying degrees, is paradoxically the life-force of his great work.

The poems added to the *Comento* after 1486 have very strong thematic links with the *Stanze.* This fact, as well as other cogent arguments based on an examination of the manuscripts, leads the editor of the *Stanze* to conclude that they were written at the same time as the *Comento* and that, contrary to Martelli's conclusions but supporting Bigi's, there was no early version of them.[28] She locates them entirely in the period 1486–92. The date of *Ambra* is difficult to ascertain; it may fall anywhere between 1474 (the date now established for the purchase of Poggio a Caiano) and 1485. Not enough work has so far been done in the fairly confused area of Lorenzo's *canzoni a ballo* and *canti carnascialeschi*, but Martelli has dated some with certainty to the carnival of 1489 and two more to February 1490.[29] He also reads "Giacoppo" as a political rather than as a love story, thereby uncovering clues that suggest 1488 as the date of its composition.[30] It is virtually impossible to date Lorenzo's *capitoli religiosi*, but the *laude* seem to have been written in the years 1489–92, "Ben arà duro cuore" perhaps being one of the last of them.

In the matter of dating, then, we are on a roundabout, and the exits still cause debate; one can but hope that the signposts to some of them will not be changed. What cannot be stressed enough is that we are dealing with a writer whose work reflects two types of change. Lorenzo, no literary dilettante, subjected his work to revision to meet the demands of his sophisticated stylistic self-consciousness, and returned to it in no systematic manner, but with rigorous professionalism, aiming at some final version that in several cases we have not been privileged to receive. But change was not simply stylistic; the work also absorbed the intellectual development of the man and reflected spiritual and psychological change. Orvieto expresses this succinctly, taking his cue from the *Comento* and moving outwards to embrace Lorenzo's entire output:

> Niente può costituirsi come definitivo: ogni nuova acquisizione tecnica o filosofica, ogni minima mutazione etico-spirituale, ogni progresso culturale si riversa inesorabilmente nell'opera di Lorenzo, determinando nel contempo la perenne mobilità di quanto già composto. Tanto che ogni sua opera o ogni mutazione d'una sua opera funziona in questo senso da vero e proprio sismografo registrante ogni scossa letteraria e filosofica non solo dell'uomo Lorenzo, ma ancor piú dell'ambiente circostante.[31]

Before we proceed to a detailed presentation of the works in this selection, brief mention needs be made of those excluded, so that the reader is helped to form an idea of the entire range of Lorenzo's rich literary activity.

The *Simposio* is an unfinished poem in *terza rima*, the metre being one of its several Dantesque features; it comprises seven *capitoli* of some 120 lines each, and an interrupted eighth one of 57. Niccolò Valori, in his life of Lorenzo written in 1494, relates that the young poet improvised this humorous satire when he met a group of revellers;[32] but while it started out as "una rassegna di beoni" it was to become "un poemetto di grande impegno [...], che sotto le vesti di un'opera comica cela un fondo di serietà, a volte di tragicità estrema".[33]

De summo bono is also in *terza rima*, divided into six *capitoli* of some 150 lines each, except that the last has 208. The first *capitolo* follows the pattern of the genre of the altercation (hence the former title) between a countryman, Alfeo, and a city-dweller, Lorenzo, who thinks that by escaping from the ambition, envy and other vices of city life he will find peace in the idyllic countryside; the realistic Alfeo dispels the illusion rather quickly. There is a major change after this initial *capitolo* as Ficino arrives and the work becomes thoroughly imbued with his religious philosophy, as expounded in his *De felicitate*. Lorenzo asks to be shown "il ver cammino,/e se le nostre vite han vero buono" (II. 59–60), nor is this the only Dantesque parallel. Ficino argues that Fortune's gifts are "apparenti ben" (II. 157), as are also man's physical attributes. Value attaches to the virtues acquired by the rational soul, and true happiness is to be found in contemplation, hence the soul needs to be freed of the body. Such contemplation through will and love leads to God, in Whom resides the supreme good, the only one that can give satisfaction. The final *capitolo* is a mystical panegyric on the supreme good and virtually a translation of Ficino's *Oratio ad Deum theologica*. *De summo bono* is, in all, a fine poem with some intensely dramatic sections showing the power that Lorenzo could infuse into his friend's influential ideas. Though unfinished, this work, like several others of Lorenzo's, reflects his evolution from an early formation deep-rooted in the philosophical theories of the *stilnovisti* to an expansion and absorption of Ficinian neo-Platonism, without rejection of the earlier ideas.

Ficino's indoctrination may have influenced, but it failed to inspire, Lorenzo's seven religious *Capitoli* or *Inni religiosi*, which are poems in *terza rima* that vary in length from 34 lines to four times that length. The first five remain strongly attached to their sources: Boethius, the hermetic texts *Asclepius* and *Pimander* (considered by

Quattrocento humanists to be the earliest theological writings) and Psalm 1; the last two would seem to be original and may not belong to the same period. These precious, refined poems cannot be dated, but they are generally assigned to the early 1470s, when Lorenzo was apparently assimilating Ficino's ideas but as yet not using them creatively.

The unfinished story "Ginevra", with its tediously verbose speeches, is mainly a vehicle for Lorenzo's particular blend of *stilnovismo ficiniano*. Not surprisingly, the doctrinal positions, the psychological observations and the very images are to be found in the *Comento*, and Martelli posits "Ginevra" as "l'antefatto, se cosí possiamo esprimerci, di quelle dotte prose esplicative, delle quali fu forse proprio essa a suscitare in Lorenzo la prima idea".[34] The companion story "Giacoppo" succeeds as a *novella* as much as "Ginevra" fails: it is racily narrated and holds the reader's attention. The dominant influence is obviously Boccaccio as exponent of the cult of intelligence, in that Giacoppo is a Calandrino-like figure, a fool to be exploited. Of great interest is the fact that it is an antecedent of Machiavelli's *Mandragola*; not only do Messer Nicia, Fra Timoteo and Callimaco find their prefiguration in Giacoppo, Frate Antonio della Marca and Francesco, but the language, mood and *mores* of Lorenzo's tale anticipate Machiavelli, though the latter, *da bravo repubblicano*, would not have wished to advertize the fact.

Apollo e Pan belongs, like its companion *Corinto*, to the genre of the mythological eclogue in *terza rima*, which was popular in the Quattrocento. It represents a poetic contest (though somewhat short on poetry) between the two gods, but Apollo's part was never written, and some manuscripts call it more appropriately *Capitolo del canto di Pan*. It is regrettable that Lorenzo similarly failed to complete his *Furtum Veneris et Martis*, a much more promising fragment, also in *terza rima*, where a moral exposure of adultery is dulled by the enticement of sensuality:

> Vien, ch'io t'invito nuda in mezzo il letto:
> non indugiar, che 'l tempo passa e vola:
> coperto m'ho di fior vermigli il petto.   (lines 37–39)

The *Stanze*, which occasion our last and possibly greatest sin of omission, are a fascinating albeit problematical work which has been viewed from two extreme standpoints. It was described by Carducci as an "open" text, meditative, wandering as if in a wood with no way out,[35] and is seen by Martelli essentially in the same way, as a Catherine wheel and a "caleidoscopio di frasi, di rime, di versi, di allegorie, di spunti, che sembrano sempre gli stessi e sono sempre diversi";[36] but it is read much more as a "closed" text by the editor of the critical edition, who finds it "organico, unitario e in sé conchiuso".[37] Castagnola publishes its two parts in the order opposite to the traditional one, thereby supporting Orvieto, who has suggested reasons why the text would be more fruitfully read in this order.[38] What is now Part I comprises 141 octaves followed by a short *madrigale*, while the new Part II contains 30 octaves followed by a *canzone*-stanza, the closing and contrasting item of each section being a song in praise of the beloved. In Part I the first rung on the ladder of love—the meeting with the woman and the vision of her exceptional beauty—is attained; in Part II there is the higher attainment of the supreme good and the woman's transfiguration in God. The movement is an upward one, from suffering in a situation of earthly love to the finding of happiness in a transcendental experience—an obviously Ficinian philosophical position. Much anthologized, and with justification, are the octaves that anticipate the arrival of the lady. As she will mean the passage to a new life, her coming is expressed through the arrival of spring (I. 22–29), and one may enjoy a finely observed Laurentian depiction of Nature's reawakening.

Nencia is a text fraught with difficulties, and if an editor were to omit it from a selection of Lorenzo's poetry his decision would certainly be understood, though possibly not applauded. There are two reasons for omitting it, and both are of substance: we have no evidence that Lorenzo wrote it, and we are unsure of the status of the drafts—for drafts they are—that have come down to us. This textual problem is summarized in the Appendix, and it is hoped that the account there of the *questione nenciale*, giving a measure of its complexity and unresolved state, may protect the reader's sanity by satisfying rather than whetting his curiosity.[39] For reasons there expounded, the A-text has been chosen for this edition. It is a composition of *rispetti continuati* that holds together and tells successfully, with a measure of economy, the story of the sensible Vallera and his day-dream, Nencia. But whose dream were they both? To this tantalizing question we have no certain answer. The detailed textual analysis of the four versions carried out by Bessi leads her to conclude that *Nencia* is the work of one author, not of many hands, as some have surmised. But who was he? The very name Nencia recalls Lorenzo, as it is a diminutive of his name (or of Vincenza?); but no manuscript attributes the poem to him, and the first edition to do so is the one of 1568 (Florence, Giunti). It must be added that Pulci's *Beca* is also attributed to Lorenzo in that edition, thereby diminishing the reliability of the evidence. By the same token *Nencia* and *Beca* were together attributed to Pulci in two of the three earliest editions (the Erlangen one publishes only *Nencia*). The attribution to Lorenzo remained firm for centuries, and was generally accepted until 1934 and thereafter, when Patetta strongly argued against it.[40] His iconoclastic writings generated a lengthy and vigorous debate with the forceful and cogent Fubini leading the partisans of Lorenzo as author,[41] while others have since argued in favour of attributing the text to a minor poet, Bernardo Giambullari (1450–1529),[42] and the remainder have accepted that while there is no proof that Lorenzo wrote *Nencia*, there is also none to the contrary.

Interpretative arguments used by Lorenzo's supporters, though valid, cannot constitute evidence because they are subjective. The very choice of a country theme and the manner of its handling are characteristic of Lorenzo, the outdoor poet. Fubini found similarities between this disputed work and Lorenzo's *Stanze* and *Ambra*, in that they reveal "quell'interesse, simpatico nello stesso tempo ed ironico per la vita elementare, rude, schietta della gente campagnola, che informa tutte le ottave della *Nencia da Barberino*".[43] Rochon expresses something of the same idea: "The ease with which the author of *Nencia* could enter into the *persona* of an enamoured countryman is characteristic of Lorenzo's ability to take on the personality of others".[44] There has been much study of an eclogue and of two letters (one of them purporting to be from Nencia to Lorenzo) by Bartolomeo Scala (1430–97), chancellor of Florence in the late Quattrocento. These throw interesting light on the matter, but they are unfortunately open to differing interpretations, which has resulted in their being used by Patetta to demolish the pro-

Lorenzo thesis, but by Fubini as "una testimonianza di valore unico per l'attribuzione della *Nencia* a Lorenzo".[45] Lorenzo spent many a happy sojourn with the Medici *brigata*—the circle of capable, cultured, allegedly carefree youths who surrounded him—in the villa of Cafaggiolo; and Cafaggiolo, in the Mugello area, is only a few miles from Barberino, home of Nencia and Vallera; but such observations provide only circumstantial evidence as tenuous as the rest. Is there any firmer evidence for attributing the poem to Lorenzo? The fact that two mid-Cinquecento authors, Gabriello Simeoni in 1549 and Benedetto Varchi in 1560, write unequivocally of the poem as Lorenzo's, taken together with the attribution in the 1568 edition, is evidence of a tradition that saw no reason to doubt the attribution of *Nencia* to Lorenzo, and this commands respect. Tradition may indeed be reliable.

Dating has some relevance in all this. A date we possess is 1476 for the P-text; Scala's letters can be dated to mid-1474; and Lorenzo was in Barberino in the summer of 1473, which originally led scholars to date *Nencia* to this period. In 1963, however, Domenico De Robertis found a previously unknown *Nencia*-type *ballata* dated 1470, which presupposes the existence of the texts known to us.[46] This earlier dating helps us to understand why Poliziano did not mention *Nencia* (if it is by Lorenzo) among Lorenzo's other works in his *Nutricia*; its exclusion is a fact much used by the "not-Lorenzo" group. Bigi however makes it clear that Poliziano joined the Medici household in the latter half of 1473, and cannot have known of all the activities of the youthful *brigatella* in the late 1460s.[47] The fact that *Nencia, Beca* and *Nencia*-type verses were in circulation by 1470 gives Martelli substantial misgivings: can such a sophisticated work have been written by a teenager?[48] With the evidence at present available, no definite conclusions can be drawn.

Whatever the problems it raises, *Nencia* is an important poem for linguistic and literary reasons, as it gave the impetus to a substantial flowering of *poesia rusticale*, or eclogues in the vernacular in which both persons and environment are characterized through dialect. It is also a sophisticated piece with exceptional charm that well merits the reader's attention. Once met, Nencia with her "occhi tanto rubacuori" (5. 1), who "se lancia com' una capretta" (8. 2), is never forgotten. Nor is Vallera, whose love knows no limits, but is subject to the needs of his herd. What remains above all, however, long after reading, is the sustained dance rhythm through which the poem lives. It is a commonplace that poetry should be read out loud, as the effect of its sounds and rhythms on the aural imagination is intrinsic to the meaning of the whole. *Nencia* is a poem with as strong a dance rhythm as a *ballata*. No matter how hastily one casts one's eye down the text, one sees it move in measure. In keeping with the nature of the *rispetto*, each octave is a unit in itself, with the last line rounding it off with some force. Occasionally the final line is given additional emphasis by being stressed in a different way from its companion in the rhyming couplet. For example, the seventh line of Octave 2 has stresses on syllables 6 and 10 (as have five of the preceding lines) but is followed by a final line stressed on 4, 8 and 10. This change makes the line slower and draws attention to it—which is appropriate, as it gives us for the first time the name of the beloved and her place of residence: "è Barberin, dov' è la Nencia mia". The predominance in the poem (two-thirds) of hendecasyllables that carry only two main stresses, on the sixth and tenth syllables, gives speed to the octaves, and the clever intercalation of lines with three main stresses (on syllables 4, 7 or 8, and 10) is used to effect. For example, seven lines of Octave 17 have two stresses, while line 5, which changes the rhythm, is the one where Vallera bids Nencia think carefully about his gifts: "Procura ben quel ch'i' posso recare." In Octave 15 the "different" line is the second: "col cane innanzi e colle pecorelle", which creates an idyllic image of a pastoral Nencia in a *tableau vivant*. Sometimes this type of line is used to demolish that same idyllic effect, as in 10. 8: "morbido e bianco, che pare un sugnaccio". The first and last octaves of the poem use mainly hendecasyllables with three stresses, which is appropriate to the seriousness of the opening and the valediction. This is a composition that could easily be sung, and it makes one think of the *stornelli fiorentini* that are still quite popular today. (The reader may be reminded of the *stornello* in Mascagni's *Cavalleria rusticana*, "Fior di giaggiolo".) As a verse-form the *stornello* is different from the *rispetto*, but the two are similar in that the statements are contained generally within units of two lines, which is mainly the case in *Nencia*.

A popular misconception about *Nencia* has been that it is "realistically" bucolic—that Vallera is a genuine herdsman of the Mugello. Comparisons with verses belonging to a rustic vernacular tradition show how untenable this is, and an alert reading of the poem reveals its literary sources. Its author was well versed in the classical tradition of the pastoral, and it is his astute handling of that tradition that results in the poem's charm. Another source is Cielo d'Alcamo's "Contrasto", written in the first half of the thirteenth century and itself not without satirical intent. It is an exchange between a boastful, brazen lover and a haughty woman, who holds her own but finally yields abruptly to his pressure. The first two octaves of *Nencia* have both structural and lexical similarities with the "Contrasto", among which critics point particularly to the list of faraway places in which the lover claims to have searched for a lady as beautiful as his beloved. Giustiniani rightly reminds us that this is no more than a braggart's boasting, as it is most unlikely that the minstrel could have visited them all.[49] On the other hand, Vallera's list sets the tone for the whole poem, following an opening octave which, in terms of parody, does not fully show its hand. It is only when the generic "città e 'n castella" is expanded that we realize that the localities are very close to each other, with Barberino not much more than twenty miles from Florence. The parody of lovers who have searched high and low lies in Vallera's topographical limitation. He has not put himself out unduly.

A further literary link is with the story of the priest and Madonna Belcolore in *Decameron*, VIII. 2, which, like *Nencia*, is set in the Florentine *contado*—in Varlungo, very close to Florence.[50] The priest tries to win Belcolore's favours by sending her fresh garlic, broad beans and onions that he has grown himself ("a sue mani"); he wants to pay for her compliance with items of dress similar to what Vallera is willing to buy for Nencia. The forms *Nenciozza* and *Gigghiozzo* lead Umberto Bosco to observe that "i suffissi in -*azzo*, -*ozzo* e simili costellano tutta la novella della Belcolore" and to cite numerous cases as evidence; but, he adds, "quel suono è una costante di tutta la poesia italiana di stile 'comico'" from the time of Guinizelli, Cavalcanti and Dante.[51] There are other specific links with Boccaccio; for example, Octave 11 strongly recalls *Filostrato*, IV. 160. But Boccaccio is most important in this context because his pastoral works occupy an intermediate position between the Graeco-Roman pastoral tradition and the overt parody of the late Quattrocento. Bosco calls him "bifronte", meaning that he was (to use Petrarch's epithets) both "nobilis" and "popularis".[52] There is already in Boccaccio what Orvieto calls an "abbassamento" of linguistic register and of the level of terms of comparison.[53] When carried to extremes, such "abbassamento" (or "degradazione", to use Bessi's word)[54] results in parody. This is readily illustrated by the example under consideration, that of the priest's offerings to Madonna Belcolore. The pastoral tradition has led us to expect gifts of the fruits of the earth, but items such as strawberries and honey, not garlic and onions. The reader has expectations that are not met, and out of the incongruity comes hilarity. This technique is applied throughout *Nencia*.

The poem relies for its comic effect on a knowledge of the genre that it parodies, but one should hesitate to define *Nencia* as a parody *tout court*, because the laughter it generates is of the genial, not the derisive, kind. While there is parody of features of the pastoral, Nencia and Vallera are not caricatures, and the A-text lacks those octaves of the V-text that could be seen as going overboard. The same is true of the obscene, of which there is only the merest hint in A while it is to be found in greater abundance in the longer version. However the A-text was put together, it is remarkable for its subtle balance; whoever is responsible for it knew the meaning of *aurea mediocritas*.

It will be obvious to the reader that in *Nencia* there are skilful stylistic manoeuvres which expose a tradition that could take itself too seriously. The unexpected constantly surprises us. The poetic is made prosaic: Vallera can call the love awakened in him by Nencia "fiaccole d'amore" (1. 6), redolent of the *stile aulico* of the love tradition, but he can also dismiss it as a "baloccar" (20. 3). There is distortion of patterns and a lowering of tone. The offer of gifts is a topos of lyric poetry, but we do not expect a shopping-list of trinkets that belong to vernacular parlance, to excise records as goods subject to tax, or to the popular *canti carnascialeschi*. Nencia is offered no gold or diamonds but "squilletti" (17. 8), a strongly onomatopoeic word that conveys the lightness of tinsel; and of these Vallera limits the quantity to a mere "quattrino", thereby creating an entirely comic effect. While there is indulgence in the hyperbole intrinsic to the genre—"e mai ne vidi ignuna tanto bella" (1. 8) and "che non si vide mai sí bella cosa" (4. 8) are quite stock-in-trade expressions—, a greater effect is obtained through the re-duction of the bombastic element to expose its absurdity, as in the

example mentioned above: "o de squilletti o d'agora un quattrino".
Possibly the greatest source of parody is to be found in the terms of
comparison. It is commonplace to praise the whiteness of the
beloved, and Bessi cites Galatea, who, for Theocritus (*Idylls*, XI. 19),
is whiter than *ricotta* (or curd, if one prefers); for Ovid (*Metamorphoses*, XIII. 789) she is whiter than the petals of the snowy colum-
bine; for Virgil (*Eclogues*, VII. 37) she is brighter than any swan. For
Vallera (10. 8) she is soft and white like lard (and poorish-quality
lard at that).[55] Parody is also to be found in the selection of words
that are inappropriate though cognate ones are poetically acceptable. That the loved one's heart is as hard as rock is commonplace;
Vallera chooses a cognate and gives us a cobble-stone (5. 4), thereby
creating an entirely different effect. There are several further examples, among which one might single out Nencia's dimple (and
the dimple as an attribute of beauty belongs to the classical tradition) being redefined as a hole (9. 3).

The last stanza (20) is problematical, with its strong Theocritan
echoes revealing the parodist's true literary base. It comes as a
surprise, as does virtually everything in this poem. Giustiniani
suggests that this stanza was written after the rest, because it
"impone al discorso una brusca virata e sorprende il lettore, che
logicamente non si aspettava il Vallera chiamare una perdita di
tempo i suoi spasimi e i suoi lamenti: l'effetto delle cose sin qui dette
è eliminato."[56] But is it really eliminated? Is not this last stanza, with
its revealing "baloccar", a clue as to how we should read the whole
poem? May not Vallera be laughing at himself, creating an image of
himself as a languid *spasimante* idolizing a creature who is unattainable because *he* makes her so? He is totally in control of a Nencia
who can be, in the one octave (10), both a "fioraliso sanza foglie"
and a cuddly mass of desirable flesh comparable to "sugnaccio".
She is a figment—and what a figment!—of his day-dream. He
creates her within a world limited by his own experience, a world
of *ritortole*, *marroni* and *mulini*, a world which determines his
emotions and healthy desire; but at the same time he can move with
self-irony into the world of the lovelorn lover and his *sospiri*. The
female reality of the poem is Mona Masa, and all she stands for is
likewise real. Real, too, is Vallera's concern for "le bestie mie" (20).
Like the best of shepherds he will not let even one go astray. Vallera
may belong to the line of "pastoral heroes" that will produce Percy

French's farmer, whose amatory decisons hang on the price of a heifer: "A girl she might lose her good looks anyhow,/And a heifer might grow into an elegant cow."

If it is found unacceptable that Lorenzo may be the author of *Nencia* mainly because it is too sophisticated a poem to come from the pen of a mere youth, then one will have similar reservations about the *Uccellagione di starne*, another "piccolo capolavoro" that we cannot attribute with certainty to Lorenzo.[57] Vittorio Rossi, writing without the information now available, assumed that both poems were written at the end of the poet's life because of their high level of artistry.[58] The *Uccellagione* must have been written before 1478, the year of the Pazzi conspiracy, as Guglielmo de' Pazzi is clearly still in the inner circle of friends. Rochon suggests 1476 as a date *ante quem*, because in that year the renowned falconer Pilato joined the Medici household, and he would surely have been mentioned otherwise.[59] A most important piece in this jigsaw is Orvieto's identification of Poliziano as the *compare*, which gives 1473 as the date *post quem*.[60] The evidence shows, then, that the poem was not written at the time of *Nencia* but later, in the period 1473–76, when Lorenzo was a more experienced poet. But was he the author? There is, again, no decisive evidence for or against him. The *Uccellagione* has thankfully given rise to less controversy than *Nencia*, with no great name to champion either side. It has generally been found in editions of Lorenzo's poetry since its first appearance in 1795 in William Roscoe's selection of Laurentian poetry with the title *La caccia col falcone*.[61] Roscoe's text was transcribed from codex Laurenziano XLI, 25, which contains a text that is similar to those of four other manuscripts; there is also, however, the very different version of MS Riccardiano 2599, first printed by Alberto Chiari in 1958[62] and attentively examined and reconstructed by Martelli, who shows (beyond doubt, I am tempted to add) that Roscoe's oft-reprinted version was a draft of which the Riccardiano text is a revised and possibly definitive redaction.[63] Above all, the revisions in the Riccardiano version, all of which seem to be authorial, give it a strict logical sequence that is lacking in the earlier text and eliminate a number of anomalies and obscurities. Only two manuscripts bear a title, and this is *Uccellagione di starne*, so it is reasonable to adopt this in favour of Roscoe's. That Lorenzo was an *appassionato* of *cacce col falcone* is attested by his correspondence; and that he should have written a poem in celebration of many such hunts, no doubt blending together different occasions, is not surprising. One is tempted to adapt what Fubini said of *Nencia*, borrowing a phrase from art historians: that if the work is not by Lorenzo then it is by an *amico di Lorenzo*.[64] Most tantalizing, why the anonymity? If the poem is indeed by Lorenzo, was the anonymity deliberate? So far there are only questions, and the rest is silence.

One question that can be answered without hesitation relates to the merit of reading this poem. The reader may be assured that only delight awaits him: it is a sophisticated poem which evokes atmosphere, weather, mood, companionship, interaction, and a host of other aspects of a merry *compagnia* in an evidently carefree summer day's sport, flavoured and embellished by conversation, with more sport planned for the morrow. The language of the *Uccellagione* is a challenge with its difficult colloquialisms, but its colourful sharpness makes a lasting impression on the reader. A *focaccia* will bring to mind the sorry fate of the hawk belonging to Dionigi, who calls himself a *cucciotto*; and one is tempted to speak not of a fish out of water, but of "in su la nona un barbagianni" (10. 8). Some images have exceptional figurative force, like "'l ciambellotto ha già presa la piega" (39. 1), or disappearing "per arte di maiolica" (44. 5), or "scuote il pesco" (15. 6). Characters come alive with a brief but sure touch: Giovan Francesco in his complete ineptitude, Giovan Simone when "gli tocca un certo grillo" (38. 5), or the unforgettable Dionigi—"il mio Dionigi", as the author calls him (34. 1), appropriating his special creation with a mixture of affection and pride in having perfectly captured the essence of this character. His sluggishness is understated—"la sua dama è la poca fatica" (6. 8)—but reflected in his being overweight. This chubby creature falls rolling "come un sasso tondo" (7. 4) and later perspires in the heat like an "uovo fresco" (34. 2)—which recalls, through the rhyme, "le pocce al fresco" (7. 7) of his earlier rambling thoughts of sleep, relaxation and shade. His yearning to be "scalzo e scinto" (35. 1) no doubt arises from his discomfort in tight-fitting clothes. It is his easy nature that enables him to proffer soothing words in an effort to dispel the ill feeling between Guglielmo and Foglia, as the fray between their hawks has reflected something of the tension between their respective owners—and so discordant a note would have ruined the harmony that ultimately encapsulates the poem.

Martelli, perceptive as ever, sees the changes made in the later draft as reflecting a tendency both to "accentuare il realismo di certi tratti" and also to develop the sense of "armoniosa gentilezza" and "raffinata stilizzazione"; from this apparent contradiction "nasce l'incanto dell'*Uccellagione,* che è quello di una realtà quotidiana e casalinga e dimessa, ma pur trasfigurata in una leggiadra aria di fiaba".[65] The poem is a perfect balance of the two, with precise details that help us to visualize the scene and its characters as if it were clearly before us like Benozzo Gozzoli's fresco in the chapel of Palazzo Medici-Riccardi, and yet, just like that fresco, creating not one specific occasion but a scene that gathers together both one and many experiences and holds them suspended away from reality, so that the characters remain "for ever panting, and for ever young". The atmospheric conditions, I would suggest, are instrumental in creating this "non-real reality" with the superb opening light:

> Era già rosso tutto l'oriente
> e le cime de' monti parean d'oro; [...]
> netta era l'aria, fresca e cristallina.   (1. 1–2; 2. 7).

The freshness and bright light gradually give way to a sun that, in an effective personification, at first gently warms "al monte [...] le spalle" (13. 1) but finally plays havoc with the shadows: "stremando [...] le raccorcia" (33. 2). The heat increases until "'l mondo ardea, come fussi una torcia" (33. 6) and "parea appiccato il fuoco in ogni stoppia" (35. 8). The choreographed movements also add to the stylized effect: the party sets out respecting a decorum dictated by this regal sport, and finds its "gentil valletta" (12. 1), the perfect *locus amœnus* (desirable place). The poet's touch is sure in his blending of this with observations of a reality that we might call *spicciola* and that is conveyed partly by the vocabulary (expressions like *cicalare, centellino, straccar la coltrice*) and partly by details like the silence at the beginning of the meal when the need for food overcomes all other needs ("Il primo assalto fu sanza romore:/ognuno attende a menar le mascella", 42. 1–2).

Much of this poem's vivacity lies in its oral quality, with direct speech not of a declamatory nature but reflecting the raciness of colloquial exchange. Some of the speaking seems collective: Octaves 16–19 are more likely to be an accumulation of statements and exhortations made by different participants than the speech of a single individual. The abundant repartee makes the poem fast-moving and creates a dramatic effect, engaging the reader as spectator, almost as participant. Orvieto calls this poem "una registrazione dal vivo d'una battuta di caccia; un testo che utilizza in larga misura la tecnica del discorso indiretto libero".[66] Indeed the direct speech often blends into the free indirect variety, and one is conscious of the voice of the narrator from his first definite entry at the opening of Octave 3—"Quando io fu' desto"—to his concluding remarks to his *compare*. The blending of tenses and moods in the last octave conveys on the one hand the sense that the event happened in the past, and on the other the impression that it is merely the activity of that one day before the company sets off for Sieve; it is both particular and universal. Nor is the poem's aural quality conveyed solely by human speech: from the outset there is an awareness of other sounds, a sort of background music to the action, whether it be the *schiamazzar* of the bird at the opening, or the sound of hawk-bells or cries to the hounds, or the final line which evokes the evening's entertainment with popular poetry and song.

Poetry in abundance is to be found in Lorenzo's *Canzoniere*. It comprises 166 poems, all of them sonnets except sixteen which are *sestine* (written prior to 1473), *canzoni* or *ballate*; forty-one of the sonnets are included in the *Comento*. Lorenzo produced his lyric poetry intermittently throughout his creative life. The sonnet "Temendo la sorella del Tonante" must be one of his earliest, as it can be dated confidently to June 1465; it shows that the sixteen-year-old was writing—predictably—Petrarchan sonnets, but not slavishly. We can date certain poems reliably enough to know that he was adding to his collection periodically during the next twenty years. And as we can establish that "Quando morrà questa dolce inimica" was written in 1486–87, it seems reasonable to suppose that the eighteen sonnets that follow it in print also did so in order of composition. Zanato's investigation of texts and dating leads him to conclude that "su tale *Canzoniere* Lorenzo non riuscí a scrivere la parola *finis*, sicché il sopravvenire della morte interruppe un'opera ancora aperta, non conclusa."[67]

While it has never been doubted that in his early lyrics Lorenzo psychologically and stylistically models himself on Petrarch, it was not conceded until recently that the collection, predominantly concerned with the experience of love, has organic unity. This, however, is strongly argued by Zanato on the basis of his work on the critical edition, which results in his finding "un'opera, per contenuto, modelli e forme metriche, fortemente unitaria, e che come tale vuole proporsi al fruitore".[68] There is a conscious adherence to Petrarch in the very notion of a *libro delle rime* (hence, in part, Zanato's change of the work's traditional title); in the first seventy-one poems he points to evidence of Petrarchan borrowings not just in the metres used and their frequency but in the "mossa iniziale del 'libro'" and the "filosofia erotica che lo anima".[69] The early Petrarchan phase (but some features were to remain constant) is well described by Domenico De Robertis: "Petrarca piú che modello letterario, è una lezione di vita, una via di scoperta interiore, un esercizio di chiarezza [...], e piú che il mito da lui creato importa la possibilità di un'ulteriore elaborazione e variazione di quei temi: la ricerca di una verità."[70] Lorenzo's philosophy of love will expand beyond its Petrarchan formation (love as suffering and distraction from divine concerns) to embrace the philosophico-theological interpretations of love of the *stilnovisti*, especially Cavalcanti and Dante (who also exercised a strong influence on Lorenzo's view of the *volgare*). As it was never the Thomist-Aristotelian aspect of the earlier poets that captured Lorenzo, his mind was disposed to move outwards into the sphere of the harmonious system offered by neo-Platonism. Ficino, in *El libro dell'Amore*, written in or very shortly after 1469, shows direct links between parts of his "system" and that of Cavalcanti, the philosopher who "tutte queste cose artificiosamente chiuse ne' sua versi" (VII. 1).[71] We therefore speak of Lorenzo's poetic myth as *stilnovismo ficiniano*; and there is no doubt that after 1473 he espoused "la fede platonica [...] con assoluta dedizione e sincerità".[72] Part of that creed was the belief that human experience is theologically significant because man can find God through it, for He is within our souls. External realities in their beauty reflect the totality of beauty which is God; hence, in the contemplation of the beauty of the beloved, man may find his Creator. The poet becomes abstracted from the reality of the experience, while the loved object recedes and becomes what has been aptly defined a "non-personaggio".[73] Love is an instrument of salvation to bring man back to God, whence all, including the experience of love, emanates. The love experience of the *Canzoniere* needs to be read in these terms.

Who was the beloved? There is ample evidence to show that she was Lucrezia Donati (1449–1501), who married Niccolò Ardinghelli in 1465, also the year of Lorenzo's possible *innamoramento*. If one is looking for the transposition of great passion from private life to poetic narration, one is completely disappointed. Lucrezia's very name is evocative of the beauty and goodness of Tarquin's Lucretia, and also of Lorenzo's much-loved mother, herself a poet. Lorenzo's muse inspired a love that was an essential premise for a poetry of exquisite sophistication, both stylistic and philosophical, and was based on a system which demanded that she become a *non-personaggio*. In a number of poems the love experience is lived evanescently, through a dream, which makes its subject all the more unreal.

Inevitably linked to the notion of love is that of fortune, together with its profound effect on human affairs. Dante, Petrarch and Boccaccio had all expressed themselves strongly on *fortuna*; it matters not that she be viewed as a God-controlled force, His "general ministra e duce" (*Inferno*, VII. 78); men know (and Lorenzo was rather dramatically aware) that there is a greater power than we can contradict. In the early Lorenzo, Fortune is almost fossilized in a tradition where she is seen as a cruel goddess of strong and wilful ways who loses no chance to harass the lover; but when the poetry changes under Ficino's influence after 1476, love is seen by the poet as no longer within the power of a fickle fortune. What remains, nonetheless, is an awareness that fortune is a dominant force in our lives—much more dominant than Machiavelli was willing to admit in his famous chapter on the subject. (When he states that fortune allows us to govern half our lives, he knows that it is what we like to think but secretly know not to be true. He then adds the unobtrusive though equally false "o presso"—if not quite half, then almost. But reality proves that it is infinitely less.) In Lorenzo's view we control precious little; as Webster put it, "we are merely the stars' tennis-balls", though those same stars, Lorenzo asserts in his play, are subject to God. Man certainly has no control over his life-span, and the notion of Fortune generates reflections on the brevity of life, on its purpose, on the wisdom of many of our concerns, on the imperative need to live today to the full for tomorrow may never come. "Che quanto piace al mondo è breve sogno" is a Petrarchan theme (*Canzoniere*, I. 14) that Lorenzo metamorphoses into various guises. (He also took from Petrarch the feature of ending a sonnet with an aphoristic final line, though this is also not infrequent in popular poetry.) An epithet that he makes very much his own is the Petrarchan *vano*, though it also has strong Dantesque connotations in this context, as Dante dismisses what fortune gives and takes as "li ben vani" (*Inferno*, VII. 79). This worthlessness, in transcendental terms, of our human concerns is a constant in Lorenzo's poetry, whether it be the "Vana è ogni mortal nostra fatica" that we find in the early *sestina* "Amor tenuto m'ha di tempo in tempo", or Giuliano's anguished cry in the closing octave of Lorenzo's play: "Fallace vita! oh nostra vana cura!" Another Petrarchan feature, the rhyme *fugge/strugge*, was to become Lorenzo's leitmotif in his immortalizing of time's headlong flight, running ahead of us, wreaking destruction on its way. Whither time's breathless race? To the only certainty in man's life: "sola sta ferma e sempre dura Morte" (see page 108). Death is implicit in many of Lorenzo's most successful poems. The *Canzoniere* may be uneven, and some of it is undoubtedly inferior to the great poetry on which it was modelled—that of Petrarch and of the *stilnovisti* in that chronological order—, but if we accept that "the word is man's most precise and inclusive tool; and poetry is the using of this most precise and inclusive tool memorably",[74] then Lorenzo's collection contains poetry in abundance.

It is hoped that the eight poems selected will prove this, though they cannot, of course, do justice to a collection that spans some twenty-five years. The first, "Fortuna, come suol, pur mi dileggia", is an early reflection on the commonplace theme of Fortune's mockery. In the second, the dream sonnet "Piú che mai bella e men che già mai fera", Lorenzo achieves exquisite lyricism in a diaphanous vision that appeases him, albeit momentarily. It contrasts strongly with the next poem, "Quanto sia vana ogni speranza nostra", with its dramatic reminder of the imperative certainty of death. In "Lascia l'isola tua tanto diletta", with its rarefied virginal atmosphere, Lorenzo sets forth in idyllic terms the conflict between chastity and love (Diana versus Venus)—a theme which dominates Boccaccio's *Caccia di Diana* and *Ninfale fiesolano*, underlies Lorenzo's

Corinto and is central to *Ambra*. In harsh contrast with the realm of Venus is "Bastava avermi tolto libertate", a poem as intensely dramatic as the preceding one is delicately idyllic, not least because it is open to a political interpretation. "Non de' verdi giardini ornati e colti", based on the myth of the white roses turned to red by the blood of Venus, hides a theological meaning in its sweetly elegiac tone. The last two sonnets, "O bella violetta, tu se' nata" and "Quando a me il lume de' belli occhi arriva", are neo-Platonist in their formulation, and in the latter in particular the love experience assumes transcendental significance. The selection, albeit limited, cannot be charged with lack of variety.

Although it is usual to speak of Lorenzo's single most important work as his *Comento*, in the manuscripts it is untitled. Martelli has suggested that it be called *Comento de' sonetti*, as this is how Piero da Bibbiena styles it in a letter to Lorenzo of 1486,[75] and its most recent editor (Zanato) has inserted *miei* into that title. The *Comento* is an unfinished work comprising a substantial "Proemio" and forty-one love sonnets, each followed by a detailed prose commentary in which the experiences related in the poetry are minutely described; this prose serves as a vehicle for an exposition of a complex doctrine and psychology of love. Much that has been said above about Lorenzo's *Canzoniere* applies equally to the poetry of the *Comento*, as the sonnets were not composed specifically for an independent work but belong to the body of *rime* written throughout Lorenzo's life. The poetry he selected for the *Comento* has cohesion only in so far as it is based on a neo-Platonist understanding of the love experience: the soul is released from the bondage of earthly love through its understanding of physical beauty and its progression to the contemplation of supreme beauty, God. The sonnets illustrate various moments of this experience, and among the recurrent motifs in Lorenzo's descriptions there are three—"gli occhi della donna amata che lo avvincono, il suo cuore fugge, la mano della donna lo ingentilisce"—which, Martelli reminds us, "tornano fin quasi alla sazietà" in the works under discussion.[76] The first sonnet selected bears this out: "Belle, fresche e purpuree viole", on the floral gift and therefore thematically linked to "O bella violetta, tu se' nata", reflects on the healing power of the lady's hand. In

"Datemi pace omai, sospiri ardenti" the poet yearns for the respite of sleep with its ensuing dreams, and the sonnet offers a variation on the theme encountered already in "Piú che mai bella e men che già mai fera". Equally, the much-loved sonnet "Cerchi chi vuol le pompe e gli alti onori" evokes an idyllic natural scene similar to the one in the poet's invitation to Venus. This poem has appealed to generations of readers because in it Lorenzo expresses admirably his yearning to leave the cares of public life and find peace among the simple joys of nature, where he can pursue his amatory thoughts; it is not an idea of love that we take away from this sonnet, but rather one of our need for inner tranquillity in a world that is too much with us. "Ove madonna volge li occhi belli", on the life-giving force of the lady's presence, has an aura that is both ethereal and ineffable as something almost cinematic is created: a still gently comes to life, emanating sounds and irradiating colours, with diaphanous creatures who gradually awake to the power of love. We think of Botticelli's Graces with the central one usually identified as Castitas. High melodic achievement is very much the hallmark of Lorenzo's best lyric output and, it will be agreed, the lyrics chosen in this section are outstanding examples of this.

There is much less agreement over the dating of the prose commentary and "Proemio". One relevant fact is that the first four elegiac sonnets and prose passages arise from the death in April 1476 of the much celebrated Simonetta Vespucci, a central figure in Poliziano's *Stanze*. This love is then, fictionally, followed by another, for the same Lucrezia Donati who is the object of the poet's affection in the *Canzoniere*. The fiction requires Lorenzo to date his love for Lucrezia from 1476, though we know it to have begun more than a decade earlier—all of which is unhelpful as far as chronology is concerned. Bigi and Rochon narrow the time-span of the *Comento*,[77] but Martelli cogently argues for various phases in the composition of this work, which, more than others by Lorenzo, was subject to extensive revision and possibly destined for radical rethinking under Savonarolan influence. The "Proemio" was written after the commentaries, but whereas Martelli originally dated its composition, or profound revision, to 1490–91, convincing even critics of different persuasion like Bigi,[78] he has since withdrawn this dating as a result of his research into the cultural changes in Florence in the last two years of Lorenzo's life.[79] Zanato has recently concluded (with seemingly good reasons) that the prose commentary cannot be dated before March 1480 and that only illness and death interrupted it.[80] It seems that greater precision is impossible.

In writing a prose commentary on his own work, Lorenzo was doing something quite uncommon in his day; he was following, rather, the example set by Dante in his *Vita nuova* and *Convivio*. He was just as philosophical as Dante in his approach, though in Dante's writings the allegory and mysticism are overt. Lorenzo's commentary, on the other hand—or *paraphrasis*, as Pico called it—,[81] does not make the allegory's terms of reference explicit; this is in keeping with the tenets of the neo-Platonists, for whom the truth hidden in poetry should be revealed only to initiates. It is not solely Plato's *Symposium* that moulds Lorenzo's allegory of love: Scripture also plays a formative role, and Martelli shows how some of the Pauline epistles (Corinthians and Hebrews) are particularly important in our correct interpretation of the woman "intesa come simbolo della bellezza intellettuale, anche se, necessariamente, contemplata ancora con l'interposizione della materia. Essa era [...] la somma Bellezza calatasi in terra e dentro ad un corpo; e poiché la Somma Bellezza, cioè Dio, s'incarna nella persona di Cristo, questa seconda donna era da interpretare come figura del Dio incarnato, e cioè di Gesú."[82] Hermeneutics is essential for the *paraphrasis* to yield all the richness of its content, but it would be regrettable if this were to daunt the reader who may quite reasonably find *stilnovismo ficiniano* becoming something of a straitjacket. Moving freely through the pages of the *Comento* one finds passages that reveal a private, unknown Lorenzo, engaging us with their humanity and emotion, and justifying us in rising to the challenge of the work's philosophical difficulty. Familiarity will breed reward.

The *Comento* has never been a particularly popular work, and—surprisingly—despite the neo-Platonist atmosphere of the early Cinquecento had to wait until 1554 for its first printing. *Inter alia*, this may have been for reasons of both content and style. Highly philosophical, rarefied and elitist poetry could not be of general appeal, as Pico had recognized,[83] and Lorenzo's prose, though a landmark in the development of Italian, was decidedly out of fashion in a period when Bembo dictated that good prose be modelled on Boccaccio.[84] Nor has the work attracted much critical interest over the centuries, and its reputation was not enhanced by the authoritative but damaging "Nota" (as it was appropriately entitled) elicited from Fubini by Spongano's appraisal of Lorenzo's prose.[85] Fubini found the prose laboured in its attempt to express a "ragionamento scolastico, a cui l'autore volontariamente si piega" with even an "insistenza fastidiosa di certe formule stilistiche" common to scholasticism.[86] The champion of *Nencia* was the strongest detractor of the commentary, and he remained unchallenged until Zanato's serious critical study of Lorenzo's prose appeared in 1979 and showed that Fubini's note may have been superficial. That Lorenzo's exposition is fundamentally scholastic cannot be doubted, and what Lorenzo took from Dante in this respect, is reinforced by the practice of Ficino, Pico and Landino.[87] Of the first of these three Kristeller has written: "The medieval, scholastic element is very noticeable in Ficino's writings. It appears in his terminology, in his method of arguing, in the ontological principles on which he bases his demonstrations."[88] Is it any wonder that it appears in Lorenzo? The point at issue is one of power: who is in control? That it is Lorenzo, dexterously using the tools of scholasticism, and not scholasticism manipulating Lorenzo, is amply illustrated by the careful analysis of the prose undertaken by Zanato. Lorenzo argues by syllogisms, moving from the general to the particular, with subtle distinctions and frequent exemplification; but he adheres rigidly to no schema. Lorenzo makes effective use of a number of variations, even changing from deductive to inductive argument. The rhetorical devices of medieval prose abound but the imitation is genial, not slavish. Lorenzo uses repetition effectively, stating a point and repeating it in different terms that seek to clarify it and to increase its impact. This effect is also achieved by the use of nouns and adjectives in pairs; these may differ in meaning or be synonyms. The technique has classical antecedents and is frequent in the Tuscan authors who were Lorenzo's models. It was overused in the religious plays of the Quattrocento but Lorenzo's *Rappresentazione* will show a less mechanical exploitation of the device. In the *Comento* it achieves phonic and rhythmic effects as well. Zanato notes a sophisticated use of the gerund to give balance to long and complex sentences with their "orchestrazione classicheggiante",[89] while we find this in the *Vita nuova* it is more extensively used by Latin authors. The strongly Latinate elements do not suffocate Lorenzo's prose; rather they are "assunti con notevole incidenza e sapientemente amalgamati alla natura sintattica del volgare, senza stravolgimenti o stridori".[90] Sparing use is made of rhetorical questions, and while there is occasional dialogue he does not descend to the colloquial register. As alliteration and repetition of a word or its cognates are features of Lorenzo's poetry, they are equally of his prose, thereby giving it a poetic quality. Zanato's examination of the vocabulary shows the presence of many Latinisms, several of which had already been used by Dante, Petrarch and Boccaccio, while others, linked to aspects of *romanitas*, had only recently entered the *volgare*. Technical terms belonging to specific linguistic registers, like medicine, the law or the visual arts, add to the scientific rigour of the prose. All of this proves the point that Lorenzo made in defence of the *volgare*: it could express with precision the most sophisticated thinking and do so harmoniously.

As the fragmentary, no matter how impressive, is never satisfactory, it has been decided to include the whole of the "Proemio" to the *Comento* in this edition, while excluding all the commentaries on individual sonnets. As well as being highly indicative of Lorenzo's thinking on a number of issues pertaining to the work as a whole, the "Proemio" will suffice as a good example of the complexity and erudition of his prose, as well as its elegance and incisiveness. It is very much a defensive piece, and the classical antecedent for a defence of both subject-matter and the use of the mother tongue is probably Cicero's *De finibus*.[91] Lorenzo defends himself both as writer of love poetry (at the expense perhaps of more important duties) and as commentator on his own poems. He defends love, both earthly and celestial, as the former leads to the latter: the experience of love ennobles and leads to perfection and to great and worthy deeds. A defence of the *volgare* as a language suitable for expressing the highest philosophical concepts in a harmonious and moving manner is followed by a defence of the sonnet as a verse-form which he defines as "difficillimo" because of the great challenge offered by its compact brevity. Lastly, he defends himself for beginning his work with reflections on death, that singularly certain experience of mankind which is essential for our entry into life, as "il principio della vera vita è la morte della vita non vera." Lorenzo's defence of love and of the writing of love poetry may appear strange, coming as it does after a lifetime of no apologies for such a practice, but it needs to be seen in the context of contemporary polemics and particularly of Lorenzo at odds with Rome. Originally he was dangerously so because he championed Naples; but there were other reasons too, and in his last years he invited trouble through his support not just of Pico, but of Ficino as well: the latter's *De vita*, published in May 1490, had been accused of heresy while still in manuscript form. Martelli comments that "sotto accusa era tutta la cultura laurenziana, che veniva colpita nei suoi piú insigni rappresentanti", and Lorenzo was stoutly defending it.[92] When he wrote his "Proemio" he was still committed to Ficinian philosophy, and this he makes incontrovertibly clear: love is pure and sublime as it is an experience through which man can find God, and the poetry that celebrates this experience can be read as an allegory of the soul's journey to its Creator. Related to this is the reflection on death leading to eternal life which ends the prefatory section. Nothing could be more orthodox than this central Christian belief. The first four sonnets and their respective commentaries are linked to a specific death, that of Simonetta, but Lorenzo's reflections move from the specific to the general; he ends by referring to the yearning of all men for happiness and perfection within the Creator's plan. It is in this context that we must interpret Love showing his power by sending another woman of supreme beauty to take the place of the first; this new love thus symbolizes resurrection to a life of eternal happiness after the death of the body, that "muddy vesture of decay" which perforce we shed.[93]

The defence of the *volgare* is also written with passionate commitment. In this, and in the fact that some of Lorenzo's views are analogous to those of Dante, it is reminiscent of *De vulgari eloquentia*, though Lorenzo would have been familiar only with the ideas of the *Convivio* (Dante's text on language and poetry was not known until the early Cinquecento). Both authors write on the language dear to their hearts with more emotion than objectivity. Lorenzo did not know either Greek or Hebrew, so his views on these languages were second-hand. His text synthesizes the views expressed in the linguistic debates of his own century, especially those expounded by Landino in his commentary on Dante's *Commedia*; and it strongly reaffirms the validity of the Florentine *volgare*. It must be recognized as a landmark in the lengthy disputes about the language that Trissino, some decades later, was finally to call Italian.[94] Unlike the Florentine intellectuals of his circle who wrote both in Latin and in the *volgare* (some also in Greek), Lorenzo wrote his literary works exclusively in the vernacular. Something that is not surprising but in effect original in his contribution to the debate on the language is his awareness of the political dimension: the language belonged to an important community, to a city of international repute—Florence—, in whose ascendancy Lorenzo believed and to whose dominance he was committed. It is very revealing that he speaks of a Florentine empire in the context of the Roman one: and empires are made partly of literary glory. There is accuracy but no neutrality in his phrase, "Dante, il Petrarca e il Boccaccio, nostri poeti fiorentini". They were assets to Florence and to him. Originality and depth characterize his appraisal of the Tuscan writers: Lorenzo rises above the somewhat petty criticisms of Dante and Boccaccio penned by the humanists as he identifies the qualities of their excellence; his assessment of Guido Cavalcanti goes much further than the views expressed in the letter which accompanied the *Raccolta aragonese* and is indicative of further study of this poet on his part. These pages neither indulge in superficial eulogy nor pay lip-service to fashion; Lorenzo's assessments are founded on knowledge of the texts and of the complex debates that these had generated.[95] A strong element of individuality also marks Lorenzo's views on metrical forms, where the criterion for excellence, sometimes explicitly stated but always implicit, is difficulty. He singles out the sonnet as his preferred metrical composition because of its difficulty and conciseness, and cites Plato, with whom he shares the belief that there is an almost divine quality in narrating both briefly and clearly. He argues for the superiority of the sonnet not only to other verse-forms of the *volgare* but also to Latin ones, finding Latin poetry inferior because its subject-matter is less grave and because, owing to its lack of rhyme, it is metrically less difficult. Lorenzo's views on the difficulty of appropriately matching rhyme to subject-matter are expressed with a degree of feeling that will evoke sympathy from anyone who has attempted it. If any further proof were needed of his total commitment to writing in the *volgare*, and of his deep understanding of the artistry of his own craft, these pages would provide it in an incontrovertible manner. The *Comento* as a whole is not an easy text and its appeal is not immediate, but Zanato concludes that Lorenzo viewed it as his most important literary work: the "messaggio dell'autore, della vita, dell'attività poetica, della cultura sua e della sua generazione" is entrusted to it, and this makes it, apart from its other intrinsic merits, "il testo piú importante e carico di significato, quello che il Magnifico guardava con piú orgoglio, al quale aveva lavorato fino all'ultimo, prima della fine della sua terrena avventura".[96]

Corinto and *Ambra* provide a sharp contrast with the *Comento*. These two *poemetti* may be considered companion pieces in so far as they are both classical in tone and inspiration and, more importantly, they have a thematic link—though this may not be immediately apparent. The first is mainly a youthful work, written possibly *circa* 1464–65, with lines 163–80 added after 1486, when Poliziano was also working on the theme of the rose as a symbol of youth. Furthermore, the *terzina* that follows them was intended as an alternative to, or a replacement for, the lines describing the tree with its fruit (beginning "Ogni arbore ha i sua fior") which are numbered 181–93 in all the editions. Our text of *Corinto* gives the ending discovered by Messina in 1958 and reconstructed by Martelli, which is much more acceptable not only on textual grounds but also on artistic ones.[97] The poem is broadly a pastoral eclogue, and possibly even a deliberate step away from *Nencia* (if this is by Lorenzo) towards a more literary tradition.[98] That it belongs in the main to the poet's youth is clearly shown by its stylistic features, by its cultural underpinning, and also by a biographical detail.[99] Most of its manuscripts bear no title, but one calls it *Innamoramento di Lorenzo de' Medici*, which leads us to identify Corinto with Lorenzo himself and Galatea with Lucrezia Donati; this is confirmed by lines 749–50 of Poliziano's *Nutricia*. If we bear in mind Lucrezia's dates of birth (1449) and marriage (1465), we realize how appropriate it is for Corinto to say to the nymph, in lines 32–33, that she has devoted fifteen years of chaste service to Diana; and this suggests the mid-1460s as a probable date for the initial draft of the poem. It is also the period of the *Simposio*, another work written in *terza rima*, which is a verse-form not used in the late works.

A number of stylistic features that *Corinto* has in common with early sonnets of Lorenzo's have been noted by Martelli, who uses them to provide further evidence that it was a juvenile work—but not, he stresses, an unskilled one, though he himself as well as

Maier had earlier suggested this:[100] that Lorenzo chooses modes characteristic of fifteenth-century Tuscan poetry like the *cantari* , with anomalies of syntax and discordant shifts of linguistic register, reflects a stylistic decision by the young poet. An interesting link, both thematic and lexical, between *Corinto* (lines 46–48 and 100–10) and the *Comento* (sonnet XVII and accompanying commentary) is used by Martelli to provide support for an early dating of the *poemetto*—prior to 1473, when there is a marked shift towards neo-Platonism.[101] A comparison of these two texts reveals that the prose commentary would well suit as an explication of the relevant *terzine* of *Corinto*, in that it is consonant with the shepherd's Petrarchan reflections; any contradictions that seem to emerge are quickly dispelled if all the texts juxtaposed by Martelli are read in Petrarchan rather than Ficinian terms.

The cultural influences at work in *Corinto* are also those of Lorenzo's early years. In the speaker's self-appraisal (beginning at line 112) the use of hyperbole and the tendency towards burlesque inevitably bring Pulci to mind, and these features contrast—not always successfully—with the classical ones in the poem. The latter are not so much borrowings—too strong a term—as reminiscences of the standard texts of a humanist education of the time.[102] They include echoes of Theocritus, *Idylls* III, VI and XI (the love of Polyphemus for Galatea), Ovid, *Metamorphoses* XIII (the same story), and Virgil, *Eclogues* II (the unrequited love of Corydon for Alexis), VI and VIII. It is worth noting that Virgil, in these the earliest of his works, was much influenced by Theocritus, so that the countryside of his poetry is more the Sicily of the Greek poet than his own Lombard plains. This is not so in the case of Lorenzo, who, even at this early stage, displays his characteristically keen eye for the natural scene. Maier was the first to note a similarity between the late section on roses (lines 163–80) and a passage in an elegy, "De rosis nascentibus", which was popular in medieval anthologies of Latin poems;[103] it was ascribed to Virgil until 1517, and subsequently to Ausonius (a fourth-century poet from Bordeaux), but in both cases incorrectly, and it remains anonymous. The linguistic similarity between "Collige, virgo, rosas" and "Cogli la rosa, o ninfa" is obvious; but equally obvious are the substantial divergences, Lorenzo's lines creating a mainly naturalistic scene quite different from the overtly symbolic Latin one.

Some of Poliziano's lines come to mind when one reads *Corinto*, as was noted by Carducci;[104] Maier suggests numerous cross-references, most of which are only casual linguistic similarities, while Martelli notes what may be an actual borrowing by Poliziano (*Stanze*, II. 7) from *Corinto* (lines 1 and 9).[105] The use of myths like that of Polyphemus is too common in the genre to be of significance, and much the same can be said of the image of the rose as a symbol of the ephemeral. One cannot speak of influences or borrowings between the two poets because we cannot be sure who wrote what first; and while they express the same commonplace sentiments, they do so in distinctly different styles, similar only in being memorable. Poliziano's famous octave "Trema la mammoletta verginella" (*Stanze*, I. 78) or his *ballata* "I' mi trovai, fanciulle, un bel mattino" or his *Serenata* will exemplify this at once. The Petrarchan image of flowers growing where the beloved walks has been much used by poets, and Poliziano's superb octave (*Stanze*, I. 55) is quite different from lines 68–72 of *Corinto*. And what is to be gained by noting verbal similarities like Lorenzo's "i bei crin d'oro" (line 73) and Poliziano's "i be' crin d'auro" (*Stanze*, I. 105), especially a century after Laura was so described? When two poets are drawing closely on the same tradition, such finds are quite predictable.

Lorenzo's "tecnica ad intarsio" (Orvieto's apt phrase for the poet's technique of juxtaposing pieces from different sources to create a unified inlay)[106] is particularly evident in *Corinto*, which blends, with varying degrees of success, the classical bucolic tradition with two native Italian ones, that of the *stilnovisti* and Petrarch, and that of popular rustic poetry.[107] Each contributes something noteworthy. The myth of Echo underlies some fine lines that through their assonance and alliteration express Corinto's melancholic, plaintive mood; similarly the myth of Narcissus is the background to lines where the motif of water and its inevitable association with tears are first exploited for self-pity and then used to lead into a totally different scene of self-congratulatory satisfaction. The exquisitely drawn scene in which Galatea is imagined dancing on the grass, with the luxuriant blending of golden hair and varied colours of flowers and vegetation in a harmony of nature, expressed in the rhythms of water and birds, is completely *stilnovista* with touches of Petrarch. The diametrical opposite of this delicacy is the grotesque bragging of Corinto as superman; this is a curious piece of inlay work where, in a classical context of Pan,

Diana and Jove and against a background of Theocritus and Ovid, we have the jocular tone of rustic hyperbole, with touches of Vallera, and the sensible voice of the successful Tuscan farmer appraising his produce. Corinto emerges as a psychologically contradictory character, a mixture of well-read, wan and weeping lover (in current terminology, a wet), of gentle person caring for the welfare of his beloved, of conceited boaster and sensible realist. If the poem has a touch of the autobiographical, then perhaps the young Lorenzo is reflected in the composite nature of his created character.

Both *Corinto* and the *Uccellagione* open with *luminosità*, one lunar, the other solar, giving us memorable lines. Lorenzo repeatedly surprises us with details of the natural scene. *Corinto* is no exception, and what Carducci found in the *Stanze* is also present here: "amore alla descrizione, quasi scientifica, quasi a catalogo, delle produzioni diverse della natura".[108] The poet excels himself in the description of roses, written some twenty years after the preceding section—hence the noticeable change of mood at this point. Corinto's words have been harsh, and there is cruelty in the story of Philomela; but he then slips into a reflection on roses revealing a meditative and sophisticated self that is most unlike the swarthy braggart of the earlier lines. There is no originality in taking the rose as a symbol of the speedy passing of youth and beauty; we find it as far back as *Idylls*, XXIII. 27 (ascribed until recently, albeit incorrectly, to Theocritus): "Fair is the rose also, yet time withers it."[109] But Lorenzo creates an unforgettable version. In the rarefied atmosphere between dawn and sunrise, reinforced by the exquisite elegance of "vaghe ciglie" (no plain *occhi* here), the gold of dawn gives way to white and red, and later green, and the rosebuds become animated as in a ballet sequence. The poet sets the scene in the past tense but as soon as he begins to describe the transformation of the roses in minute detail he switches to the present ("spiega"), thereby giving timelessness to the phenomenon of transience. There is hardly a more severe and yet poignant statement on the passing of youth than "che vana cosa è il giovenil fiorire", and the *terzina* that follows it, if chilling in its truth, is one of the most beautiful that Lorenzo ever wrote.

To enjoy to the full Lorenzo's high poetic achievement at the end of *Corinto* it is necessary to read the reconstructed text. The traditional text with both roses and fruit-trees has been negatively criticized, and the matter is well expressed by the finest reader of the poem, Bruno Maier. On the subject of the lines which begin with the garden and then zoom in on details of individual rosebuds, he writes: "La rappresentazione si fa subito minuta e precisa, con un procedimento che vorrei definire *cinematografico*, per il passaggio graduale dalla visione complessiva e distante al primo piano ed allo scorcio vicino."[110] The "venatura di sincera e delicata malinconia" running through the passage is crystallized in line 180 ("che vana cosa è il giovenil fiorire"), which Maier describes as "tra i [versi] piú intensi che Lorenzo abbia scritto, come poeta della giovinezza e dell'inesorabile trascorrere dell'umana esistenza". But in the ensuing autumnal variation on the scene (the fruit-trees) he finds a "palese sintomo di scadimento dell'arte sua [...]. Un pezzo di bravura, non di poesia."[111] His assessment is unduly harsh, but his sense of a disharmony between the sections is valid; and, we might add, there is also an unnecessary repetition. Much the same thinking prompted Martelli to examine the traditional ending of the poem in the light of the *terzina* that had not been incorporated into the text. The poem's last line—the imperative "Cogli la rosa, o ninfa, or che è il bel tempo"—provided a strong clue. When this line is printed after the variation on autumn fruits (formerly lines 181–92) it is dislocated in terms of imagery and detached from the subdued thinking from which it emanates; it seems an aphoristic, independent ending. Martelli's textual restoration shows how Lorenzo, removing the lines on the fruit-trees, turned this line "da semplice frase proverbiale, una delle tante impiegate con valore di massima conclusiva nei sonetti del tirocinio" into "un punto d'arrivo d'un tema che colmava di sé gli ultimi versi".[112] The "second" example, of trees and flowers turned into fruits, is poetically discordant with the previous lines, and does not make a good sequence as it labours the point; but it remains, *pace* Maier, a fine piece. It was a good enough ending until Lorenzo found a better one—a fact that he recognized.

Whichever ending of *Corinto* we take, it is one of desolation as nature completes its cycle in death. The rosebud opens to reach full bloom, then its petals fall and languish on the ground; the fruits ("i dolci pomi") are picked from the tree and the boughs "di frutti e

fronde alfin si spogliono." *Ambra* begins precisely at this point:
"Fuggita è la stagion, che avea conversi/i fiori in pomi già maturi
e colti"; the similarity of language matches the similarity of mood,
as the chill of autumn develops into the cold of winter. This latter
season dominates the first twenty-two octaves out of a total of forty-
eight, and it is not surprising that, along with manuscripts which
leave it untitled, we have some that call the poem *Descriptio hiemis*,
and *Descritione del verno* ("Description of Winter"). It was first
printed privately in 1791, by William Roscoe, who gave it the title
Ambra, from the story told in its second half. By this title it has
remained known, though the editor of the 1985 critical edition
(Bessi) gives it both titles; and that perhaps best reflects the enigma
of the poem. Certain features of the manuscripts, especially the
variants, leave open the possibility that the poem is not in a
definitive form, that Lorenzo considered it an "open" text, to be
revised[113]—perhaps even, as Martelli suggests,[114] to be incorporated in some final version of the *Stanze*. Orvieto regards it as a
fragment,[115] and Martelli had previously expressed the same view,
adding nonetheless that it is "una delle piú belle liriche laurenzia-
ne".[116] I have argued elsewhere that the poem has thematic cohesion,[117] while the detailed textual work carried out by Rossella
Bessi indicates that it is equally possible to read it as two sections
written at different times.[118] This raises the familiar and disconcerting
problem of dating. The evidence used by scholars in establishing
1486 as the date *post quem* for *Ambra* rests on two of Poliziano's
Sylvæ, the third and fourth. To the former belongs Poliziano's own
poem *Ambra* (1485), in which he refers to Lorenzo's villa Ambra as
"mei Laurentis amor" (line 518), and tells a different version of the
nymph's story; to the latter belong his *Nutricia* (1486) with the
famous list of poems by Lorenzo, which does not include the one
under discussion—presumably, but not necessarily, because it had
not yet been written. The other line of argument adopted is that the
poem must have been written after the villa was built in 1485–86.
None of this convinces Bessi, especially since recent research has
shown that Lorenzo acquired the property at Poggio a Caiano as
early as 1474 (not in 1479 as traditionally accepted) and that his
plans for an estate of substantial size took shape over several years.
It is reasonable to surmise that the poem's gestation may also have
lasted some time. Ambra was the name of the house, of the estate,

and of the brook that flowed into the river Ombrone, itself a tributary of the Arno: it is not therefore necessary to assume that in the poem the name refers specifically to the first of these. In the story the chaste nymph Ambra, when bathing in the waters of the Ombrone, arouses the passion of the river god; he pursues her and as she flees his embraces he calls upon the Arno to help him; in flight from two gods, Ambra prays to Diana for safety and is turned into a rock. The Ombrone was prone to flooding and Lorenzo had a dam built in August–September 1485, which was certainly completed by November; it seems incongruous to Bessi that Lorenzo should have written the story of Ambra beginning in the present tense (see Octave 23) if the possibility of flooding no longer existed.[119] On the other hand, the story is told retrospectively, and while it may be logical to write a poem on a flood only while the threat of the event is real, poetic imagination works differently. Regrettably, the inevitable conclusion is that none of these arguments is strong enough to help us to date *Ambra* with any degree of precision.

Like *Corinto* and the *Uccellagione, Ambra* has a striking opening with details that evince sharp observation of the natural scene, while in the second octave the fabulous world of classical mythology is introduced. There is careful interplay of these two elements in the ensuing stanzas, with frequent personification of features of the Tuscan countryside. The harsh season of winter, when the omnipotent forces of nature are unleashed against powerless man, turns into a drama with the elemental forces of the universe as *personæ*, and finds expression in many powerful and memorable lines. The transition from the description of winter to the story of Ambra is smooth: the victorious waters have seized space formerly denied them, and Ombrone embraces the "piccola isoletta" Ambra (Octave 23). This is the cue for Lorenzo to tell a love story as unreal as the existence of river gods but realistic in its features and details, as he excels in giving concrete expression to the elemental emotions in man, as deep and as strong as the uncontrolled forces of nature. Equilibrium is maintained between the two parts: the increasing intensity of Ombrone's desire is comparable to the increasing momentum of the flood; he burns with love as the earth burns in its volcanic activity. The animal world present in the first part reappears in the second in three fine similes that describe the fleeing nymph (Octaves 27, 38, 43). Ambra in her chastity is as cold as the ice of winter, and this ultimately annihilates her humanity. The story culminates in a surrealistic, totally frozen, lifeless scene.

When we consider the theme of *Ambra* we can read the poem, as Martelli does, in a manner that is "strettamente dottrinale: come l'amore dei sensi porti alla morte dell'oggetto stesso del nostro amore"; it can then be linked to the end of the "Proemio" to the *Comento* with its allegorical interpretation of the myth of Orpheus, "nel senso che chi non sappia morire alla vita della materia, non riesce a raggiungere la perfezione della felicità."[120] But the poem may also be read in a completely different manner, compatible with Lorenzo's awareness of life's brevity and of man's compelling need for physical immortality through reproduction. If read in this manner, the poem acquires cohesion and the various elements that may otherwise seem disparate are brought together: the winter scene, the intense sexual passion, the devastation caused by rejection. Support for this reading is provided by the poem's literary allusions, which take us to sources that have in common with Ambra's story the lack of a happy fulfilment of love. The very nature of the story brings to mind Ovid's *Metamorphoses*, and in particular the transformations of Daphne, Aglauros and Arethusa: each of these narratives has a tragic ending and a background of frustrated love. Virgil's Camilla (*Æneid*, VII. 806ff) is a loveless warrior maiden. Dante's "Io son venuto al punto de la rota", a poem that underlies the first eighteen octaves of *Ambra*, is a wintry poem on the intensity of frustrated passion, and the cranes evoke their fellows in the canto of Dante's ill-fated lovers, Paolo and Francesca. There is a link with Aristeo's lament in Poliziano's *Orfeo*, and Octave 45 evokes the same poet's sad *ballata* "Dolorosa e meschinella". Other poems of Lorenzo's echoed here are also ones of unhappiness, be it his desolate sonnet "Dolci pensier, non vi partite ancora", in which he regrets the departure of his thoughts of love, or his "Amor, poi ch'io lasciai tuo gentil regno", where the poet laments his loveless state. Octave 46 recalls "Non de' verdi giardini ornati e colti", the sonnet of a distraught Venus running to a dying Adonis. The rhyme *fugge/ strugge* of Octave 35 reflects the prominent use Lorenzo made of it, as in "Donna, vano è il pensier" and "Chi tempo aspetta", where it is associated with the transience of life. These poems invite one to love while one has youth and beauty, a message identical to that of *Corinto*. There the appeal to love is in a context of fertility, something wholly negated in the Ambra story: because Ambra rejects the appeal, she is turned neither into a tree, as Daphne was, nor into a fountain, like Arethusa (and both are images of life), but into a rock round which the waters freeze. Life is negated in all its aspects. The fiery passion, comparable to the turbulent force of winter, and developed in the heat of summer, leads to a chilling finale of wintry congealment in "rigidi cristalli", the objective correlative of the frigidity of the nymph. The portrayal of Ombrone is charged with sexuality, the image of the horn being a symbol of the river's fertilizing power, and the nakedness of the nymph and her pursuer being mentioned six times in the space of eight octaves. As the passion of the river god is frustrated, its fire yields to ice, as life to death. Ombrone's lament brings the poem to its climactic close. The god, with his deeply human range of feelings, mourns the loss of life brought about by the rejection of love, and his lament is set not in the seasons of love and fertility, banished from the start, but in the destructive and alien one of winter. The wheel has come full circle. We have moved from Corinto's Galatea and her scorn of love, to Ambra's rejection of Ombrone in her faithfulness to Lauro and the virginal Diana; but the negation of love means the negation of life.

An exuberant celebration of life, and of love because it engenders life, is to be found in Lorenzo's *canzoni a ballo* and *canti carnascia-leschi*, two genres that are almost indistinguishable as they share themes and metrical intricacies. The *canzone a ballo*, or *ballata*, was by definition inextricably linked to dance music, and its ancestry was both popular and literary. The *stilnovisti* took it from its rural home and altered it into a highly polished and stylish product, as is evident in the *ballate* written by Dante, Guido Cavalcanti and Cino da Pistoia. But this did not endanger the popular strain that "smacked of the soil and the streets, of bucolic pranks and primitive banter, of pungent ribaldry and unashamed appetites."[121] Lorenzo— and Poliziano as well—blended the two, combining the popular with the sophisticated. Lorenzo left us thirty-two *canzoni a ballo* of very great variety, though nearly all focus on the theme of love; in many cases it is sheer sexual indulgence, but nonetheless a joyous life-giving force that men are unwise to reject, as the spring of man's life comes but once. Many of the songs are humorously ribald and characterized by a healthy celebration of the elemental forces of nature heralded by Boccaccio, though these same songs were also called the dregs of "oscenità plebea" by a stern De Sanctis.[122] This may perhaps be applicable to "Ragionavasi di sodo" in the present selection. Some of these poems, however, contain thoughtful reflections, tinged with varying degrees of sadness, on the brevity of youth, beauty and the pleasures they give. Lorenzo's writing on this quite hackneyed theme is memorable and haunting. There is an urgency that must have sprung from an awareness that his own life would be brief, what with conspiracies when he looked death in the face, his failing health and family history in this respect, and family bereavements like the untimely death of Clarice in 1488. This is the mood most characteristic of Lorenzo's poetry, and it generated two outstanding poems in "Donna, vano è il pensier" and "Chi tempo aspetta".

Of the first of these, one of Lorenzo's last (1490) and arguably his best, Martelli has written:

> Può rivelarci, forse come nessun' altra [poesia], a quale livello di perfezione giungesse ed in quale clima spirituale si muovesse l'ultimo Lorenzo.
>
> Nella brevità stessa della ballata sta gran parte della sua bellezza: e, piú che nella sua brevità, nel giro compatto dello schema metrico (ABbC dEED AFfC), che, ricollegando e per le rime e per l'identità della struttura l'ultima alla prima strofa, riesce a creare una sorta di magico spazio, entro il quale si compone armonicamente il profondo dolore, che pur costituisce la materia del canto.[123]

The poem opens with the assertion of a truth we cannot escape: "Donna, vano è il pensier che mai non crede/che venga il tempo della sua vecchiezza." There is an arresting initial vocative— "Donna"—that both singles out the beloved and yet removes all identity from her, as she is emblematic of the totality of womankind to whom the message is addressed. This opening is stark and sombre, and we miss the gaiety common in these songs, where the poet's usual audiences consist of "donne belle" or "donne gentil, giovani adorni". The belief in the eternity of youth is dismissed as "vano", a richly Petrarchan epithet that also reminds us of Dante's Fortuna dispensing "li ben vani" ("vani" because, be they good or bad, they are useless in relation to life's ultimate purpose). It is an epithet Lorenzo uses forcefully, whether in the opening line of his sonnet "Quanto sia vana ogni speranza nostra" or in his *sestina* "Amor tenuto m'ha di tempo in tempo", where he writes:

> Vana è ogni mortal nostra fatica [...]

> Le nostre passion' quanto sien vane,
> quanto il pianto e 'l dolore è fermo e certo,
> e quanto invano ogni mortale sdegno,
> quanto è perduta ogni umana fatica,
> mostra quel che a fuggir mai non è stanco,
> che ogni cosa ne porta e fura, il tempo.

> Passa via il tempo, e le mie opre vane
> conoscer fammi, e ch'io son stanco e certo
> di mia fatica e me medesmo ho a sdegno.   (lines 19, 31–39)

In "Donna, vano è il pensier" alliteration links several key words: *vano, vecchiezza, venga, vola, vita, vivere*. The rhyme *vecchiezza/giovinezza* polarizes two high points of human existence: the exuberance of youth and the decay of old age. *Giovinezza* is in the same position in lines 3 (where it ends the *settenario*) and 12 (where it ends the first hemistich, which is a *settenario*); it also rhymes internally with *bellezza*, the condition to which it is inextricably linked. Indeed the poem is full of what Orvieto terms "persistenze foniche e variazioni polifoniche"; but Orvieto, by limiting his appreciation to the sheer artistry of the poem, greatly reduces Lorenzo's extraordinary achievement in matching content with sound and rhythm.[124] The meditation of line 4 ("Abbi sempre a star ferma in una tempre") recalls "sola sta ferma e sempre dura Morte", the final line of "Quanto sia vana ogni speranza nostra"; it reminds us that it is not youth but death that is the one unchanging and constant factor in man's life. *Vola, fugge,* and *presto*—all pithy, incisive words— emphasize the speed with which the fulness of manhood wanes and the futility of our trying to resist. The Dantesque *nostra vita* shifts the poem from the individual *donna* of the opening, and from the 1490 carnival, to an occasion "sanza tempo tinta" involving all mankind. The image of the flower must be read in terms of the "giovenil fiorire" of *Corinto* as the message here is that addressed to Galatea. The word *merzede* shares not only its rhyme with *crede* in line 1 but also its religious overtones: woman has a duty to love, as denial of love will mean a denial of life itself—the message of *Ambra*. The final word of the poem, *sempre*, reduces the image of youth and beauty created by the words accompanying it, by bringing us back to the first quatrain: it rhymes with *tempre*, which in turn rhymes internally with *sempre*; and these words recall Lorenzo's inescapable statement on death.[125]

The rhyme *fugge/strugge* is effectively used in this poem and, like *vano*, it has a strong Petrarchan link, appearing at least eight times in Petrarch's verse. It conveys effectively the transitory and destructive nature of time; Lorenzo uses it for the *ripresa* of "Chi tempo aspetta", where the two words end alternate stanzas, thereby giving additional unity to the composition and increasing its haunting musicality. There are several verbal echoes between "Donna, vano è il pensiero" and "Chi tempo aspetta", poems which have fundamentally the same theme and exemplify Lorenzo's ability to devise very different variations on it. "Chi tempo aspetta" consists entirely of hendecasyllables, and each of the four stanzas elaborates the existential points baldly stated in "Donna, vano è il pensier", where the mood's incisiveness depended on brevity. Here the poet relishes the joys of youth: "Oh quante cose in gioventú si prezza! / Quanto son belli i fiori in primavera!" There is no greater sorrow than to bear the guilt of having misused our time; the Dantesque echo here (Francesca) serves to increase the idea of guilt. There is always intensity coupled with a sense of urgency in Lorenzo's bidding us to make the most of our time as "giovinèzza passa a poco a poco". Here the urgency is created by a clever use of short, incisive words and fast rhythms following slow ones, as in the line "di usare il tempo ben, che vola e fugge". The intensity is conveyed by anaphora, "questo è quel mal che" opening two consecutive lines. A hint of *stilnovismo* in the "gentil core" of "Donna, vano è il pensier" is expanded in this poem to embrace an image of youths and ladies singing and dancing, which we may also connect to the *ballata* Fiammetta sings at the end of the tenth day of the *Decameron*.

Fiammetta's "gelosia", the "gentil core" and the "foco d'amore" all reappear in "Chi non è innamorato", where the dance rhythm is at its strongest. The dance is a rite in love-making, reserved exclusively for the inner circle of those initiated in love. Others are excluded, and the poet propounds a set of hypotheses to strengthen the resolve of those within the circle. Of this poem Bowra writes: "Lorenzo is certain that it is right for men to love in this way and wishes the movement of the dance to stir their lurking, shy desires into confidence and action."[126] The movement of the dance is conveyed by a clever combination of hendecasyllables and *settenari*, the latter predominating. Lorenzo achieved the much more reflective mood of "Donna, vano è il pensier" partly by a dominant use of hendecasyllables and the intercalation of the shorter lines to give a sense of urgency. This metrical difference between the two poems also reflects a difference of theme: Love and those in his bondage predominate in "Chi non è innamorato", and there is only a slight hint that the opportunity to love will not return, at the poem's close:

> Non ha dato Natura
> tanta bellezza a voi
> acciò che poi sia il tempo male usato.

Orvieto somewhat unsympathetically finds "una persistente banalizzazione della tematica erotica" in the dance songs, and "un fittissimo reticolo di doppi sensi" in the carnival ones; in both cases he believes that if we had access to the choreography of the street festivals that were so much a feature of Florentine public life "la banalità del testo verrebbe cosí ampiamente riscattata dai prolungati effetti musicali."[127] We certainly diminish their impact by removing them from the music and spectacle to which they belong. The festivities that incorporated the *canti carnascialeschi* either preceded Lent, in the period known as *carnevale* (still celebrated in Italian cities), or ushered in the feast of the patron saint of Florence, John the Baptist, which was celebrated on 24 June, midsummer's day. On these occasions *trionfi* and *carri* passed through the streets and squares: *trionfi* were floats bearing the personifications of mythological beings or allegorical virtues, while *carri* were highly decorated wagons bearing representatives of different trades and crafts. Another popular festival was *Calendimaggio* (May Day), when it was customary for young men to serenade their ladies and offer them a *maio* (garland of flowering branches). The young men generally went around masked (often as women), hence the name *mascherate*. Those *canti carnascialeschi* which celebrate a particular trade or craft (often with *doppi sensi*) were presumably sung all year round.[128] There is no evidence that the *canto carnascialesco* was perceived as a genre before Anton Francesco Grazzini (1503–84), known as Lasca, used the term in his famous collection entitled *Trionfi, carri, mascherate o canti carnascialeschi,* in which he attributes the development of this type of composition to Lorenzo, though it was in fact less innovatory than Lasca stated.[129] There is such confusion in the textual tradition of both dance and carnival songs that today only eleven *canti carnascialeschi* are ascribed with some certainty to Lorenzo. These include the "Canzona di Bacco" and the "Canzona de' sette pianeti", composed for the 1490 carnival, which are more correctly termed *trionfi* or *carri*—a genre that did not make use of sexual metaphor. The nine *mascherate* or *canti carnascialeschi* proper belong to a more popular tradition; they have an average of about fifty lines each, and all but one use fairly explicit sexual metaphor as a comic expedient. Some, like the "Canzona de' confortini", given in our selection, can be dated to 1474–78 (it is worth bearing in mind that public celebrations were forbidden in the decade following the Pazzi conspiracy). It is obvious from Lasca's title that he uses the term *canto carnascialesco* generically, to include compositions for the first three specified types of spectacle, which are not synonymous. Manuscripts and incunabula call these songs *canzone per andare in maschera,* and their distinctive characteristic, in so far as we can detect one, was a link with spectacle. Song had a natural place in celebratory spectacle, and we know that Lorenzo had a marked interest in music; it is not surprising, then, that he should have raised the status of what must have been popular but rudimentary rhyming jingles and given them a new sophisticated character. Lasca tells us that "il primo canto, o Mascherata, che si cantasse in questa guisa fu d'huomini che vendevano berriquocoli e confortini [sweetmeats], composta a tre voci da un certo Arrigo Tedesco."[130] This, as we know already, is the Italian name of Heinrich Isaac, the musician whom Lorenzo invited to Florence in 1484. We know that Antonio Squarcialupi, the cathedral organist, also set a number of Lorenzo's poems to music, and from Lorenzo's letters it is clear that he also employed other musicians for the same purpose. Some of Lorenzo's *laude* were set to the same melodies as some of these profane songs, and it is through the music extant for one of the *laude* that Rubsamen has plausibly suggested what may have been the music for "Quant' è bella giovinezza", otherwise known as the "Canzona di Bacco".[131]

This is one of the two *canti* chosen here, as is *di rigore* in any anthology that limits selection even to only one poem by Lorenzo. Whether it is his best is largely a matter of personal taste; what is undisputed is that it is a most successful poem juxtaposing the contradictory moods of assertive merrymaking and a hauntingly melancholic refrain: "Chi vuol esser lieto, sia,/di doman non c'è certezza." Olga Zorzi Pugliese traces this ambiguity to the very myth of Bacchus as interpreted in the Renaissance—a Bacchus drawn not just from Ovid (*Metamorphoses* XI) but also from Anacreon and Euripides. She writes: "Sempre ambiguo, anche una volta cresciuto, egli rimane giovane e di apparenza effeminata [...] dispensatore ai mortali sia di gioia che angoscia."[132] It is easy to visualize the float to which Lorenzo's song belonged, with Bacchus and Ariadne surrounded by merry-making nymphs and young satyrs indulging in a ritual of love. These would be followed by a comically drunken Silenus, and by Midas, serving as a stern reminder that gold is not the source of happiness. The poem moves in a series of circles with its theme stated at the beginning and repeated at the end of each stanza. There is a crescendo of frenzy typical of Bacchanalia, conveyed by the fast rhythm, which explodes in the strong beats of:

> Ciascun suoni, balli e canti,
> arda di dolcezza il core,
> non fatica, non dolore!

All thought of the morrow must be hounded away with drink and loud music; but subtly, persistently and quite audibly we are reminded of the morrow's uncertainty. Bowra writes: "The figures of Bacchus and Ariadne might have been used for an occasion of unclouded delight, but Lorenzo uses them to shape his own anxieties about the fleeting character of youth and the uncertainty of tomorrow"; while Orvieto finds the poem "non solo pregna di teosofia ficiniana ma anche parafrasi scritturale e, se si vuole, un tragico canto di appressamento alla morte"[133]

In the manuscripts our second *canto carnascialesco* bears the title "Canzona de' sette pianeti". The seven planets, or heavenly bodies (the Moon, Mercury, Venus, the Sun, Mars, Jupiter and Saturn), in a direct address to their listeners, after attributing to themselves all human types and all the achievements and failures of mankind, advise mortals to follow the bidding of Venus, goddess of love. The poem expresses views that are not inconsistent with Lorenzo's basic position on astrology; a clear statement of this is to be found in his religious play, where Jupiter indeed moves his heaven but is in turn subject to God (*Rappresentazione*, 130. 7–8). Although the exhortation of this song is similar to that of the preceding one, with which it also has linguistic links, the mood is more serious, less frenzied, and more suited to expression in hendecasyllables. Spring, the season of Venus, bids us love—"ciascun s'allegri, ciascun s'innamori"—, but we cannot escape the fact that we do this in full awareness of the transience of "questa brieve vita". The central stanza, on Venus, implies that in love there may be more sorrow than joy, and Martelli, who reads this carnival song in the light of *De summo bono* and of Lorenzo's belief that an unerring God has made the way to perfection dark and difficult (*Comento*, IV), percep-tively writes:

> Il cammino dell'uomo toccato dal fuoco della dolce stella s'innalza dal sereno, originario uniformarsi agl'istinti della natura delle fiere, dei pesci e degli uccelli, fino alla chiara, ma malinconica-mente lontana luminosità degli astri: ed è strada oscura e difficile, una lunga storia di patimenti e d'errori, confortata soltanto dalla remota luce di Venere, pegno e fine dell'umana ascesi.[134]

One is reluctant to disappoint the reader whose anxiety about dating matches that of Laurentian scholars, but justice cannot be done to the intricacies of dating these compositions without boring even the most determined. There is enough evidence to sustain the view that Lorenzo wrote *canzoni a ballo* from the mid-1460s,[135] and we know from Poliziano's *Nutricia* that he had certainly done so by 1486, though they are mentioned in the same breath as Lorenzo's juvenilia. Additional proof lies in the fact that "Chi non è in-namorato" was included in the *Raccolta aragonese*, which precedes Poliziano's poem by a decade. Zanato's inclusion of "Donna, vano è il pensier" among the early poems of the *Canzoniere* creates a new problem and suggests a different history for a poem which had been dated with some degree of certainty. It is a salutary reminder that hypotheses fill the disconcerting gaps in the documentary evi-dence. Martelli linked the writing of "Donna, vano è il pensier" to the 1490 carnival, and because of its thematic and linguistic links with "Chi tempo aspetta" he was inclined to place the latter with it, and both of them with the two *trionfi* here selected. The evidence Martelli used for associating these carnival songs with February 1490 has not so far been contested.[136]

Another dating that has been challenged, however, is that of the next poem in our selection, the *lauda* "O Dio, o sommo Bene". It has generally been seen as later than the 1490 carnival, but according to its most recent editor, Toscani, while it remains a late work it precedes that carnival.[137] Although it has the same metrical form as the "Canzona de' sette pianeti" it is not sung to the melody of any carnival song by Lorenzo, from which Toscani deduces that it must have been already written or Lorenzo would have re-used the tune of his own song. Toscani has collated nine *laude*, or religious hymns, of certain authorship from manuscripts and early printed sources. The evidence suggests that this was a late activity of Lorenzo's, no doubt belonging to the phase when Savonarolan influence had caused him to move away from his *stilnovismo ficiniano*. It is reasonable to suppose that "Quant' è grande la bellezza", "O maligno e duro core" and "Peccator', su tutti quanti" were written after the carnival of 1490; and from a letter to Pietro Dovizi da Bibbiena we learn that Lorenzo wrote *laude* in Holy Week 1491.[138] Toscani suggests that "Ben arà duro core" may have been written in 1492, and thus in the closing months of Lorenzo's life.

As was the case with *canzoni a ballo* and *canti carnascialeschi*, there was an intimate relationship between *laude* and music. They were sung by religious confraternities, which were groups of lay persons committed to piety and works of charity. Lorenzo was associated with several of these throughout his life, and he wrote his play for one to which his children belonged.[139] All his *laude* but one are preceded by the rubric "Cantasi come [...]", as the music of these hymns was generally taken from a popular song. Moreover, not just the metre and rhyme-scheme but even some of the concepts of the song were re-used. Expressions of love for a lady could be turned into a hymn in praise of the Virgin. It is not difficult to see on which *trionfo* Lorenzo based his *lauda* "Quant'è grande la bellezza", and a comparison between the "Canzona di Bacco" and the opening of the hymn makes the relationship all the clearer:

Quanto è grande la bellezza
di te, Vergin santa e pia!
Ciascun laudi te, Maria;
ciascun canti in gran dolcezza!

Colla tua bellezza tanta
la Bellezza innamorasti.
O Bellezza eterna e santa,
di Maria bella infiammasti!
Tu di amor l'Amor legasti,
Vergin santa, dolce e pia.
Ciascun laudi te, Maria;
ciascun canti in gran dolcezza.

Both compositions are in *ottonari*, rhyming xyyx ababbyyx, with identical rhythm. It is the printed rather than the manuscript tradition that gives the rubric referring to a known song, but, as Toscani shows, this is not always reliable.[140] For three hymns wrong sources were given, though they went unchallenged down the centuries until Toscani made alternative and more plausible suggestions. "Vieni a me, peccatore" has the rubric "Cantasi a modo proprio composto per Isaac", which is unusual in that as a rule music was not specially composed for these hymns.

Only two of Lorenzo's hymns consist entirely of hendecasyllables: for four he used *ottonari* and for the other three, an alternation of hendecasyllables and *settenari*. As with the *canzoni a ballo*, those entirely in hendecasyllables are the more reflective ones, since the shorter line better suits liturgical songs of praise or penance. The meditative nature of "O Dio, o sommo Bene" is immediately apparent from both its format and its title; the latter recalls Lorenzo's philosophical-religious poem *De summo bono*, and the hymn draws considerably on the sixth *capitolo* of that poem in its expression of the belief that only God can give the peace for which the soul yearns. This is interwoven with the familiar *tema laurenziano* of the insatiable desire for something beyond our grasp as life flees and the promises of youth are not fulfilled. Like another of Lorenzo's *laude*, "Vieni a me, peccatore", "O Dio, o sommo Bene" gives expression to Christ's statements, "If any man thirst, let him come to me, and drink" (John 7. 37), and "He that shall drink of the water that I will give him shall not thirst for ever" (John 4. 13). Toscani has shown that the most direct influence on "O Dio, o sommo Bene" is St Augustine;[141] and, given the theme of the poem, it will not be difficult to link it to the much-quoted line from the opening of the *Confessions*, "Our hearts find no peace until they rest in You." Carducci, of whom one hardly thinks as a poet sympathetic to religious faith, wrote sensitively on this hymn, taking it together with "Poi ch'io gustai, Iesú": "Pare prorompere dall'intimo seno il dolore e l'affetto, come d'uomo stanco de' piaceri e de' triboli, del desiderare infinito e del posseder travaglioso. Nelle quali [laude] è anche da notare la ben temperata fusione delle idee platoniche con le cristiane."[142]

A change was taking place in Lorenzo's interests, and it is reflected both in the *laude* and in the religious play—works which are as rich in Biblical references as they are lacking in classical ones. The cultural substratum of Lorenzo's final works is no longer the literature of antiquity, revered by the humanists, but Scripture, as preached by Savonarola. It was this fervent Dominican who induced Lorenzo to move away from Ficinian neo-Platonism in favour of a less ambiguous religious belief. A crucial document is the friar's *Apologeticus*, sent to the press in 1491, in which he asserts that it was sheer calumny to accuse him of being an enemy of literary and philosophical studies; he did not condemn these, rather it was the misuse of such studies that he found reprehensible. His thinking in this tract is summarized thus by Martelli:

> Filosofia e poesia, inutili o dannose alla fede cristiana quando si ispirino alla vanagloria del secolo, possono essere utili, se non necessarie, quando siano subordinate a Dio, unico amore ed unico scopo del vero cristiano; [...] veri poeti, veri filosofi cristiani sono solo coloro per la bocca dei quali parla la scienza di Dio, non quella, ventosa e fumosa, dell'uomo.[143]

Lorenzo responded to these distinctions, as his hymns and play testify, and in the closing months of his life there developed between him and the friar "una oggettiva coincidenza d'interessi e di proponimenti".[144] The two men were to some extent interdependent: Savonarola needed Lorenzo as the secular channel for his God-given mission, and Lorenzo wished to strengthen his position with what he had often lacked, ecclesiastical approval. Not that it was difficult for Lorenzo to accept the friar's ideas; they were, in essence, those of Ficino in his *De christiana religione* of 1473–74. But there was a difference, and it was one of priorities. The motto of the "inquietante figura di santo mondano", as Martelli aptly describes Ficino, was "Miscere poetica philosophicis" ["Mingle poetic things with philosophical things"].[145] He created a myth that blended poetry, with its strong appeal to the senses, and philosophy, with its strong appeal to the intellect; but it was not clear exactly how the two were to be combined. For Lorenzo the balance was different; his was a philosophical poetry rather than a poetic philosophy. Savonarola occasioned further evolution in the same direction, leading to a view of poetry as acceptable within certain terms but nonetheless the last and lowest of the rational sciences.

Many a writer on Lorenzo has mused on the depth and sincerity of his religious commitment, though why one should doubt it any more than, say, Michelangelo's is puzzling. There was nothing so evil or treacherous in his life as to lend credence to the notion that his religion was all a hypocritical covering-up of tyrannical rule. On the other hand religion could certainly bring political advantages. Savonarola himself wrote that "molte volte il tiranno, massime in tempo d'abbondanza e quiete, occupa il popolo in spettacoli e feste, acciocché pensi a sé e non a lui"—though this has to be read as a zealot's rhetoric, not a historian's objective record.[146] The score between Lorenzo and his God must be long settled, and his sincerity is both inscrutable and immaterial to us as readers of his poetry. We shall never know the depth, if any, of his religious belief, but what we know with certainty is the depth of his religious knowledge, established in part by the study of the language of the *Rappresentazione di san Giovanni e Paolo* undertaken by Martelli. Martelli shows how "la Scrittura invade in forze il tessuto dell'opera", from which it is evident that "almeno i testi sacri, non solo [Lorenzo] li aveva mandati a memoria, ma quella memoria doveva averli gelosamente custoditi con una lettura forse quotidiana, certo con una intensa loro meditazione."[147]

The *sacra rappresentazione* (approximately, "mystery play") was an important form of drama in Renaissance Italy. Its popularity in fifteenth-century Florence is attested by the number of surviving texts and by records of performances; but this popularity rested more on the perceived need for public expressions of religious devotion mixed with spectacle than on poetic merit, of which the plays are generally devoid. Nearly all the religious plays are, like Lorenzo's, in *ottava rima*, but an attempt at recitation of these texts reveals their inadequacy, with their clumsy, frequently end-stopped lines and their staccato quality as the *ottava* is broken up between various speakers. Recurring stock phrases, semantic reinforcement and commonplace sententiousness are other features of the texts, which are generally anonymous; it is quite likely that the organizers drew on stock texts which were adapted to suit the occasion. Lorenzo's play has most of the features of contemporary religious drama, but its style, content and construction are so sophisticated that an abyss separates it from other texts of its kind. The plays were often staged very elaborately, with appropriate musical accompaniment and dazzling spectacle, which no doubt compensated for the poverty of the texts. Lorenzo's play was staged in the most beautiful manner possible, as was recorded by one of the actors, Bartolomeo Masi, in his diary.[148] Masi's account of the event, delightful for its liveliness and important for its details, gives us a definite date of performance: Thursday, 17 February 1491, the second day of Lent (not the first, because the sets were not ready).[149] For the crispness of this information many a scholar is sincerely grateful.

These religious plays were usually performed by youths belonging to lay confraternities, and Lorenzo wrote his for the *compagnia* of St John the Baptist, to which his sons belonged. As the diarist records that all members of the *compagnia* were on stage, it is reasonable to assume that the Medici brothers themselves acted in the play; their father and other noteworthy citizens were in the audience. Some of the actors were probably younger than the statutory age for membership of such groups (thirteen), and boys played the parts not only of grown men but also of women—hence the text's request for forebearance (Octave 3). This request follows another for silence, "massimamente quando si canta" (1. 6), from which it is clear that music forms an integral part of the play. The stage directions specify that Octave 58 is to be sung, and it is possible that the other prayers (in Octaves 68 and 132) were sung as well. Where appropriate a musical interlude must have been used to represent the passing of time; music is implied by criers and heralds; and Constantine's call to "buffoni e cantator, chi suoni e danzi" (24. 8) is another cue for musical entertainment. Such moments may have been deliberately contrived by the playwright to allow some of the young actors to display their particular talents. Heinrich Isaac composed the music for this *rappresentazione*, and it is possible that his extant piece "A la bataglia" belongs to it—an opinion held by both Pirro and Ghisi.[150] The latter describes the piece as "un complesso ideale, per sonorità e timbro che si prestava soprattutto a esecuzioni all'aperto e al carattere eroico e guerresco del pezzo", and it seems therefore very suitable music for the rumbustious section of the fight against the Dacians.[151]

That the performance of Lorenzo's play outshone that of run-of-the-mill plays is not surprising, and may be seen as an external manifestation of the superior quality of the text itself. Yet again, Lorenzo picked up a well-established genre and transformed it into something distinctive. While the title leads one to expect the martyrdom of John and Paul (beheaded in Rome in 362 by order of Julian the Apostate), we come to realize that they are minor characters with small speaking parts, and only memorable—if at all—for their unquestioned commitment to martyrdom. Contrary to the established practice of having the stage occupied by divine personages or the eponymous saint, Lorenzo's play is dominated by characters who are not specifically "religious"—Constance, Gallican, Constantine, and Julian the Apostate, who has some of the best lines. John and Paul serve as a link between parts that would otherwise be disconnected, and make this highly episodic play a series of *tableaux*; but their martyrdom did not inspire Lorenzo. If turmoil and doubt ever gripped these saints, the struggle is over; the very texture of the speeches of John and Paul, redolent of Biblical songs of praise, reveals that they are not of this world.

The anomalies and inconsistencies in the plot may indicate hasty composition, but on the other hand the very nature of the *sacra rappresentazione* meant that its credibility did not lend itself to close scrutiny. Suspension of disbelief is vital in a genre based on faith in an omnipotent divinity. To demand historical accuracy is also to court disaster: the play reflects a source which was not historical at all but Jacopo da Varagine's *Legenda sanctorum*. This text, known popularly in English as the *Golden Legend*, had been composed around 1266 and had become extremely important throughout Western Europe. Lorenzo used stories from four separate chapters of it, appropriating not just the broad outlines but also several details,[152] and a comparison between his text and Jacopo's Latin prose reveals interesting linguistic similarities. One of the most obvious of many possible examples is the play's last line, "O Cristo Galileo, tu hai pur vinto", which renders Jacopo's "vicisti Galilæa, vicisti." Though similar linguistically, the two texts are markedly different in dramatic terms. Lorenzo, for instance, had enough artistic sensitivity to make the play end on this note. Not so Jacopo, with his morbid passion for torture, whether punishment for sin or martyrdom. He adds: "With these words he [Julian] died in much misery and his own people left him without burial. The Persians skinned him and his skin was turned into a rug for their king." The difference springs from the divergence of their purposes, Jacopo the devotional writer emphasizing retribution for wrongdoing, and Lorenzo the artist aiming at a good play albeit within the parameters of the religious performance. It is probably for this reason that the play lacks the usual ending with an angel dismissing the audience in an appropriate manner. The fact that Lorenzo follows the practice of having an angel open the play and outline its plot reveals his awareness of tradition; his decision to omit the angel's customary valediction can only be interpreted as a touch of fine artistic insight on his part: the dramatic finale thus retains its full impact, with the acknowledgement that life is brief and perfidious and that Christ, the Laurentian *sommo bene,* has won.

Christ's victory, manifested in the triumph of good over evil, is the foregone conclusion of all *sacre rappresentazioni,* and Lorenzo's, like the rest of them, has its measure of "devozion", "martíre" and "vendetta", as the angel announces in the second octave. And vengeance there certainly is, explicitly sanctioned by a robust and warlike Virgin Mary whose bidding to Mercury is: "Da te sien le mie ingiurie vendicate" and "Il cristian sangue vendicato sia" (Octave 141). The rise and fall of the younger Constantine cannot but strike us as a bizarre example of the speed of the Almighty in matters of retribution. A more Christian Christianity is shown by Constantine the elder in his sparing of the captive king's life (Octave 85), though the religious persuasion of the Emperor poses a problem in that in the earlier section of the play he is pagan, while this seems not to be the case later. In all of this Lorenzo can be said to be following the dictates of the genre, but his *Rappresentazione* is virtually unique in its political statements and its exploration of what Martelli has called a "grande tema: il rapporto tra teologia e politica, tra vita contemplativa e vita attiva".[153] Constantine's abdication speech and Julian's policy statements have received the most attention, in part because they have lent themselves to auto-biographical interpretation. Yet it is not in these passages that we find the real political crux, the conflict between total commitment to an inhuman Christianity and the human demands of daily survival. This is found quite early in the play, in the exchange between Constance and her father. Constantine's dilemma is that *ragion politica* demands that he give Gallican his daughter, thereby ensuring the state's safety and his own honour, whereas the moral obligation—the vow made by Constance when cured of leprosy—makes this impossible. It is she who solves it by advising her father to play for time, and to send Gallican on a long and difficult campaign (a worthy one, though possibly unnecessary), from which—she quite clearly implies—he might never return. The matter is sealed with a pledge which obviously lacks sincerity. This shrewd Constance co-exists with the gentle, loving creature whose healing and conversion are expressed in a language so full of Biblical connotations that the change in her, physical and spiritual, must be seen as an "allegoria *in factis* dell'intera storia dell'umanità, che, precipitata nella desolazione del peccato e nel dolore della deiezione, torna ad emergere mediante la grazia divina alla beati-tudine ed alla salvezza".[154] Such apparent contradictions are not oversights on Lorenzo's part, rather they arise from his clear knowledge that such is the fabric of human existence.

That all three parties—father, daughter and captain—come out of the *impasse* respectably is due to a "divinity that shapes our ends" as it obligingly eliminates the problem. The problem is not solved: its solution would require an impossible reconciliation of opposites, as Lorenzo knew. So did Machiavelli, who quoted approvingly from Lorenzo's *Rappresentazione* (99. 7–8) in his *Discorsi* (III. 19), and could have cited other lines from the play's political speeches to support his own viewpoints. This is less surprising than it may at first seem if one examines the tradition of political tracts on which both writers drew. Martelli has quite clearly shown that Lorenzo depended on "un àmbito di luoghi comuni della trattatistica poli-tica, da Platone ed Aristotele fino a Platina e a Patrizi".[155] His

reflections on government are not remarkable for innovative thinking, but they are striking for their common sense and for being
based on what Machiavelli was later to call "la verità effettuale della
cosa" (*Il principe* xv). Lorenzo was no theorist and wrote from the
standpoint of the practitioner of power rather than of the secretary
at the dispatch desk—hence his awareness of the unresolved
dilemma posed by political success. Of great interest is the abdication
speech. Constantine implies that he has lived by the highly moral
code that he now professes, but it has not obviated his need of the
sword. The "affanno e doglia" (101. 7) that are the ruler's lot are
caused not simply by the vicissitudes of life but also by the struggle
of conscience. Lorenzo may be voicing a weariness that is more than
physical, and intimating a desire to relinquish what has given no
inner peace; one could rule by moral principles only "se li uomini
fussino tutti buoni" (*Il principe* xviii), and Lorenzo did not need
Machiavelli to tell him that they are not. The historical Constantine
did not abdicate, and the political views of his fictional counterpart
could have been equally well expressed by a dying king. The fact
that he does abdicate, thereby following in the footsteps of Gallican,
indicates the victory of a *vita contemplativa* over a *vita attiva*—and
this may be of much autobiographical significance.

Certainly autobiographical is the paternal love, of which there
is no shortage in the play, be it that of Constantine, of Gallican or of
the captured king. Although Lorenzo has been interpreted in
contradictory fashions in virtually all matters, one aspect of his
personality—his attachment to his children—has never been
doubted. In this feature lies the play's emotional appeal. The
portrayal of the bond of love that ties daughter and father is one of
the play's major strengths. The *Rappresentazione* was written not
long after the death of Lorenzo's daughter Luisa, whom for reasons
of expediency he had betrothed to his cousin Giovanni. Similar
considerations had dictated the marriage of his beloved Mad-
dalena to Franceschetto Cibo, an alliance he had negotiated with
many misgivings. Into the creation of Constance, to whom he gives
deeply moving lines, Lorenzo seems to have put his heart.

Although this *Rappresentazione* is *sacra* and decidedly Biblical in
many of its features, there is not on Lorenzo's part a total abandon-
ment of his humanist formation, as is attested by the play's resonant
evocation of *romanitas*. Toschi, who reads the text *in chiave romana*,

writes that "reggia e fasto imperiale, templi degli antichi iddii, partenze e ritorni di eserciti, contrasti di potenza, tramonti di grandi fortune, ambiente e vicende concorrono a creare quell'atmosfera di storia antica di cui si compiacevano gli spiriti imbevuti di umanesimo."[156] Later in 1491, for the feast of St John the Baptist, Lorenzo gave full expression to his *romanitas* by organizing fifteen *trionfi* depicting the consul Æmilius Paullus triumphing in Rome after conquering the East. This sumptuous spectacle may have been the first non-Christian show performed on the feast of Florence's patron saint, and may also have had political implications, emphasizing the city's international character and Lorenzo's own authority.[157] The *Rappresentazione*, then, with its religious, political and Roman elements, cannot be defined in any one single manner; it is contradictory and enigmatic, thus reflecting the essence of its author.

In one matter Lorenzo was certainly constant: in his lack of trust in our "fallace vita". He was not to abdicate either his literary or his political activity; death freed him of such decisions, *in medias res*, while he was still writing, re-writing and revising. The *Rappresentazione* is exceptional among Lorenzo's later works in that it is finished (it was performed); but the poet worked tirelessly at the others, battling against time, and aware as ever that

> nostro solo è quel poco che è presente,
> né 'l passato o il futuro è nostro tempo:
> l'un non è piú, e l'altro è ancor niente.

NOTES

1 Lorenzo, *Opere*, edited by Martelli, pp. xi–xii.
2 See Rubinstein, *The Government of Florence under the Medici*. Part III (pp. 174–228) is specially relevant.
3 See the entry "Florence" in *A Concise Encyclopaedia of the Italian Renaissance*, edited by J. R. Hale (London, Thames and Hudson, 1981), pp. 136–37.
4 See *Federico da Montefeltro: lo stato; le arti; la cultura*, 3 vols (Rome, Bulzoni, 1986); C. H. Clough, *The Duchy of Urbino in the Renaissance* (London, Variorum Reprints, 1981).
5 Hook, *Lorenzo*, p. 72.

6   F. de' Nerli, *Commentarj dei fatti civili occorsi dentro la città di Firenze dall'anno 1215 al 1537* (Trieste, Coen, 1859) vol. I, p. 95.

7   See R. de Roover, *The Rise and Decline of the Medici Bank* (Cambridge, Mass., Harvard University Press, 1968).

8   See E. H. Gombrich, "The Early Medici as Patrons of Art", in *Italian Renaissance Studies: A Tribute to the Late Cecilia M. Ady*, edited by E. F. Jacob (London, Faber, 1960), pp. 279–311; D. S. Chambers, *Patrons and Artists in the Italian Renaissance* (London, Macmillan, 1970).

9   See Hook, *Lorenzo*, Chapter 6, "Lorenzo as Patron of Art and Letters", and in particular p. 128.

10   On the ousting of Pulci see P. Orvieto, *Pulci medievale* (Rome, Salerno, 1978), Chapter 6 (pp. 213–43).

11   See P. O. Kristeller, *The Philosophy of Marsilio Ficino*, translated by V. Conant (New York, Columbia University Press, 1943).

12   Lorenzo, *Canzoniere*, edited by Orvieto, p. xviii.

13   Martelli, "La politica culturale dell'ultimo Lorenzo", p. 1062.

14   See Martelli, "La politica culturale dell'ultimo Lorenzo" on the relationship between Lorenzo and Savonarola, but note the adverse criticism of some of Martelli's points by R. Ridolfi, "Il Savonarola e il Magnifico", *Bibliofilía* 83 (1981), 71–78; see also D. Weinstein, *Savonarola and Florence: Prophecy and Patriotism in the Renaissance* (Princeton, Princeton University Press, 1970).

15   Orvieto, *Lorenzo*, p. 71.

16   See M. Martelli, "I pensieri architettonici del Magnifico", *Commentari*, 17 (1966), 107–11; P. E. Foster, *A Study of Lorenzo de' Medici's Villa at Poggio a Caiano*, 2 vols (New York, Garland, 1978), I, 290. Foster seems to misunderstand Martelli's contribution.

17   Foster, *A Study of Lorenzo de' Medici's Villa*, p. 293.

18   W. Roscoe, *The Life of Lorenzo de' Medici, Called the Magnificent*, fourth edition, 3 vols (London, Cadell-Davies and Edwards, 1800), II, 182–87. Roscoe quotes from a description of the demesne by the contemporary Michele Verino.

19   Lorenzo, *Scritti scelti*, pp. 659–60.

20   N. Machiavelli, *Lettere*, edited by F. Gaeta (Milan, Feltrinelli, 1961), p. 374.

21   V. Lee, "The Outdoor Poetry", in her *Euphorion*, 2 vols (London, Fisher Unwin, 1884), I, 111–66.

22   William Roscoe (1753–1831) was a Liverpool historian, barrister and writer, who published a famous life of Lorenzo in 1795, and one of his son Leo X in 1805. His biography of Lorenzo went into several editions and countless printings, and was translated into Italian, French and German; for a period it won warmer acclaim for Lorenzo the poet in

the English-speaking world than he enjoyed among Italians. Roscoe also edited the works of Alexander Pope, and was a botanist of some standing (an order of the scitaminean plants is named after him). See H. Roscoe, *The Life of William Roscoe* (London, Cadell, 1833).

23 Started by a group of literary figures in 1582, the Florentine *Accademia della Crusca* soon espoused the protection of the purity of the Italian language, and was responsible for the publication of an important *Vocabolario*.

24 Lorenzo, *Scritti scelti*.

25 E. Bigi, "Sulla cronologia dell'attività letteraria di Lorenzo il Magnifico", *Atti dell'Accademia delle scienze di Torino*, 87 (1952–53), 154–69.

26 Lorenzo, *Canzoniere*, edited by Zanato, I, 281.

27 Lorenzo, *Opere*, edited by Martelli, p. xxviii; Orvieto, *Lorenzo*, p. 67.

28 Lorenzo, *Stanze*, pp. lxxi–lxxxvii; Martelli, *Studi laurenziani*, pp. 135–78; Bigi, "Sulla cronologia".

29 Martelli, *Studi laurenziani*, pp. 37–49.

30 Martelli, "Il 'Giacoppo' di Lorenzo", p. 124.

31 Orvieto, *Lorenzo*, p. 48.

32 In *Diario de' successi più importanti seguiti in Italia, e particolarmente in Fiorenza dall'anno 1498 in fino all'anno 1512 raccolto da Biagio Buonaccorsi, con la Vita del Magnifico Lorenzo de' Medici il Vecchio scritta da Niccolò Valori patrizio fiorentino* (Florence, Giunti, 1568), p. 17 (unnumbered).

33 Lorenzo, *Simposio*, p. 96.

34 Lorenzo, *Opere*, edited by Martelli, p. xviii.

35 G. Carducci, *Delle poesie di Lorenzo de' Medici* (Florence, Barbèra, 1859), p. xxix, cited in Orvieto, *Lorenzo*, p. 54.

36 Martelli, *Studi laurenziani*, p. 138.

37 Lorenzo, *Stanze*, p. lxxxi.

38 Orvieto, *Lorenzo*, pp. 54–59.

39 See pp. 253–56 ; the Appendix contains further bibliographical information.

40 F. Patetta, "Un terzo testo della *Nencia da Barberino* attribuita a Lorenzo de' Medici", *Rendiconti della Classe di scienze morali, storiche e filologiche dell'Accademia dei Lincei*, 6, x (1934), 129–63.

41 M. Fubini, "I tre testi della *Nencia da Barberino* e la questione della paternità del poemetto", now in his *Studi sulla letteratura del Rinascimento*, second edition (Florence, La Nuova Italia, 1971), pp. 66–116.

42 A. Chiari and I. Marchetti, *L'autore della "Nencia da Barberino"* (Milan, Marzorati, 1948).

43 Fubini, "I tre testi della *Nencia*", p. 110.

44 Rochon, *La Jeunesse de Laurent*, p. 382.

45 Fubini, "I tre testi della *Nencia*", p. 99.

46 D. De Robertis, *Editi e rari: studi sulla tradizione letteraria tra Tre e Cinquecento* (Milan, Feltrinelli, 1978), pp. 137–47.

47 E. Bigi, *La cultura del Poliziano e altri studi umanistici* (Pisa, Nistri-Lischi, 1967), pp. 44ff.

48 Lorenzo, *Opere*, edited by Martelli, pp. xviii–xix.

49 Giustiniani, *Il testo della "Nencia"*, p. 43, n. 27.

50 Noted first by Roscoe (*The Life of Lorenzo*, I, 395), and subsequently by Carducci, De Sanctis and others.

51 U. Bosco, *Saggi sul Rinascimento italiano* (Florence, Le Monnier, 1970), p. 41.

52 Bosco, *Saggi sul Rinascimento italiano*, p. 42.

53 Orvieto, *Pulci medievale*, p. 116.

54 *La Nencia da Barberino*, p. 63 and passim.

55 *La Nencia da Barberino*, p. 40.

56 Giustiniani, *Il testo della "Nencia"*, p. 52.

57 So defined by E. Bellorini, editor of Lorenzo de' Medici, *Scritti scelti* (Turin, UTET, 1944), p. 222, and by Martelli in Lorenzo, *Opere*, edited by Martelli, p. xix.

58 V. Rossi, *Il Quattrocento*, second edition (Milan, Vallardi, 1932), p. 337.

59 Rochon, *La Jeunesse de Laurent*, p. 437.

60 P. Orvieto, "Angelo Poliziano 'compare' della brigata laurenziana", *Lettere italiane*, 25 (1973), 301–18.

61 Roscoe first published Lorenzo's poems privately in 1791, in Liverpool, with the title *Poesie del Magnifico Lorenzo de' Medici, tratte da testi a penna della Libreria mediceo-laurenziana e finora inedite*; in 1795 he included them in the first edition of his life of Lorenzo.

62 A. Chiari, "Sul testo della laurenziana *Uccellagione*", *Rinascimento*, 9, i (1958), 11–41.

63 M. Martelli, "La tradizione manoscritta dell'*Uccellagione di starne*", *Rinascimento*, 5, ii (1965), 51–58.

64 *Atti del convegno sul tema: "La poesia rusticana nel Rinascimento"* (Rome, Accademia Nazionale dei Lincei, 1969), p. 42.

65 Martelli, "La tradizione manoscritta dell'*Uccellagione*", p. 76, n. 2.

66 Orvieto, *Lorenzo*, p. 19.

67 Lorenzo, *Canzoniere*, edited by Zanato, I, 285.

68 Lorenzo, *Canzoniere*, edited by Zanato, I, 282–83.

69 Lorenzo, *Canzoniere*, edited by Zanato, I, 282.

70 D. De Robertis, "Lorenzo lirico", in *Storia della letteratura italiana*, edited by E. Cecchi and N. Sapegno, 9 vols (Milan, Garzanti, 1966), III, 495–513 (p. 496).

71 All quotations from this text are from the critical edition: M. Ficino, *El libro dell'Amore*, edited by S. Niccoli (Florence, Olschki, 1987).

72　Lorenzo, *Canzoniere*, edited by Orvieto, p. xviii.

73　Orvieto, *Lorenzo*, p. 42.

74　J. Fowles, *The Aristos* (London, Triad Panther, 1981), p. 195.

75　Martelli, "Per l'edizione critica del *Comento*", p. 59.

76　Martelli, *Studi laurenziani*, pp. 139–40.

77　Lorenzo, *Scritti scelti*, p. 295; Rochon, *La Jeunesse de Laurent*, pp. 140–41.

78　Zanato, *Saggio sul "Comento"*, p. 318, n. 73.

79　Martelli, "La politica culturale dell'ultimo Lorenzo", p. 1065; but the entire article is fundamental to our understanding of the major change in Lorenzo's policies in the last two years of his life.

80　See Lorenzo, *Comento*, pp. 123–29.

81　*Prosatori latini del Quattrocento*, edited by E. Garin (Milan-Naples, Ricciardi, 1952), p. 803. Pico's letter was written in July 1484 and is an important document for establishing dates.

82　Martelli, "La politica culturale dell'ultimo Lorenzo", pp. 1051–52.

83　Orvieto, *Lorenzo*, p. 50.

84　Zanato, *Saggio sul "Comento"*, pp. 280–81.

85　R. Spongano, *Un capitolo di storia della nostra prosa d'arte: la prosa letteraria del Quattrocento* (Florence, Sansoni, 1941).

86　M. Fubini, "Nota sulla prosa di Lorenzo il Magnifico: a proposito di un libro sulla prosa del Quattrocento", in his *Studi sulla letteratura del Rinascimento* (see note 41 above), pp. 117–25 (pp. 119–20).

87　Zanato, *Saggio sul "Comento"*, p. 240.

88　Zanato, *Saggio sul "Comento"*, p. 245, citing P. O. Kristeller, "The Scholastic Background of Marsilio Ficino", in his *Studies in Renaissance Thought and Letters* (Rome, Storia e Letteratura, 1956), pp. 35–97 (p. 38).

89　Zanato, *Saggio sul "Comento"*, p. 255; but see the entire section "Caratteri stilistici della prosa", pp. 239–81, for a thorough analysis of the prose of the *Comento*.

90　Zanato, *Saggio sul "Comento"*, p. 257.

91　Zanato, *Saggio sul "Comento"*, p. 13.

92　Martelli, "La politica culturale dell'ultimo Lorenzo", p. 928.

93　Martelli says something analogous in "La politica culturale dell'ultimo Lorenzo", p. 1049.

94　For Lorenzo's views on the *volgare* see Zanato, *Saggio sul "Comento"*, pp. 11–44.

95　Zanato, *Saggio sul "Comento"*, p. 32.

96　Zanato, *Saggio sul "Comento"*, p. 321.

97　M. Messina, "Alcuni manoscritti sconosciuti delle rime di Lorenzo de' Medici il Magnifico: appunti per una edizione critica", *Studi di filologia italiana*, 16 (1958), 275–342; pp. 320–25 deal specifically with *Corinto*.

98　Suggested by M. Martelli, "Preistoria (medicea) di Machiavelli", *Studi di filologia italiana*, 29 (1971), 377–405 (p. 397).

99   Noted in Martelli, "Per la storia redazionale del *Corinto*", pp. 221–22.

100 Martelli, "Per la storia redazionale del *Corinto*", p. 233, n. 5.

101 Martelli, "Per la storia redazionale del *Corinto*", pp. 224–30.

102 "Reminiscenze poetiche" is the phrase used by B. Maier, *Lettura critica del "Corinto"*, p. 11.

103 Maier, *Lettura critica del "Corinto"*, pp. 50ff. "De rosis nascentibus" may be read in *Appendix vergiliana*, edited by W. V. Clausen et al. (Oxford, Clarendon Press, 1966), pp. 177–78.

104 See G. Carducci, *Delle poesie toscane di messer Angelo Poliziano* (Florence, Barbèra, 1863), pp. 187–88 and passim for links between Poliziano's and Lorenzo's texts.

105 Martelli, "Per la storia redazionale del *Corinto*", p. 237.

106 Orvieto, *Lorenzo*, p. 66.

107 See Maier, *Lettura critica del "Corinto"*, pp. 57ff. Throughout his study Maier traces in *Corinto* the drawing together of three traditions: "il classicismo della tradizione bucolica grecolatina; l'accento di schiettezza e di rusticana semplicità mutuato [...] dalla poesia popolare italiana; ed il riecheggiamento dei modi aulici e dotti della nostra lirica amorosa, dallo *stil novo* al Petrarca."

108 Carducci, *Delle poesie toscane di messer Angelo Poliziano*, pp. 72–73.

109 *Theocritus*, edited with a translation and commentary by A. S. F. Gow, 2 vols (Cambridge, Cambridge University Press, 1950), I, 179.

110 Maier, *Lettura critica del "Corinto"*, p. 47.

111 Maier, *Lettura critica del "Corinto"*, pp. 54–55.

112 Martelli, "Per la storia redazionale del *Corinto*", p. 239.

113 Lorenzo, *Ambra*, p. 52.

114 Martelli, *Studi laurenziani*, p. 178.

115 Orvieto, *Lorenzo*, p. 83.

116 Martelli, *Studi laurenziani*, pp. 177–78.

117 Salvadori Lonergan, "Lorenzo de' Medici's *Ambra*".

118 Lorenzo, *Ambra*, pp. 7–33.

119 Lorenzo, *Ambra*, pp. 29–33. Charles Dempsey, in "La data dell'*Ambra* (*Descriptio hiemis*) di Lorenzo de' Medici", *Interpres*, 10 (1990), 265–69, argues for 1491 as a date for *Ambra* on the grounds that the flood described in the poem has features in common with the one described in Landucci's *Diario fiorentino*. The dam built by Lorenzo proved too weak for the flood of 1491.

120 Lorenzo, *Opere*, edited by Martelli, p. xxxiii.

121 Bowra, "Songs of Dance and Carnival", p. 331.

122 F. De Sanctis, *Storia della letteratura italiana*, edited by N. Gallo, 2 vols (Turin, Einaudi, 1958), I, 422.

123 Martelli, *Studi laurenziani*, p. 46.

124 Orvieto, *Lorenzo*, p. 71.

125 For a full analysis of this poem see Salvadori Lonergan, "Lorenzo de' Medici: proposta per una lettura di 'Donna, vano è il pensier'".

126 Bowra, "Songs of Dance and Carnival", p. 335.

127 Orvieto, *Lorenzo*, p. 70.

128 See R. C. Trexler, *Public Life in Renaissance Florence* (New York, Academic Press, 1980).

129 See A. F. Grazzini (Lasca), *Tutti i trionfi, carri, mascherate o canti carnascialeschi andati per Firenze dal tempo del Magnifico Lorenzo vecchio de' Medici; quando egli ebbero prima cominciamento, per infino a questo anno presente 1559* (Florence, Torrentino, 1559); Lorenzo, *Canti carnascialeschi*, p. 14.

130 Lasca, *Tutti i trionfi*, quoted by Orvieto in Lorenzo, *Canti carnascialeschi*, p. 12.

131 W. H. Rubsamen, "The Music for 'Quant' è bella giovinezza' and Other Carnival Songs by Lorenzo de' Medici", in *Art, Science and History in the Renaissance*, edited by C. S. Singleton (Baltimore-London, Johns Hopkins University Press, 1967), pp. 163–84.

132 O. Zorzi Pugliese, "Ambiguità di Bacco nel 'Trionfo' laurenziano e nell'arte rinascimentale", in *Letteratura italiana e arti figurative*, edited by A. Franceschetti, 3 vols (Florence, Olschki, 1988), I, 397–404 (p. 399).

133 Bowra, "Songs of Dance and Carnival", p. 351; Lorenzo, *Canti carnascialeschi*, p. 9.

134 Martelli, *Studi laurenziani*, p. 44.

135 Lorenzo, *Canzoniere*, edited by Zanato, I, 278.

136 Martelli, *Studi laurenziani*, pp. 37–49.

137 This information was supplied to the editor of the present volume in a letter dated 19 February 1991 by Bernard Toscani, who is engaged in further research on the dating of the *Laude*.

138 Rochon, *La Jeunesse de Laurent*, p. 599.

139 See R. F. E. Weissman, *Ritual Brotherhood in Renaissance Florence* (New York, Academic Press, 1982).

140 Lorenzo, *Laude*, pp. 63–66.

141 Lorenzo, *Laude*, p. 79.

142 Carducci, *Delle poesie di Lorenzo* (see note 35 above), p. lxi.

143 Martelli, "La politica culturale dell'ultimo Lorenzo", p. 936.

144 Martelli, "La politica culturale dell'ultimo Lorenzo", p. 938.

145 Martelli, "La politica culturale dell'ultimo Lorenzo", pp. 1044–45.

146 G. Savonarola, *Trattato circa il reggimento e governo della città di Firenze*, edited by L. Firpo (Rome, Belardetti, 1965), p. 459.

147 Martelli, "Politica e religione", pp. 200 and 206.

148 See *Ricordanze di Bartolomeo Masi calderaio fiorentino dal 1478 al 1526*, edited by G. O. Corazzini (Florence, Sansoni, 1906), pp. 15–16.

149 On the dating see H. A. Mathes, "On the Date of Lorenzo's *Sacra*

rappresentazione di S. Giovanni e Paolo: February 17, 1491", *Ævum*, 25 (1951), 324–28. For further details on the staging of this play and for an analysis of it, see Salvadori Lonergan, "A Lorenzo il leon d'oro?"

150 A. Pirro, "Leo x and Music", *Musical Quarterly*, 21 (1935), 1–16; F. Ghisi, "Le musiche di Isaac per il *San Giovanni e Paulo* di Lorenzo il Magnifico", *Rassegna musicale*, 8–12 (1943), 264–68.

151 Ghisi, "Le musiche di Isaac per il *San Giovanni e Paulo*", p. 267.

152 These are Chapters xxiv, xxx, lxxxvii, and cxxv in J. da Varagine, *Legenda aurea*, edited by T. Graesse, third edition (Bratislava, Koebner, 1890).

153 Martelli, "Politica e religione", p. 214.

154 Martelli, "Politica e religione", pp. 203–04.

155 Martelli, "Politica e religione", p. 209.

156 P. Toschi, *L'antico teatro religioso italiano* (Matera, Montemurro, 1966) p. 157.

157 See R. Trexler, *Public Life in Renaissance Florence*, p. 452.

A WORD ABOUT LORENZO'S LANGUAGE

Linguistic alertness on the part of the reader will solve most problems arising from Lorenzo's Italian, which differs somewhat in orthography, morphology and syntax from current usage. There is, furthermore, no consistency in Lorenzo's practice, and his considerable oscillation reflects the linguistic anarchy of the Quattrocento (it was not until the following century that some codification was achieved). There must be a willing suspension of belief in today's rigorous grammatical rules, and Lorenzo's seemingly quixotic approach to gender agreements will endear him to the average undergraduate; that *gente* is often a plural must also delight anglophones. The following notes are neither exhaustive nor scientifically presented, and they aim solely to help the reader in a treasure hunt. Lorenzo's form is followed by the modern equivalent where this may not be immediately obvious.

The modern Italian word will generally be found by making some minor alteration like changing or transposing or eliminating a vowel or consonant. Look out for: interchange of *e* and *i* as in *destrutto/distrutto, nimico/nemico*; interchange of *e* and *ie* as in *mel/miele, queta/quieta, brieve/breve, niega/nega*; the omission of posttonic *e* or *i* as in *merto/merito, carco/carico, medesmo/medesimo, spirto/spirito*; interhcange of *u* and *o* as in *singulare, surgere, romore, officio*; interchange of *uo* and *o* as in *pruova/prova, truova/trova*, with the ubiquitous heart being *core* as well as *cuore*; *-ue* for *-ú* as in *virtue, giue, piue* and *Gesue*; *-ii* or *-li* for *-i* as in *misterii, ampli*; *-zia* for *-za* as in *esperienzia, sentenzia, adolescenzia, potenzia, constanzia/costanza* (the retention of *n* in this last example and in similar words makes them like their modern English equivalents); the full form of apocopated words: *caritate/carità, virtute/virtú*; intervocalic *c* for *z* or vice versa as in *giudicio, offizio, spezie/specie*; *gn* for *ng* as in *giugnere/giungere, ristrignersi/ristringersi, cigne/cinge*. The numeral two appears as *duo, dua* or *due*. Nouns and adjectives in -*e* are often left unchanged in the plural, so *ape, notte, valle* etc. will be found as plural forms, as well as *errante chiome, cose deforme, tutte le gente* etc.; irregular plurals may differ from their current forms: *ciglie/ciglia, miglie/miglia*.

Ingenuity will be required in the case of verb + pronoun combinations, as the pronoun often follows the verb in cases where it now precedes, and the different position causes changes of spelling. Examples, in a range of tenses and moods: *sonvi/vi sono, conviemme/mi conviene, hamme/mi ha, truovansi/si trovano, eranvi/vi erano, sentími/mi sentii, duolsi/si duole, ruppegli/gli ruppe, contentisi/si contenti, bastiti/ti basti, daratti/ti darà*. The opposite happens occasionally, as in *non vi vedendo/non vedendovi*.

Characteristic of Lorenzo's style is his fondness for diminutives, generally in -*etto*, -*ello* or -*ino*, as in modern Italian: *fioretti, pecorelle, collarino* etc.

ARTICLES: *il* for *lo* and vice versa; *'l* for *il*; *li* for *i* and *gli*. This also applies to cases where the article is combined with another part of speech and to words which behave like the definite article: *quelli soldati, alli due fratelli* etc. Articles and prepositions are not necessarily combined according to modern usage.

POSSESSIVE ADJECTIVES: *mia* for *miei/mie* etc. Example: *i mia pianti, i sua capelli*. Also *mie* for *mio*: *il mie cuor*.

PRONOUNS: Subject: *e'* for *egli* and *essi*; *ei* for *essi*; *la* for *lei*. Direct object: *il* for *lo* (*nol = non lo*); *gli* for *li*; *li* for *le*. Indirect object: *me* for *mi* etc.; *li* for *gli* and *le*; *ne* will be used as well as *ci* for "us". With preposition *con*: *meco/con me, teco/con te* etc.

PRESENT INDICATIVE: -*ono*/-*ano*: *cantono, restono, cercono, trovono* etc.; omission of -*isc*-: *pate/patisce; debbo* predominates over *devo; de'* and *dee* are found for *deve*; other common forms are *veggo/vedo, veggono/vedono, aggio/ho, può/puoi, puote/può, fo/faccio, baste/basta*.

PASSATO REMOTO: -*orno* is found for -*arono*: *entrorno/entrarono*; -*ío* for -*irono*: *sentío/sentirono*; -*on(o)* or -*eno* for third person plural -*ero*: *fêron/fecero, vennon/vennero, ebbono/ebbero, stieno/stettero; fûrno, fûro* and *fôro* appear for *furono; fue/fu, fe'/feci* or *fece, diè/diede, messi/misi*.

IMPERFECT: The characteristic consonant *v* is often omitted: *dicea/diceva, avea/aveva, ardea/ardeva, venía/veniva, parean/parevano* etc. The first person singular will often end in -*a* (*aveva* or *avea* for *avevo*).

FUTURE: Third person of *essere*: *fia/sarà, fieno/saranno; avere* is conjugated without *v* in all its persons: *arò/avrò* etc., with the shortened *aran* often to be found for *avranno*. Occasionally (usually where there is *r* before the end of the stem) a doubling may be found: *doverrà/dovrà, crederrà/crederà, proverrà/proverà*. Syncopated forms are *merrai/menerai, ricorrai/raccoglierai*.

CONDITIONAL: As in the case of the future, the stem for *avere* is *ar*-: *arei/avrei* etc. Third person singular: *-ia/-ebbe*, as in *saria/sarebbe, staria/starebbe, potria* or *porria/potrebbe*; or *-e'/-ebbe*: *trafiggere'/trafiggerebbe*. Third person plural: *-ieno/-ebbero, -ebbono/-ebbero*, as in *sarieno/sarebbero, sosterrieno/sosterrebbero, farieno/farebbero, potrebbono/potrebbero*. Doubling of *r* is to be found: *proverrei/proverei*. *Dovere* may retain *e*: *doverrei/dovrei, doverre'/dovrebbe*.

PRESENT SUBJUNCTIVE: *-i/-ia* and *-ino/-ano*: *abbi/abbia, conoschi/conosca, piacci/piaccia, possino/possano*. Note: *sieno/siano, chiegga/chieda*.

IMPERFECT SUBJUNCTIVE: *-ssi/-sse*: *avessi/avesse, sognassi/sognasse; u/o* in forms of *essere*: *fussi/fosse* etc.; *-ino/-essero*: *fussino/fossero, potessino/potessero*. Note also: *fesse/facesse*.

REFLEXIVES: Some verbs are used reflexively where in modern usage they are not: *si muore, ritornavansi/ritornavano, partissi/partí*. Reflexives will not necessarily be conjugated with *essere*.

PAST PARTICIPLES: There are short forms in *-o* (properly called verbal adjectives) for many *-are* verbs: *cerco/cercato, mostro/mostrato, tocco/toccato*. Some *-ere* verbs have a regular participle unknown to modern Italian: *renduto/reso*; and some irregular forms differ from current ones: *suto/stato, sparto/sparso, rimaso/rimasto, nascoso/nascosto*. Some *-ire* verbs have *-uto*: *conceputo/concepito*. Agreements with the auxiliary *avere* will be found, contrary to modern practice: *rendute ho grazie/ho reso grazie, ha convertite le tue figlie, hanno condotta la famiglia*.

CONTRACTED VERBAL FORMS: These are often indicated by a circumflex (^). Examples: *tôrre/togliere, côrrei/coglierei, fêsse/facesse*.

SUGGESTED ANCILLARY READING

LORENZO DE' MEDICI: TEXTS AND EDITIONS

Opere, edited by A. Simioni, second edition, 2 vols (Bari, Laterza, 1939)

Opere, edited by M. Martelli (Turin, Caula, 1965)

Scritti scelti, edited by E. Bigi, second edition (Turin, UTET, 1965)

Uccellagione di starne, in M. Martelli, "La tradizione manoscritta dell'*Uccellagione di starne*", *Rinascimento*, 5, ii (1965), 51–85 (pp. 71–85)

Simposio, edited by M. Martelli (Florence, Olschki, 1966)

La Nencia da Barberino, edited by R. Bessi (Rome, Salerno, 1982)

Canzoniere, edited by P. Orvieto (Milan, Mondadori, 1984)

Ambra (Descriptio hiemis), edited by R. Bessi (Florence, Sansoni, 1986)

Stanze, edited by R. Castagnola (Florence, Olschki, 1986)

Laude, edited by B. Toscani (Florence, Olschki, 1990)

Canti carnascialeschi, edited by P. Orvieto (Rome, Salerno, 1991)

Canzoniere, edited by T. Zanato, 2 vols (Florence, Olschki, 1991)

Comento de' miei sonetti, edited by T. Zanato (Florence, Olschki, 1991)

Lettere, edited by N. Rubinstein et al., in progress (Florence, Giunti-Barbèra, 1977–)

[In English translation] *Selected Poems and Prose*, edited by J. Thiem, translated by J. Thiem et al. (Pennsylvania, Pennsylvania State University Press, 1991)

SECONDARY MATERIALS

C. Ady, *Lorenzo dei Medici and Renaissance Italy* (London, English Universities Press, 1955)

M. Bowra, "Songs of Dance and Carnival", in *Italian Renaissance Studies: A Tribute to the late Cecilia M. Ady*, edited by E. F. Jacob (London, Faber, 1960), pp. 328–53

V. R. Giustiniani, *Il testo della "Nencia" e della "Beca" secondo le più antiche stampe* (Florence, Olschki, 1976)

J. R. Hale, *Florence and the Medici: The Pattern of Control* (London, Thames and Hudson, 1977)

J. Hook, *Lorenzo de' Medici* (London, Hamish Hamilton, 1984)

B. Maier, *Lettura critica del "Corinto" di Lorenzo de' Medici* (Trieste, Zigiotti, 1949)

M. Martelli, *Studi laurenziani* (Florence, Olschki, 1965)

M. Martelli, "Per l'edizione critica del *Comento de' sonetti* di Lorenzo de' Medici: restauri preliminari al testo vulgato", *Rinascimento*, 7 (1967), 55–138

M. Martelli, "Per la storia redazionale del *Corinto*", *Studi di filologia italiana*, 33 (1975), 221–40

M. Martelli, "La politica culturale dell'ultimo Lorenzo", *Il ponte*, 35 (1980), ix, 923–50 and x, 1040–69

M. Martelli, "Il 'Giacoppo' di Lorenzo", *Interpres*, 7 (1987), 103–24

M. Martelli, "Politica e religione nella sacra rappresentazione di Lorenzo de' Medici", in *Mito e realtà del potere nel teatro: dall'antichità classica al Rinascimento* (Rome, Coletti, s.d.), pp. 189–216

M. Martelli, "Firenze", in *Letteratura italiana: storia e geografia*, 3 vols, edited by A. Asor Rosa (Turin, Einaudi, 1988), ii, 25–201

P. Orvieto, *Lorenzo de' Medici* (Florence, La Nuova Italia, 1976)

A. Rochon, *La Jeunesse de Laurent de Médicis (1449–1478)* (Paris, Les Belles Lettres, 1963)

N. Rubinstein, *The Government of Florence under the Medici, 1434 to 1494* (Oxford, Clarendon Press, 1966)

C. Salvadori Lonergan, "Lorenzo de' Medici's *Ambra*: due poesie diverse?", *Hermathena*, 121 (1976), 159–68

C. Salvadori Lonergan, "Lorenzo de' Medici: proposta per una lettura di 'Donna, vano è il pensier che mai non crede'", *Civiltà italiana*, 4, i–iii (1980), 164–71

C. Salvadori Lonergan, "A Lorenzo il leon d'oro? A Global Look at the *Rappresentazione di San Giovanni e Paolo*", in *Writers and Performers: Exploring Italian Drama*, edited by J. Dashwood and J. Everson (Lampeter, Edwin Mellen, 1991), pp. 33–51

S. Sturm, *Lorenzo de' Medici* (New York, Twayne, 1974)

G. Tanturli, "Sul *Comento* di Lorenzo de' Medici", *Studi medievali*, III, 23 (1982), 339–59

P. Ventrone, "Note sul carnevale fiorentino di età laurenziana", in *Il carnevale: dalla tradizione arcaica alla traduzione colta del Rinascimento*, edited by M. Chiabò and F. Doglio (Rome, Coletti, 1990), pp. 321–66

T. Zanato, *Saggio sul "Comento" di Lorenzo de' Medici* (Florence, Olschki, 1979)

LA NENCIA DA BARBERINO

1   Ardo d'amore, e conviemme cantare
per una dama che me strugge el cuore;
ch'ogni otta ch'i' la sento ricordare,
el cor me brilla e par ch'egli esca fuore.
Ella non truova de bellezze pare,
cogli occhi gitta fiaccole d'amore.
I' sono stato in città e 'n castella,
e mai ne vidi ignuna tanto bella.

2   I' sono stato ad Empoli al mercato,
a Prato, a Monticegli, a San Casciano,
a Colle, a Poggibonzi e San Donato,
a Grieve e quinamonte a Decomano;
Fegghine e Castelfranco ho ricercato,
San Piero, el Borgo e Mangone e Gagliano:
piú bel mercato ch'ento 'l mondo sia
è Barberin, dov' è la Nencia mia.

3   Non vidi mai fanciulla tanto onesta,
né tanto saviamente rilevata:
non vidi mai la piú leggiadra testa,
né sí lucente, né sí ben quadrata;
con quelle ciglia che pare una festa
quand' ella l'alza, ched ella me guata:
entro quel mezzo è 'l naso tanto bello
che par propio bucato col succhiello.

4   Le labbra rosse paion de corallo:
ed havvi drento duo filar de denti,
che son piú bianchi che que' del cavallo;
da ogni lato ve n'ha piú de venti.

Le gote bianche paion di cristallo
sanz' altro liscio, né scorticamenti,
rosse ento 'l mezzo, quant' è una rosa,
che non si vide mai sí bella cosa.

5   Ell' ha quegli occhi tanto rubacuori,
ch'ella trafiggere' con egli un muro.
Chiunch' ella guata convien che 'nnamori;
ma ella ha 'l cuore com' un ciottol duro;
e sempre ha drieto un migliaio d'amadori,
che da quegli occhi tutti presi fûro.
La se rivolge e guata questo e quello:
i', per guatalla, me struggo el cervello.

6   La m'ha sí concio e 'n modo governato
ch'i' piú non posso maneggiar marrone,
e hamme drento sí ravviluppato
ch'i' non ho forza de 'nghiottir boccone.
I' son come un graticcio deventato,
e solamente per le passione,
ch'i' ho per lei nel cuore (eppur sopportole!),
la m'ha legato con cento ritortole.

7   Ella potrebbe andare al paragone
tra un migghiaio di belle cittadine,
ch'ell' apparisce ben tra le persone
co' suoi begghi atti e dolce paroline;
l'ha ghi occhi suoi piú neri ch'un carbone
di sotto a quelle trecce biondelline,
e ricciute le vette de' capegli,
che vi pare attaccati mill' anegli.

8   Ell' è dirittamente ballerina,
ch'ella se lancia com' una capretta:
girasi come ruota de mulina
e dassi della man nella scarpetta.
Quand' ella compie el ballo, ella se 'nchina,
po' se rivolge e duo colpi iscambietta,
e fa le piú leggiadre riverenze,
che gnuna cittadina da Firenze.

9 La Nencia mia non ha gnun mancamento:
l'è bianca e rossa e de bella misura,
e ha un buco ento 'l mezzo del mento,
che rabbellisce tutta sua figura.
Ell' è ripiena d'ogni sentimento:
credo che 'n pruova la fêsse natura
tanto leggiadra e tanto appariscente,
ch'ella diveglie il cuore a molta gente.

10 Ben se potrà chiamare avventurato
chi fie marito de sí bella moglie;
ben se potrà tener in buon dí nato
chi arà quel fioraliso sanza foglie;
ben se potrà tener santo e biato,
e fien guarite tutte le suo' doglie,
aver quel viso e vederselo in braccio
morbido e bianco, che pare un sugnaccio.

11 Se tu sapessi, Nencia, el grande amore
ch'i' porto a' tuo' begli occhi tralucenti,
e la pena ch'i' sento e 'l gran dolore,
che par che mi si svèglin tutti i denti;
se tu 'l pensasse, te creperre' el cuore,
e lasceresti gli altri tuo' serventi,
e ameresti solo el tuo Vallera,
ché se' colei che 'l mie cuor disidèra.

12 Nenciozza, tu me fai pur consumare
e par che tu ne pigli gran piacere.
Se sanza duol me potessi cavare,
me sparere' per darti a divedere
ch'i' t'ho 'nto 'l cuore e fare'tel toccare;
tel porre' in mano e fare'tel vedere:
se tu 'l tagghiassi con una coltella,
e' griderebbe: "Nencia, Nencia bella!"

13 Quando te veggo tra una brigata,
convien che sempre intorno mi t'aggiri:
e quand'i' veggo ch'un altro te guata,
par propio che del petto el cor me tiri.

Tu me se' sí 'nto 'l cuore intraversata,
ch'i' rovescio ognindí mille sospiri,
pien de singhiozzi tutti lucciolando,
e tutti quanti ritti a te gli mando.

14   Non ho potuto stanotte dormire;
mill' anni me parea che fusse giorno,
per poter via con le bestie venire,
con elle insieme col tuo viso adorno.
E pur del letto me convenne uscire:
puosimi sotto 'l portico del forno;
e livi stetti piú d'un'ora e mezzo,
finché la luna se ripuose, al rezzo.

15   Quand'i' te vidi uscir della capanna
col cane innanzi e colle pecorelle,
e' me ricrebbe el cuor piú d'una spanna
e le lacrime vennon pelle pelle;
e poi me caccia' giú con una canna
dirieto a' miei giovenchi e le vitelle,
e avvia'gli innanzi vie quinentro
per aspettarti, e tu tornasti dentro.

16   I' me posi a diacer lungo la gora,
abbioscio su quell' erba voltoloni,
e livi stetti piú d'una mezz' ora,
tanto che valicorno e tuo' castroni.
Che fa' tu entro, che non esci fuora?
Vientene su per questi valiconi,
ch'i' cacci le mie bestie nelle tua,
e parrem uno, eppur saremo dua.

17   Nenciozza mia, i' vo' sabato andare
sin a Firenze a vender duo somelle
de schegge, ch'i' me puosi ier a tagghiare,
mentre ch'i' ero a pascer le vitelle.
Procura ben quel ch'i' posso recare,
se tu vuo' ch'io te comperi cavelle:
o liscio o biacca into 'n cartoccino
o de squilletti o d'agora un quattrino.

18   Se tu volessi, per portare a collo,
      un collarin de que' bottoncin rossi
      con un dondol nel mezzo, recherollo:
      ma dimmi se gli vuoi piccini o grossi.
      S'i' me dovessi tragli del midollo
      del fusol della gamba o degli altr' ossi,
      o s'i' dovessi vender la gonnella,
      i' te l'arrecherò, Nencia mie bella.

19   Che non me chiedi qualche zaccherella?
      so che n'aopri di cento ragioni:
      o uno 'ntaglio per la tuo' gonnella,
      o uncinegli o magghiette o bottoni,
      o vuoi pel camiciotto una scarsella,
      o cintol per legarti gli scuffioni,
      o vuoi, per ammagghiar la gamurrina,
      de seta una cordella cilestrina?

20   Gigghiozzo mio, tu te farai con Dio,
      perché le bestie mie son presso a casa.
      I' non vorrei che pel baloccar mio
      ne fusse ignuna in pastura rimasa.
      Veggo ch'ell' hanno valicato el rio,
      e odomi chiamar da mona Masa.
      Rimanti lieta: i' me ne vo cantando
      e sempre Nencia ento 'l mie cuor chiamando.

UCCELLAGIONE DI STARNE

1   Era già rosso tutto l'oriente
e le cime de' monti parean d'oro;
la passeretta schiamazzar si sente
e 'l contadin tornava al suo lavoro;
le stelle eran fuggite, e già presente
si vedea quasi quel ch'amò l'alloro;
ritornavansi al bosco molto in fretta
l'allocco e 'l barbagianni e la civetta.

2   La volpe ritornava alla sua tana
e 'l lupo ritornava al suo deserto:
era venuta e sparita Diana,
però forse saría suto scoperto;
avea già la sollecita villana
alle pecore e porci l'uscio aperto;
netta era l'aria, fresca e cristallina,
e da sperar buon dí per la mattina.

3   Quando io fu' desto da certi romori
di buon sonagli e allettar di cani:
"Or su, andianne presto, uccellatori,
perché gli è tardi e ' luoghi son lontani;
el canattier sia el primo ch'esca fuori
acciò che i piè de' cavalli stamani
non ci guastassin di can qualche paio.
Deh! vanne avanti presto, Cappellaio."

4   Adunque el Cappellaio 'nanzi cammina.
Chiama Tamburo e Pezzuolo e Martello,
La Foglia, la Castagna e la Guercina,
Fagiano, Fagianin, Rocca e Cappello,

e Frizza e Biondo e Balocco e Rossina,
Ghiotto, la Corta, Viuola e Pestello,
Zambracco e Sacco e 'l mio Buontempo vecchio
e Staccio Burattel, Fuso e Pennecchio.

5   Quando i cani han di campo preso un pezzo,
quattro seguiron con quattro sparvieri:
Guglielmo, che per suo antico vezzo
sempre quest' arte ha fatta volentieri,
Giovan Francesco, e Dionigi è 'l sezzo,
ch'innanzi a lui cavalca il Foglia Amieri.
Ma, perch' egli era a buon' or la mattina,
per riverenza Dionigi inchina.

6   E la Fortuna, che ha sempre piacere
di far diventar brun quel ch'è piú bianco,
dormendo Dionigi fa cadere
appunto per disgrazia al lato manco,
sicché, cadendo addosso allo sparviere,
ruppegli un'alia e macerogli 'l fianco;
questo gli piacque assai, benché nol dica,
ché la sua dama è la poca fatica.

7   Non cadde Dionigi, anzi rovina,
e, come debbi creder, toccò fondo,
ché, come un tratto egli ha preso la china,
presto lo truova come un sasso tondo.
Disse fra sé: "Meglio era stamattina
restar nel letto come fe' Gismondo
scalzo e 'n camicia in su le pocce al fresco:
ma non c'incappo piú, se di questa esco.

8   "Io ebbi pure un poco del cucciotto
a uscire staman per tempo fuori,
ché, s'io mi stavo, come il Birria, sotto,
facea per me e per gli uccellatori,
ché si saría meglio ordinato e cotto
e la tovaglia coperta di fiori:
meglio è straccar la coltrice e 'l piumaccio
che 'l cavallo e guastar l'uccello in braccio."

9   Intanto lo sparvier vuol rimpugnare,
      ma egli è sí rotto che non può far l'erta,
      perché i frascon cominciano a cascare
      e da l'un lato pendea la coverta;
      pur Dionigi il voleva aiutare;
      ma, rassettando la manica aperta,
      la man ghermigli, onde sotto se 'l caccia,
      saltogli addosso e fanne una cofaccia.

10   Restano adunque tre da uccellare;
      e drieto a questi andava molta gente,
      chi per piacere e chi pur per guardare:
      Bartolo e Ulivier, Braccio e 'l Parente,
      che mai non vide piú starne volare;
      e io mi messi con lor; similmente
      Piero Alamanni e 'l Portinar Giovanni,
      che pare in su la nona un barbagianni.

11   Strozzo drieto a costor, come maestro
      di questa gente, andava scosto un poco,
      come colui ch'all'arte è molto destro
      e molte volte ha fatto simil giuoco.
      E tanto va, chi a caval, chi pedestro,
      che finalmente ei son venuti al loco,
      il qual per uccellar fe' sol natura,
      con tutta l'arte e ordine e misura.

12   E' si vedea una gentil valletta,
      un fossatel con certe macchie in mezzo,
      da ogni parte rimunita e netta:
      sol nel fossato star posson al rezzo;
      era da ogni lato una piaggetta,
      che d'uccellar faría venir riprezzo
      a un gottoso e cieco, tanto è bella:
      el mondo non ha una pari a quella.

13   Scaldava il sole al monte già le spalle
      e 'l resto della valle è ancora ombrosa,
      quando giugnea la gente in su quel calle;
      prima a vedere e disegnar si posa

e poi si spargon tutti per la valle;
e, perché a punto riesca ogni cosa,
chi va co' can, chi alla guardia o a getto,
sí come Strozzo ha ordinato e detto.

14   Era da ogni lato uno sparviere,
alto, in buon luogo da poter gittare;
l'altro a capo ne va del canattiere,
ch'a la brigata la vorrà scagliare;
era Bartolo al fondo; ed Uliviere
ed alcuni altri, per poter guardare,
a mezza piaggia, in una bella stoppia.
El canattiere a' can leva la coppia.

15   Non altrimenti, quando la trombetta
sente alle mosse il lieve barberesco,
parte correndo o, vuoi dir, vola in fretta;
cosí quei can, che sciolti son di fresco;
e, se non pur che 'l canattier gli alletta,
chiamando alcuno e a chi scuote il pesco,
sarebbe il seguitargli troppa pena;
ma la pertica e 'l fischio gli raffrena.

16   "Tira, buon can! Su, tira, su, cammina!
Andianne! andianne! Torna qui, te', torna!
Ah! sciagurato, Tamburo e Guercina!
Abbiate cura a Sacco, che soggiorna:
ah! bugiardo! ah! poltron! Volgi, Rossina!
Guata buon can, guata brigata adorna!
Te', Fagianino... oh! che volta fu quella!
Vedila qui, quella starnina, vella!

17   "State avveduti a Staccio... frulla! frulla!
ecco e' leva cacciando, l'amor mio;
ma io non veggo però levar nulla,
e n'ha pur voglia, e n'ha pur gran disio.
Guarda la Corta là che si trastulla.
Oh! che romor faranno, già 'l sent' io:
chi salta e balla, e chi la leverà
di questi cani il miglior can sarà.

18   "Io veggo che Buontempo è in sulla traccia;
      ve' che le corre: e' le farà levare;
      abbi cura a Buontempo, che le caccia;
      parmi vederle e sentirle frullare;
      benché sia vecchio, ancor non ti dispiaccia,
      ch'io l'ho veduto e so quel ch'ei sa fare:
      i' so che 'l mio Buontempo mai non erra.
      Ecco, a te, Ulivier, guardale a terra!

19   "Guarda quell' altra all'erta, una al fossato:
      non ti dissi io che mi parea sentile?
      Guardane una alla vigna, all'altro lato
      guardane due e tre, guardane mille!"
      Alla brigata prima avea gittato
      Giovan Francesco, e riempiea le ville
      di grida e di conforti: "Ah! buono uccello!",
      ma, per la fretta, gittò col cappello.

20   "Ecco, Guglielmo, a te una ne viene:
      cava il cappello, ed alzerai la mano;
      non istar piú, Guglielmo! Ecco, a te, bene!"
      Guglielmo getta e grida: "Ahi, villano!"
      Fugge la starna, e drieto ben li tiene
      quello sparvier, che mai non esce invano:
      dettegli in aria forse cento braccia,
      poi cadde in terra, e già la pela e straccia.

21   "Garri a quel can" Guglielmo grida forte,
      che corre per cavargliele di piè.
      E, perch' a ciò le pertiche eran corte,
      un sasso prese e a Guercina diè,
      per riscampar sí buon uccel da morte;
      e, quando presso allo sparvier piú è,
      non lo veggendo, cheto usava stare,
      per veder se sentissi sonagliare.

22   E, cosí stando, gliel venne veduto:
      "Presto!" grida "a cavallo! E' l'ha pur presa!"
      E poi s'accosta, destro e avveduto,
      come colui che l'arte ha bene intesa;

presegli il geto e per quel l'ha tenuto;
dagli il capo e 'l cervel, ché non gli pesa;
sghermito, e l'ugne e 'l becco gli avea netto;
poi rimisse il cappello e torna al getto.

23   Giovan Francesco intanto avea ripreso
il suo sparviere e preso miglior loco;
pargli veder ch'a lui ne venga teso
uno starnone; e, com' è presso un poco,
aperta la man presto, il braccio steso,
gittò come maestro di tal giuoco;
giunse la starna, e, perch' ella è la vecchia,
si fe' lasciare e tutto lo spennecchia.

24   Invero egli era un certo sparverugio,
che somigliava un gheppio, e in un calappio
non credo che pigliassi un calderugio,
legato bene stretto con un cappio;
non avere' speranza nello indugio,
ch'a giuoco ne va poi come un fatappio;
e la cagion ch'a quel tratto non prese
fu che non v'avea il capo e non v'attese.

25   Intanto egli era uno starnone all'erta;
videlo il Foglia e fegli un gentil getto:
lo sparvier vola per la piaggia aperta
e presegnene innanzi, al dirimpetto.
Corre giú il Foglia e pargnene aver certa,
però che lo sparvier molto è perfetto:
preselo al netto, ove non era stecco
in terra, e insanguinogli i piedi e 'l becco.

26   E questo fe', ché lo sparviere è soro.
E intanto Ulivier forte chiamava:
"Chiama giú il Cappellaio, chiama costoro!
E' n'è qui una" (e col dito mostrava);
"rilega i can, però che basta loro
la Rocca, che di sotterra le cava;
vien giú, Guglielmo, non istare al rezzo,
e tu e 'l Foglia le mettete in mezzo."

27   Cosí fu fatto; e, come e' sono in punto,
        el canattier diceva: "Sotto, Rocca!
        Qui cadde, ve'. Ah! se tu l'arai giunto,
        siesi tuo; torna qui, te', pogli bocca."
        Poi dice: "Avetel voi guardato a punto?"
        E in quel lo starnon del fondo scocca.
        "Ecco, a te, Foglia!" Il Foglia grida e getta,
        e simil fe' Guglielmo molto in fretta.

28   Lasciò la starna andarne lo sparvieri
        e attende a fuggir quel che gli ha drieto.
        Disse Guglielmo: "Tu l'hai, Foglia Amieri."
        E, benché nol dimostri, ei n'è pur lieto.
        "Corri tu, che vi se' presso, Ulivieri!"
        diceva il Foglia, e Guglielmo sta cheto.
        Corse Ulivieri; e, com' egli è giú sceso,
        vide che l'uno sparvier l'altro ha preso.

29   Quel del Foglia avea preso per la gorga
        quel di Guglielmo e crede che 'l suo sia;
        par che a Guglielmo ta' parole porga:
        "La tua è stata troppa villania!
        Credo che 'l tuo sparvier massiccio scorga
        a sparvier certo; e, per la fede mia,
        tu pigli assai villani e stran trastulli;
        ma io pazzo a 'mpacciarmi con fanciulli!

30   "Questa è stata, per Dio! piacevol cosa,
        che per la gorga è preso il mio sparviere."
        Disse Guglielmo: "E' fanno alla franciosa",
        e non poteva le risa tenere,
        ché cosí fa l'allegrezza nascosa.
        Intanto piú s'accosta il Foglia Amiere;
        e, come agli sparvier n'andò, di botto
        vide che quel di Guglielmo è di sotto.

31   E getta presto il suo logoro in terra;
        e lo sparvier di súbito v'andava,
        e, come vincitor di quella guerra,
        gli fece vezzi, ché lo meritava.

Guglielmo intanto s'avvede ch'egli erra,
e lo sparvier suo guasto; onde gridava:
"Tu se' pur, Foglia, stato tu il villano!"
E mancò poco e' nol disse con mano.

32   Ma 'l Foglia innanzi alla furia si leva,
e stassi cheto, ed ha pur pazienza:
altro viso e parole non aveva
quel ch'aspettava in favor la sentenza,
e poi subitamente la perdeva.
Disse Guglielmo: "Io voglio usar prudenza:
ritroverrenci in luogo forse un tratto,
ch'io ti farò ben savio stu se' matto!"

33   Già il sole in verso mezzogiorno cala
e vien l'ombre stremando e le raccorcia;
dà lor proporzione e brutta e mala,
come a figura dipinta in iscorcia;
rinforzava il suo canto la cicala
e 'l mondo ardea, come fussi una torcia;
l'aria sta cheta e ogni fronde salda
nella stagion piú dispettosa e calda.

34   Quando il mio Dionigi tutto rosso,
sudando come fussi un uovo fresco,
disse: "Star piú con voi certo non posso.
Deh! vientene, ancor tu, Giovan Francesco!"
Pietro Alamanni ancor disse: "Io son mosso,
ché star qui piú a me stesso rincresco,
ché pazzia è, ché par la terra accesa,
aspettar piú per pascer poi di presa."

35   Diceva Dionigi: "Scalzo e scinto
a uno infrescatoio vo' starmi un'ora."
E finalmente il partito fu vinto
di partir tutti, ché 'l sol gli divora.
El Cappellaio ne va che par sospinto
co' bracchi ansando con la lingua fuora;
quanto piú vanno, il caldo piú raddoppia:
parea appiccato il fuoco in ogni stoppia.

36   Tornonsi a casa, chi tristo e chi lieto,
e chi ha pieno il carnaiuol di starne;
alcun si sta sanza esse molto cheto,
e bisogna procacci d'altra carne.
Guglielmo viene dispettoso a drieto,
né può di tanta ingiuria pace farne;
Gioan Francesco già non se ne cura,
ch'uccella per piacer, non per natura:

37   "Ov' è 'l Corona? Ov' è Giovan Simone?"
domanda. "Braccio, ov' è quel del gran naso?"
Braccio rispose: "A me consolazione
è che ciascun di costor sia rimaso.
Non prese mai il Corona uno starnone,
se per disgrazia non l'ha preso o a caso;
e piú sparvier ha morti già meschini
ch'Orlando non uccise Saracini.

38   "Egli arà forse preso qualche grillo;
lascialo andar, ché questa è poca ingiuria,
ché me' sarebbe perder, che smarrillo:
menarlo meco i' m'ho recato a ingiuria.
Gioan Simone, gli tocca un certo grillo,
sella il cavallo o, se gli ha, mula, a furia
el sacco toglie, e questo è suo mal vecchio:
per mio consiglio e' non verrà a Fucecchio;

39   "ché 'l ciambellotto ha già presa la piega
d'andarne sanza dire agli altri addio;
il cappelluccio e' vassene a bottega,
a un grembiule, ch'è 'l cucco e 'l suo desio;
lui già, quando il fiero naso spiega,
cani e cavalli aombra e fa restio;
né de' sentir della rosa l'odore,
se non conficca la punta nel fiore.

40   "Luigi Pulci anco rimaso fia:
e' se n'andò là oggi in un boschetto,
ch'aveva il capo pien di fantasia:
vorrà fantasticar qualche sonetto;

guarti, Corona, per la fede mia,
che borbottoe staman molto nel letto,
e' ricordava ogni volta il Corona,
e l'ha a cacciar in frottola o in canzona."

41   Giungono a casa, e chi ripone il cuoio,
chi i can governa e mette nella stalla;
poi, fatto cerchio a uno infrescatoio,
truovansi tutti co' bicchieri a galla.
Quivi si fa un altro uccellatoio,
quivi si dice un gru d'ogni farfalla;
e par trebbiano el vin, sendo cercone:
sí fa la voglia le vivande buone.

42   Il primo assalto fu sanza romore:
ognuno attende a menar le mascella;
ma poi, passato quel primo furore,
chi d'una cosa e chi d'altra favella;
ciascuno al suo sparvier dava l'onore,
cercando d'una scusa pronta e bella;
e chi molto non fe' col suo sparviere,
si sfoga or qui col ragionare e 'l bere.

43   Ogni cosa guastava la quistione
del Foglia e di Guglielmo finalmente;
ma Dionigi con parole buone
dicea: "Guglielmo, e' non si tiene a mente
a caccia nulla e a l'uccellagione:
basta che 'l Foglia del caso si pente;
fa' che tu sia, come fu' io, discreto,
ch'uccisi il mio e stommi in pace cheto."

44   Ora ecco il sol ne l'oceàn n'è ito,
e Luigi, e Luigi è già tornato;
e 'l Corona anche a desco è comparito;
Giovan Simone ha fatto al modo usato:
per arte di maiolica è sparito.
E, poi che molto si fu cicalato,
a letto tutti, e prima un centellino,
ché d'ogni cosa porta pena il vino.

45   Or quel che poi si sognassi la notte,
questo sarebbe bello a poter dire,
ch'io so ch'ognun rimetterà le dotte
e insino a terza vorranno dormire;
poi ce n'andreno in Sieve, a quelle grotte,
e qualche lasca farem fuori uscire.
E cosí passa, o compar, lieto il tempo,
con mille rime a zucchero e a tempo.

FROM THE *CANZONIERE*

1

Fortuna, come suol, pur mi dileggia
e di vane speranze ognor m'ingombra;
poi si muta in un punto, e mostra che ombra   3
è quanto pe' mortal' si pensa o veggia.
   Or benigna si fa et ora aspreggia,
or m'empie di pensieri et or mi sgombra,   6
e fa che l'alma spaventata aombra,
né par che del suo male ancor s'aveggia.
   Teme e spera, rallegrasi e contrista,   9
ben mille volte il dí nostra natura:
spesso il mal la fa lieta e 'l bene attrista,
   spera il suo danno e del bene ha paura,   12
tanto ha il viver mortal corta la vista.
Alfin vano è ogni pensiero e cura.

2

   Piú che mai bella e men che già mai fera
mostrommi Amor la mia cara inimica,
quando e pensier' del giorno e la fatica   3
tolto avea il pigro sonno della sera.
   Sembrava agli occhi miei propria come era,
deposta sol la sua durezza antica   6
e fatta agli amorosi raggi aprica:
né mai mi parve il ver cosa sí vera.

Prima al parlare e päuroso e lento   9
stavo, come solea; poi la päura
vinse il disio, e cominciai dicendo:
    "Madonna...": e in quel partissi come un vento. 12
Cosí in un tempo súbita mi fura
el sonno e sé e mia merzé, fuggendo.

3

Quanto sia vana ogni speranza nostra,
quanto fallace ciaschedun disegno,
quanto sia il mondo d'ignoranzia pregno,   3
la mäestra del tutto, Morte, il mostra.
    Altri si vive in canti e in ballo e in giostra,
altri a cosa gentil muove l'ingegno,   6
altri il mondo ha e le sue opre a sdegno,
altri quel che dentro ha, fuor non dimostra.
    Vane cure e pensier', diverse sorte,   9
per la diversità che dà Natura,
si vede ciascun tempo al mondo errante.
    Ogni cosa è fugace e poco dura,   12
tanto Fortuna al mondo è mal constante;
sola sta ferma e sempre dura Morte.

4

Lascia l'isola tua tanto diletta,
lascia il tuo regno dilicato e bello,
ciprigna dea, e vien' sopra il ruscello,   3
che bagna la minuta e verde erbetta.
    Vieni a questa ombra, alla dolce äuretta
che fa mormoreggiare ogni arbuscello,   6
a' canti dolci d'amoroso uccello:
questa da te per patria sia eletta.
    E se tu vien' tra queste chiare linfe,   9
sia teco il tuo amato e caro figlio,
ché qui non si conosce il suo valore.

Togli a Dïana le sue caste ninfe,   12
che sciolte or vanno e sanza alcun periglio,
poco prezzando la virtú d'Amore.

5

Bastava avermi tolto libertate
e dalla casta via disiunta e torta,
sanza volere ancor vedermi morta   3
in tanto strazio e in sí tenera etate.
    Tu mi lasciasti sanza aver pietate
di me, che al tuo partir pallida e smorta,   6
presagio ver della mia vita corta,
restai, piú non prezzando mia beltate.
    Né posso altro pensar, se non quell' ora   9
che fu cagion de' mia süavi pianti,
del mio dolce martíre e tristo bene;
    e se non fussi il rimembrare ancora   12
consolator delli affannati amanti,
morte posto avre' fine a tante pene.

6

Non de' verdi giardini ornati e cólti
dello aprico e dolce äere pestano
veniam, madonna, in la tua bianca mano,   3
ma in aspre selve e valle umbrose còlti:
    ove Venere, afflitta e in pensier' molti
pel periglio de Adon, correndo invano,   6
un spino acuto al nudo piè villano
sparse del divin sangue e boschi folti.
    Noi summettemmo allora il bianco fiore,   9
tanto che 'l sacro sangue non aggiunge
a terra: onde il color purpureo nacque.
    Non aure estive o rivi tolti a lunge   12
noi nutriti hanno, ma sospir' d'amore
l'aure son sute, e lacrime fûr l'acque.

7

O bella vïoletta, tu se' nata
ove già il primo mio bel disio nacque;
lacrime triste e belle furon l'acque   3
che t'han nutrita e piú volte bagnata.
  Pietate in quella terra fortunata
nutrí il disio, ove il bel cesto giacque;   6
la bella man ti colse, e poi li piacque
farne la mia di sí bel don bëata.
  E' mi pare ad ogni or fuggir ti voglia   9
a quella bella mano, onde ti tegno
al nudo petto dolcemente stretta:
  al nudo petto, ché disire e doglia   12
tiene in luogo del cor, che 'l petto ha a sdegno
e stassi onde tu vieni, o vïoletta.

8

Quando a me il lume de' belli occhi arriva,
fugge davanti alle amorose ciglia
de' miei varii pensier' la gran famiglia,   3
la Pietà, la Speranza semiviva.
  Parte dalla memoria fugitiva
ciascuna impressïon che 'l ver simiglia   6
e resta sol dolcezza e maraviglia,
ché ogni altra cosa occide, ovunque è viva.
  Li spirti incontro a quel dolce splendore,   9
da me fuggendo, lieti vanno, in cui
(e loro il sanno) Amor gli occide e strugge.
  Se la mia vita resta, o se pur fugge,   12
che, morta in me, allor vive in altrui,
dubbio amoroso solva il gentil cuore.

FROM THE *COMENTO DE' MIEI SONETTI*

PROEMIO

Assai sono stato dubbioso e sospeso se dovevo fare la presente interpretazione e comento de' miei sonetti, e, se pure qualche volta ero piú inclinato a farlo, le infrascritte ragioni mi occorrevano in contrario[1] e mi toglievano da questa opera. Prima, la presunzione nella quale mi pareva incorrere comentando io le cose proprie, cosí per la troppa estimazione che mostravo fare di me medesimo, come perché mi pareva assumere in me quel giudicio che debba essere d'altri, notando in questa parte l'ingegni di coloro alle mani de' quali perverranno i miei versi, come poco sufficienti a poterli intendere. Pensavo, oltre a questo, poter esser da qualcuno facilmente ripreso di poco giudicio,[2] avendo consumato il tempo e nel comporre e nel comentare versi, la materia e subietto de' quali in gran parte fussi una amorosa passione; e questo essere molto piú reprensibile in me per le continue occupazioni e publiche e private, le quali mi dovevano ritrarre[3] da simili pensieri, secondo alcuni non solamente frivoli e di poco momento,[4] ma ancora perniciosi e di qualche pregiudicio cosí all'anima nostra come all'onore del mondo. E, se questo è, il pensare a simili cose è grande errore, metterle in versi molto maggiore, ma il comentarle non pare minor difetto che sia quello di colui che ha fatto un lungo e indurato abito nelle male opere; massime perché i comenti sono riservati per cose teologiche o di filosofia e importanti grandi effetti,[5] o a edificazione e consolazione della mente nostra o a utilità della umana generazione. Aggiugnesi ancora a questo,[6] che forse a qualcuno parrà reprensibile, quando bene la materia e subietto fussi per sé assai degno, avendo scritto e fattone menzione in lingua nostra materna e volgare,[7] la quale, dove si parla ed è intesa, per essere molto comune non pare declini da qualche viltà, e in quelli luoghi dove non ne è notizia non può essere intesa,[8] e però a questa parte[9] questa opera e fatica nostra pare al tutto vana e come se non fussi fatta.

Queste tre difficoltà hanno insino a ora ritardato quello che piú tempo fa avevo proposto, cioè la presente interpetrazione. Al presente ho pure deliberato, vinto, al mio parere, da migliore ragione, metterla in opera, pensando che, se questa mia poca fatica sarà di qualche estimazione e grata a qualcuno, sarà bene collocata e non al tutto vana; se pure arà poca grazia,[10] sarà poco letta e da pochi vituperata, e, non essendo molto durabile, poco durerà ancora la reprensione nella quale possa incorrere.

E, rispondendo al presente alla prima ragione e a quelli che di presunzione mi volessino in alcuno modo notare,[11] dico che a me non pare presunzione lo interpetrare le cose mie, ma piú presto tòrre fatica ad altri; e di nessuno è piú proprio officio lo interpetrare che di colui medesimo che ha scritto,[12] perché nessuno può meglio sapere o eligere la verità del senso suo: come mostra assai chiaramente la confusione che nasce della varietà de' comenti, nelli quali il piú delle volte si segue piú tosto la natura propria che la intenzione vera di chi ha scritto. Né mi pare per questo fare argomento che io tenga troppo conto di me medesimo o tolga ad altri il giudicarmi: perché credo sia ufficio vero d'ogni uomo operare tutte le cose a benificio degli uomini, o proprio o d'altri; e perché ognuno non nasce atto o disposto a potere operare quelle cose che sono reputate prime nel mondo, è da misurare sé medesimo e vedere in che ministerio[13] meglio si può servire all'umana generazione, e in quello esercitarsi, perché e alla diversità degl'ingegni umani e alla necessità della vita nostra non può satisfare una cosa sola, ancora che sia la prima e piú eccellente opera che possino fare gli uomini: anzi, pare che la contemplazione, la quale sanza controversia[14] è la prima e piú eccellente, pasca minore numero delli uomini che alcuna delle altre. E per questo si conclude non solamente molte opere d'ingegno, ma ancora molti vili ministerii concorrere di necessità alla perfezione della vita umana, ed essere vero officio di tutti gli uomini, in quel grado che si truovono o dal cielo o dalla natura o dalla fortuna disposti, servire alla umana generazione. Io arei bene desiderato potermi esercitare in maggiore cose; né voglio però per questo mancare, in quello che sopporta lo ingegno e forze mie, a qualcuno, se non a molti, i quali, forse piú tosto per piacere a me che perché le cose mie satisfaccino a[15] loro, mi hanno confortato[16] a questo: l'autorità e grazia de' quali vale assai appresso di me.[17] E se non potrò fare altra utilità a chi leggerà i versi miei, almanco qualche poco di piacere se ne piglierà, perché forse qualche ingegno troveranno proporzionato e conforme al loro;[18] e se pure qualcuno se ne ridessi, a me sarà grato che tragga de' versi miei questa voluttà, ancora che sia piccola; parendomi, massimamente publicando questa interpetrazione, sottomettermi piú tosto al giudicio degli altri, conciosiacosa che se da me medesimo avessi giudicato questi miei versi indegni d'essere letti, arei fuggito il giudicio degli altri, ma comentandoli e publicandoli fuggo, al mio parere, molto meglio la presunzione del giudicarmi da me medesimo.

Ora, per rispondere alle calunnie di quelli che volessino accusarmi avendo io[19] messo tempo e nel comporre e nel comentare cose non degne di fatica o di tempo alcuno, per essere passioni amorose ecc., e massime tra molte mie necessarie occupazioni, dico che veramente con giustizia sarei dannato quando la natura umana fussi di tanta eccellenzia dotata, che tutti gli uomini potessino operare sempre tutte le cose perfette; ma perché questo grado di perfezione è stato concesso a molti pochi, e a questi pochi ancora molto rare volte nella vita loro, mi pare si possa concludere, considerata la imperfezione umana, quelle cose essere migliori al mondo nelle quali interviene minor male.[20] E giudicando piú tosto secondo la natura comune e consuetudine universale degli uomini, se bene non l'oserei affermare, pure credo l'amore tra gli uomini non solamente non essere represibile, ma quasi necessario, e assai vero argumento di gentilezza[21] e grandezza d'animo, e sopra tutto cagione d'invitare gli uomini a cose degne ed eccellenti, ed esercitare e riducere in atto quelle virtú che in potenzia sono nell'anima nostra. Perché, chi cerca diligentemente quale sia la vera difinizione dell'amore, trova non essere altro che appetito di bellezza;[22] e, se questo è, tutte le cose deforme e brutte necessariamente dispiaccionò a chi ama. E mettendo per al presente da parte quello amore[23] il quale, secondo Platone, è mezzo a tutte le cose a trovare la loro perfezione e riposarsi ultimamente nella suprema bellezza, cioè Dio; parlando di quello amore che s'estende solamente ad amare l'umana creatura, dico che, se bene questa non è quella perfezione d'amore che si chiama "sommo bene", almanco veggiamo chiaramente contenere in sé tanti beni ed evitare tanti mali, che secondo la comune consuetudine della vita umana tiene luogo di bene.[24]

massime se è ornata di quelle circostanzie e condizioni che si convengono a un vero amore, che mi pare siano due: la prima, che si ami una cosa sola; la seconda, che questa tale cosa si ami sempre. Queste due condizioni male possono cadere[25] se il subietto amato non ha in sé, a proporzione dell'altre cose umane, somma perfezione, e se, oltre alle naturali bellezze, non concorre nella cosa amata ingegno grande, modi e costumi ornati e onesti, maniera e gesti eleganti, destrezza d'accorte e dolci parole, amore, constanzia e fede; e queste cose tutte necessariamente convengono alla perfezione dello amore. Perché, ancora che il principio d'amore nasca dagli occhi e da bellezza,[26] nondimeno alla conservazione e perseveranza in esso bisognano quell' altre condizioni; perché se, o per infermità o per età o altra cagione, si scolorissi il viso e mancassi in tutto o in parte la bellezza, restino tutte quell' altre condizioni, non meno grate allo animo e al cuore che la bellezza agli occhi. Né sarebbono ancora queste tali condizioni sufficienti, se ancora in colui che ama non fusse vera cognizione di queste condizioni, che presuppone perfezione di giudicio nell'amante; né potrebbe essere amore della cosa amata verso colui che ama, se quello che ama non meritassi essere amato, presupposto l'infallibile giudicio della cosa amata. E però, chi propone un vero amore, di necessità propone grande perfezione, secondo la comune consuetudine degli uomini, cosí nello amato come in chi ama; e come avviene in tutte le altre cose perfette, credo che questo tale amore sia suto al mondo molto raro: che tanto piú arguisce l'eccellenzia sua.[27] Chi ama una cosa sola e sempre, di necessità non pone amore ad altre cose, e però si priva di tutti gli errori e volutà nelle quali comunemente incorrono gli uomini; e amando persona atta a conoscere e cercando in ogni modo che può di piacerli, bisogna di necessità che in tutte le opere sue cerchi degnificarsi[28] e farsi eccellente tra gli altri, seguitando opere virtuose, per farsi piú degno che può di quella cosa che lui stima sopra all'altre degnissima; parendogli che, e in palese e in occulto, come la forma della cosa amata sempre è presente al cuore, cosí sia presente a tutte l'opere sue, le quali laudi o riprenda secondo la loro convenienzia,[29] come vero testimonio e assistente giudice non solo delle opere, ma de' pensieri. E cosí, parte colla vergogna reprimendo il male, parte con lo stimolo del piacerli eccitando[30] il bene, se pure questi tali perfettamente non operano, almanco fanno quello che al mondo è reputato manco male: la quale cosa, rispetto alla imperfezione umana, al mondo per bene si elegge.

Questo adunque è stato il subietto de' versi miei. E se, pure con tutte queste ragioni, non risponderò alle obtrettazioni[31] e calunnie di chi mi volessi dannare, almanco, come disse il nostro fiorentino Poeta,[32] apresso di quelli che hanno provato che cosa è amore, "spero trovar pietà, non che perdono": il giudicio de' quali è assai a mia satisfazione. Perché, se gli è vero, come dice Guido bolognese, che amore e gentilezza si convertino e sieno una cosa medesima,[33] credo che agli uomini basti e solamente sia espettibile[34] la laude degli alti e gentili ingegni, curandosi poco degli altri, perché è impossibile fare opera al mondo che sia da tutti gli uomini laudata; e però chi ha buona elezione si sforza acquistare laude apresso di quelli che ancora loro sono degni di laude, e poco cura la opinione degli altri. A me pare si possa poco biasimare quello che è naturale; nessuna cosa è piú naturale che l'appetito d'unirsi con la cosa bella, e questo appetito è stato ordinato dalla natura negli uomini per la propagazione della umana generazione, cosa molto necessaria alla conservazione della umana spezie.[35] E a questo la vera ragione che ci debba muovere non è né nobiltà di sangue, né speranza di possessioni, di ricchezza o d'altra commodità, ma solamente la elezione naturale, non sforzata o occupata[36] da alcuno altro rispetto, ma solamente mossa da una certa conformità e proporzione[37] che hanno insieme la cosa amata e lo amante, a fine della propagazione dell'umana spezie. E però sono sommamente da dannare quelli i quali l'appetito muove ad amare sommamente le cose che sono fuori di questo ordine naturale e vero fine già proposto da noi, e da laudare quelli e quali, seguitando questo fine, amano una cosa sola diuturnamente e con somma constanzia e fede.

A me pare che assai copiosamente sia risposto a tale obietto.[38] E, dato che questo amore, come di sopra abbiamo detto, sia bene, non pare molto necessario purgare[39] quella parte che in me parrebbe forse piú repressibile, per le diverse occupazioni publiche e private: perché, s'egli è bene, il bene non ha bisogno d'alcuna escusazione, perché non ha colpa. E se pure qualche scrupoloso giudicio non volessi ammettere queste ragioni, almanco conceda questa piccola licenzia alla età giovenile e tenera, la quale non pare tanto obligata alla censura e giudicio degli uomini e nella quale non pare tanto grave qualunque errore, massime perché è piú stimulata a declinare[40] dalla via retta e per la poca esperienzia manco si può opporre a quelle cose che la natura e comune uso delli uomini persuadono.[41] Questo dico in caso che pure fussi stimato errore amare molto, con somma sincerità e fede, una cosa, la quale sforza per la perfezione sua l'amore dello amante: la quale cosa non confesso essere errore. E, se questo è, o per le ragioni dette o avuto rispetto all'età, né il comporre né il comentare miei versi fatti a questo proposito mi può essere imputato a grave errore. E dato che fussi vero[42] che non si convenissi comento a simile materia, per essere piccola e poco importante o a edificazione o a contento della mente nostra, dico che, se questo è, la fatica di questo comento convenirsi massimamente a me,[43] acciò che altro ingegno di più eccellenzia che il mio non abbia a consumarsi o mettere tempo in cose sí basse; e se pure la materia è alta e degna, come pare a me, il chiarirla bene e farla piana e intelligibile a ciascuno essere molto utile: e questo, per quello che ho detto di sopra, nessuno il può fare con più chiara espressione del vero senso che io medesimo. Né io sono stato il primo che ho comentato versi importanti[44] simili amorosi subietti, perché Dante lui medesimo comentò alcuna delle sue canzoni e altri versi;[45] e io ho letto il comento di Egidio romano e Dino Del Garbo,[46] eccellentissimi filosofi, sopra a quella sottilissima canzone di Guido Cavalcanti,[47] uomo al tempo suo riputato primo dialettico che fussi al mondo, e inoltre in questi nostri versi vulgari[48] eccellentissimo, come mostrano tutte le altre sue opere e massime la sopra detta canzone, che comincia *Donna mi prega* ecc., la quale non importa[49] altro che il principio come nasce ne' cuori gentili amore e gli effetti suoi. E se pure alla purgazione mia[50] non sono sufficienti né le sopra scritte ragioni, né gli esempi, la compassione almeno mi doverrà giustificare, perché, essendo nella mia gioventú stato molto perseguitato dagli uomini e dalla fortuna,[51] qualche poco di refrigerio non mi debbe essere negato, il quale solamente ho trovato e in amare ferventemente e nella composizione e comento de' miei versi, come più chiaramente faremo intendere quando verremo alla esposizione di quello sonetto che comincia *Se tra gli altri sospir ch'escon di fore*. Quali sieno sute le mie maligne persecuzioni, per essere assai publiche è assai noto; qual sia suta la dolcezza e refrigerio che 'l mio dolcissimo e constantissimo amore ha dato a queste, è impossibile che altri che io lo possi intendere, perché, quando bene l'avessi ad alcuno narrato, cosí era impossibile a lui lo intenderlo come a me riferirne il vero. E però torno al sopradetto verso del nostro fiorentino Poeta, che, "dove sia chi per pruova[52] intenda amore" (cosí questo amore che io ho tanto laudato, come qualche particolare amore e carità verso di me), "spero trovar pietà, non che perdono."

Resta adunque solamente rispondere alla obiezione che potessi essere fatta avendo scritto in lingua vulgare, secondo il giudicio di qualcuno non capace o degna d'alcuna eccellente materia e subietto.[53] E a questa parte si risponde alcuna cosa non essere manco degna per essere piú comune,[54] anzi si prova ogni bene essere tanto migliore quanto è piú comunicabile e universale, come è di natura sua quello che si chiama "sommo bene":[55] perché non sarebbe sommo se non fussi infinito, né alcuna cosa si può chiamare infinita, se non quella che è comune a tutte le cose. E però non pare che l'essere comune in tutta Italia la nostra materna lingua li tolga dignità, ma è da pensare in fatto la perfezione o imperfezione di detta lingua. E, considerando quali sieno quelle condizioni che danno dignità e perfezione a qualunque idioma e lingua, a me pare sieno quattro, delle quali una o al piú dua sieno proprie e vere laudi della lingua, l'altre piú tosto dipendino o dalla consuetudine e oppinione degli uomini o dalla fortuna.

Quella che è vera laude della lingua è l'essere copiosa e abondante e atta a esprimere bene il senso e concetto della mente. E però si giudica la lingua greca piú perfetta che la latina, e la latina piú che l'ebrea, perché l'una piú che l'altra meglio esprime la mente di chi ha o detto o scritto alcuna cosa.

L'altra condizione che piú degnifica la lingua è la dolcezza e armonia, che risulta piú d'una che d'un'altra; e benché l'armonia sia cosa naturale e proporzionata con l'armonia dell'anima e del corpo nostro, nondimeno a me pare, per la varietà degli ingegni umani, che tutti non sono bene proporzionati e perfetti,[56] questa sia piú presto oppinione che ragione: conciosiacosa che quelle cose che si giudicano secondo che comunemente piacciono o non piacciono, paiono piú tosto fondate nella oppinione che nella vera ragione, massime quelle, il piacere o dispiacere delle quali non si prova con altra ragione che con l'appetito.[57] E, non ostanti queste ragioni, non voglio però affermare questa non poter essere propria laude della lingua; perché, essendo l'armonia (come è detto) proporzionata alla natura umana, si può inferire[58] il giudicio della dolcezza di tale armonia convenirsi a quelli che similmente sono bene proporzionati a riceverla, il giudicio de' quali debba essere accettato per buono, ancora che fussino pochi:[59] perché le sentenzie e giudíci degli uomini piú presto si debbono ponderare che numerare.

L'altra condizione che fa piú eccellente una lingua è quando in una lingua sono scritte cose sottili e gravi[60] e necessarie alla vita umana, cosí alla mente nostra come alla utilità degli uomini e salute del corpo: come si può dire della lingua ebrea, per li ammirabili misterii che contiene, accomodati,[61] anzi necessari alla ineffabile verità della fede nostra; e similmente della lingua greca, contenente molte scienze metafisiche, naturali e morali molto necessarie alla umana generazione. E quando questo avviene, è necessario confessare che piú presto sia degno il subietto che la lingua, perché il subietto è fine e la lingua è mezzo.[62] Né per questo si può chiamare quella lingua piú perfetta in sé, ma piú tosto maggiore perfezione della materia che per essa si tratta; perché, chi ha scritto cose teologiche, metafisiche, naturali e morali, in quella parte che degnifica la lingua nella quale ha scritto pare che piú presto reservi la laude nella materia,[63] e che la lingua abbi fatto l'ufficio d'istrumento, il quale è buono o reo secondo il fine.

Resta un'altra sola condizione che dà reputazione alla lingua, e questo è quando il successo delle cose del mondo[64] è tale, che facci universale e quasi comune a tutto il mondo quello che naturalmente è proprio o d'una città o d'una provincia sola. E questo si può piú presto chiamare felicità e prosperità di fortuna che vera laude della lingua, perché l'essere in prezzo e assai celebrata una lingua nel mondo consiste nella oppinione[65] di quelli tali che assai la prezzono e stimono, né si può chiamare vero e proprio bene quello che dipende da altri che da sé medesimo: perché, quelli tali che l'hanno in prezzo potrebbono facilmente sprezzarla e mutare oppinione, e quelle condizioni mutarsi per le quali, mancando la cagione, facilmente mancherebbe ancora la dignità e laude di quella.[66] Questa tale dignità d'essere prezzata per il successo prospero della fortuna è molto appropriata alla lingua latina, perché la propagazione dello Imperio Romano l'ha fatta non solamente comune per tutto il mondo, ma quasi necessaria. E per questo concluderemo che queste laudi esterne e che dipendono dall'oppinione degli altri o dalla fortuna non sieno laudi proprie.

E però, volendo provare la dignità della lingua nostra, solamente dobbiamo insistere nelle prime condizioni e vedere se la lingua nostra facilmente esprime qualunque concetto della nostra mente; e a questo nessuna migliore ragione si può introdurre che l'esperienza. Dante, il Petrarca e il Boccaccio, nostri poeti fiorentini, hanno, nelli gravi e dolcissimi versi e orazioni[67] loro, mostro assai chiaramente con molta facilità potersi in questa lingua esprimere ogni senso. Perché, chi legge la *Commedia* di Dante vi troverrà molte cose teologiche e naturali essere con grande destrezza e facilità espresse; troverrà ancora molto attamente nello scrivere suo quelle tre generazioni di stili che sono dagli oratori laudati, cioè umile, mediocre e alto; e in effetto, in uno solo, Dante ha assai perfettamente assoluto quello che in diversi autori, cosí greci come latini, si truova.[68] Chi negherà nel Petrarca trovarsi uno stile grave, lepido e dolce, e queste cose amorose con tanta gravità e venustà trattate, quanta sanza dubbio non si truova in Ovidio, Tibullo, Catullo, Properzio[69] o alcuno altro latino? Le canzone e sonetti di Dante sono di tanta gravità, sottilità e ornato,[70] che quasi non hanno comparazione. In prosa e orazione soluta,[71] chi ha letto il Boccaccio, uomo dottissimo e facundissimo, facilmente giudicherà singulare e sola al mondo non solamente la invenzione, ma la copia[72] ed eloquenzia sua; e considerando l'opera sua del *Decameron*, per la diversità della materia, ora grave, ora mediocre e ora bassa, e contenente tutte le perturbazioni che agli uomini possono accadere, d'amore e odio, timore e speranza, tante nuove astuzie e ingegni,[73] e avendo a esprimere tutte le nature e passioni degli uomini che si trovono al mondo, sanza controversia giudicherà nessuna lingua meglio che la nostra essere atta a esprimere. E Guido Cavalcanti, di chi di sopra facemmo menzione, non si può dire quanto comodamente abbi insieme congiunto la gravità e la dolcezza, come mostra la canzone sopra detta e alcuni sonetti e ballate sue dolcissime. Restano ancora molti altri gravi ed eleganti scrittori, la menzione de' quali lasceremo piú tosto per fuggire la prolissità, che perché non ne siano degni. E però concluderemo piú tosto essere mancati alla lingua uomini che la esercitino, che la lingua agli uomini e alla materia;[74] la dolcezza e armonia della quale, a chi per essersi assuefatto con essa ha con lei qualche consuetudine, veramente è grandissima e atta molto a muovere.[75]

Queste, che sono e che forse a qualcuno potrebbono pure parere proprie laudi della lingua, mi paiono assai copiosamente nella nostra. E per quello che insino a ora massime da Dante è suto trattato nell'opera sua, mi pare non solamente utile, ma necessario, per li gravi e importanti effetti, che li versi suoi sieno letti, come mostra l'esempio per molti comenti fatti sopra la sua *Commedia* da uomini dottissimi e famosissimi,[76] e le frequenti allegazioni[77] che da santi ed eccellenti uomini ogni dí si sentono nelle loro pubbliche predicazioni. E forse saranno ancora scritte in questa lingua cose sottili e importanti e degne d'essere lette, massime perché insino a ora si può dire essere l'adolescenzia di questa lingua, perché ognora piú si fa elegante e gentile; e potrebbe facilmente, nella gioventú e adulta età sua, venire ancora in maggiore perfezione, e tanto piú aggiugnendosi qualche prospero successo ed augumento al fiorentino imperio:[78] come si debbe non solamente sperare, ma con tutto l'ingegno e forze per li buoni cittadini aiutare; pure, questo, per essere in potestà della fortuna e nella volontà dello infallibile giudicio di Dio, come non è bene affermarlo, non è ancora da disperarsene. Basta, per al presente, fare questa conclusione: che di quelle laudi che sono proprie della lingua, la nostra ne è assai bene copiosa; né giustamente ce ne possiamo dolere. E per queste medesime ragioni nessuno mi può riprendere se io ho scritto in quella lingua nella quale io sono nato e nutrito, massime perché e la ebrea e la greca e la latina erano nel tempo loro tutte lingue materne e naturali, ma parlate o scritte piú accuratamente e con qualche regola o ragione da quelli che ne sono in onore e in prezzo,[79] che generalmente dal vulgo e turba popolare.

Pare con assai sufficienti ragioni provato la lingua nostra non essere inferiore ad alcuna delle altre; e però, avendo in genere dimostro[80] la perfezione d'essa, giudico molto conveniente ristrignersi al particolare e venire dalla generalità a qualche proprietà,[81] quasi come dalla circonferenzia al centro. E però, sendo mio primo proposito la interpetrazione de' miei sonetti, mi sforzerò mostrare, tra gli altri modi degli stili volgari e consueti per chi ha scritto in questa lingua, lo stile del sonetto non essere inferiore o al ternario o alla canzona o ad altra generazione di stile volgare, arguendo dalla difficultà: perché la virtú, secondo i filosofi, consiste circa il difficile.[82]

È sentenzia[83] di Platone che il narrare brevemente e dilucidamente molte cose non solo pare mirabile tra gli uomini, ma quasi cosa divina. La brevità del sonetto non comporta che una sola parola sia vana, e il vero subietto e materia de' sonetti, per questa ragione, debbe essere qualche acuta e gentile sentenzia, narrata attamente e in pochi versi ristretta, fuggendo la oscurità e durezza. Ha grande similitudine e conformità questo modo di stile con l'epigramma, quanto allo acume della materia e alla destrezza dello stile, ma è degno e capace il sonetto di sentenzie piú gravi, e però diventa tanto piú difficile. Confesso il ternario essere piú alto e grande stile, e quasi simile all'eroico,[84] né per questo però piú difficile, perché ha il campo piú largo, e quella sentenzia che non si può ristrignere in due o in tre versi sanza vizio di chi scrive,[85] nel ternario si può ampliare. Le canzoni mi pare abbino grande similitudine con la elegia; ma credo, o per natura dello stile nostro o per la consuetudine di chi ha scritto insino a qui canzone, lo stile della canzone non sanza qualche poco di pudore ammetterebbe molte cose non solamente leggere e vane, ma troppo molle e lascive,[86] le quali comunemente si trovano scritte nelle latine elegie. Le canzoni ancora, per avere piú larghi spazi dove possino vagare, non reputo tanto difficile stile quanto quello del sonetto; e questo si può assai facilmente provare con la esperienzia, perché chi ha composto sonetti e s'è ristretto a qualche certa e sottile materia, con grande difficultà ha fuggito la oscurità e durezza dello stile; ed è grande differenzia dal comporre sonetti in modo che le rime sforzino la materia, a quello che la materia sforzi le rime.[87] E' mi pare ne' versi latini sia molto maggiore libertà che non è ne' volgari, perché nella lingua nostra, oltre a' piedi, che piú tosto per natura che per altra regola è necessario servare ne' versi, concorre ancora questa difficultà delle rime; la quale, come sa chi l'ha provato, disturba molte e belle sentenzie, né permette si possino narrare con tanta facilità e chiarezza. E che il nostro verso abbia i suoi piedi si prova perché si potrebbono fare molti versi contenenti undici sillabe, sanza avere suono di versi o alcun'altra differenzia dalla prosa. Concluderemo per questo il verso volgare essere molto difficile, e, tra gli altri versi, lo stile del sonetto difficillimo, e per questo degno d'essere in prezzo[88] quanto alcuno degli altri stili volgari. Né per questo voglio inferire li miei sonetti essere di quella perfezione che ho detto convenirsi a tal modo di stile; ma, come dice Ovidio di Fetonte,[89] per al presente mi basta avere tentato quello stile che appresso i volgari è piú eccellente, e se non ho potuto aggiugnere alla perfezione sua o conducere questo carro solare,[90] almanco mi sia in luogo di laude lo ardire d'avere tentato questa via, ancora che con qualche mio mancamento le forze mi sieno mancate a tanta impresa.

Parrà forse suto questo nostro proemio e troppo prolisso e maggiore preparazione che non è in sé l'effetto. A me pare non sanza vera necessità essere suto alquanto copioso, e, considerando la inezia di questi miei versi, ho giudicato abbino bisogno di qualche ornamento, il quale si conviene a quelle cose che per loro natura sono poco ornate; né si conveniva minore escusazione alle colpe che forse mi sarebbono sute attribuite. E però, assoluta[91] questa parte, verremo alla esposizione de' sonetti, fatto prima alquanto di argumento,[92] che pare necessario a questi primi quattro sonetti.

ARGUMENTO

Forse qualcuno giudicherà poco conveniente principio a' versi miei cominciando non solamente fuora della consuetudine di quelli che insino a qui hanno scritto simili versi, ma, come pare *prima facie*,[93] pervertendo quasi l'ordine della natura, mettendo per principio quello che in tutte le cose umane suole essere ultimo fine; perché li primi quattro sonetti furono da me composti per la morte d'una donna,[94] che non solo estorse questi sonetti da me, ma le lacrime universalmente dagli occhi di tutti gli uomini e donne che di lei ebbono alcuna notizia. E però, non ostante che paia cosa molto assurda cominciando io dalla morte, a me pare principio molto conveniente, per le ragioni che diremo appresso.

È sentenzia de' buoni filosofi la corruzione[95] d'una cosa essere creazione d'un'altra e il termine e fine d'un male[96] essere grado e principio d'un altro. E questo di necessità avviene, perché, essendo la forma e spezie, secondo i filosofi, immortale, di necessità conviene sempre si muova sopra la materia; e di questo perpetuo moto necessariamente nasce una continua generazione di cose nuove, la quale essendo sanza intermissione di tempo alcuno e con una brevissima presenzia dell'essere delle cose e dello stato d'esse in quella tale qualità o forma, bisogna confessare il fine d'una cosa essere principio d'un'altra; e, secondo Aristotile, la privazione è principio delle cose create.[97] E per questo si conclude nelle cose umane fine e principio essere una medesima cosa: non dico già fine e principio d'una cosa medesima, ma quello che è fine d'una cosa, *immediate*[98] è principio d'un'altra. E, se questo è, molto convenientemente[99] la morte è principio a questa nostra opera. E tanto piú, perché chi esamina piú sottilmente troverrà il principio dell'amorosa

vita procedere dalla morte, perché chi vive ad amore muore prima
all'altre cose;[100] e se lo amore ha in sé quella perfezione che già
abbiamo detto, è impossibile venire a tale perfezione se prima non
si muore quanto alle cose piú imperfette. Questa medesima sentenzia pare che abbino seguito Omero, Virgilio e Dante, delli quali
Omero manda Ulisse appresso agl'inferi, Virgilio Enea,[101] e Dante
lui medesimo perlustra[102] lo inferno, per mostrare che alla perfezione
si va per questa via. Ma è necessario, dopo la cognizione delle cose
imperfette, quanto a quelle morire: perché, poi che Enea è giunto a'
campi elisii e Dante condotto in paradiso, mai piú si sono ricordati
dell'inferno; e arebbe Orfeo tratto Euridice dell'inferno e condotto-
la tra quelli che vivono, se non fussi rivoltosi[103] verso l'inferno: che
si può interpretrare Orfeo non essere veramente morto, e per questo
non essere aggiunto alla perfezione della felicità sua, di avere la sua
cara Euridice. E però il principio della vera vita è la morte della vita
non vera; né per questo pare posto sanza qualche buono rispetto la
morte per principio de' versi nostri.

SONNETS

1

Belle, fresche e purpurëe vïole,
che quella candidissima man colse,
qual piaggia o qual puro äer produr volse   3
tanti piú vaghi fior' che far non suole?
Qual rugiada, qual terra o ver qual sole
tante vaghe bellezze in voi raccolse?   6
Onde il süave odor natura tolse,
o il ciel, che a tanto ben degnar ne vuole?
Care mie vïolette, quella mano   9
che vi elesse intra l'altre, ove eri, in sorte
vi ha di tante eccellenzie e pregio ornate!
Quella che il cor mi tolse, e di villano   12
lo fe' gentile, a cui siate consorte:
quella adunque, e non altri, ringraziate!

2

Datemi pace omai, sospiri ardenti,
o pensier' sempre nel bel viso fissi,
ché qualche sonno placido venissi   3
alle roranti mie luci dolenti!
    Or li uomini e le fere hanno le urgenti
fatiche e ' dur' pensier' queti e remissi,   6
e già i bianchi cavalli al giogo ha missi
la scorta de' febei raggi orïenti.
    Deh, facciàn triegua, Amor! ch'io ti prometto   9
ne' sonni sol veder quello amoroso
viso, udir le parole ch'ella dice,
    toccar la bianca man che il cor m'ha stretto.   12
O Amor, del mio ben troppo invidioso,
lassami almen dormendo esser felice!

3

Cerchi chi vuol le pompe e gli alti onori,
le piazze, e templi e gli edifizii magni,
le delizie, il tesor, quale accompagni   3
mille duri pensier', mille dolori.
    Un verde praticel pien di bei fiori,
un rivolo che l'erba intorno bagni,   6
uno uccelletto che d'amor si lagni,
acqueta molto meglio i nostri ardori;
    l'ombrose selve, e sassi e gli alti monti,   9
gli antri obscuri e le fere fugitive,
qualche leggiadra ninfa päurosa.
    Quivi veggo io con pensier' vaghi e pronti   12
le belle luci come fussin vive,
qui me le toglie ora una ora altra cosa.

4

Ove madonna volge li occhi belli,
sanza altro sol la mia leggiadra Flora
fa germinar la terra e mandar fora   3
mille varii color' di fior' novelli.

Amorosa armonia rendon li uccelli
sentendo il cantar suo, che l'innamora;   6
veston le selve i secchi rami, allora
che senton quanto dolce ella favelli.

Delle timide ninfe a' petti casti   9
qualche molle pensiero Amore infonde,
se trae riso o sospir la bella bocca.

Or qui lingua o pensier non par che basti   12
a intender ben quanta e qual grazia abonde,
là dove quella candida man tocca.

CORINTO

La luna in mezzo alle minori stelle
chiara fulgea nel ciel quieto e sereno,
quasi ascondendo lo splendor di quelle;   3
   e 'l sonno avea ogni animal terreno
dalle fatiche lor diurne sciolti:
e il mondo è d'ombre e di silenzio pieno.   6
   Sol Corinto pastor ne' boschi folti
cantava per amor di Galatea
tra ' faggi, e non v'è altri che l'ascolti: 9
   né alle luci lacrimose avea
data quiete alcuna, anzi soletto
con questi versi il suo amor piangea: 12
   "O Galatea, perché tanto in dispetto
hai Corinto pastor, che t'ama tanto?
perché vuoi tu che muoia il poveretto?   15
   Qual sieno i mia sospiri e il tristo pianto
odonlo i boschi, e tu, Notte, lo senti,
poi ch'io son sotto il tuo stellato ammanto.   18
   Sanza sospetto i ben pasciuti armenti
lieti si stanno nella lor quiete,
e ruminando forse erbe pallenti.   21
   Le pecorelle ancor drento alla rete,
guardate dal can vigile, si stanno
all'aura fresca dormienti e liete.   24
   Io piango non udito il duro affanno,
io pianto i prieghi e le parole all'ugge:
che, se udite non son, che frutto fanno?   27
   Deh, come innanzi agli occhi nostri fugge,
non fugge già davanti dal pensiero!
ché poi piú che presente il cor mi strugge.   30

Deh, non aver il cor tanto severo!
Tre lustri già della tua casta vita
† servito hai di Diana il duro impero: 33
†   non basta questo? Or dammi qualche aita,
ninfa, che se' sanza pietate alcuna.
Ma, lasso a me! non è la voce udita.   36
    Se almen di mille udita ne fussi una!
Io so ch'e versi posson, se li sente,
di cielo in terra far venir la luna.   39
    I versi fêron già l'itaca gente
in fère trasformar: ne' verdi prati
† rompono i versi il frigido serpente.   42
    Adunque i rozzi versi e poco ornati
daremo al vento; ed or ho visto come
saranno a lei li mia pianti portati.   45
    L'aura move degli arbor l'alte chiome,
che rendon mosse un mormorio suave,
ch'empie l'aere ed i boschi del suo nome: 48
    se porta questo a me, non li fia grave
portar mio pianto a questa dura femmina
per gli alti monti e per le valli cave,   51
    ov' abita Eco, che i mia pianti gemina;
o questo o il vento a lei lo portin seco:
† io so che 'l pianto in pietra non si semina.   54
    Forse ode ella vicina in qualche speco.
Non so se sei qui presso: so ben ch'io,
fuggi dove tu vuoi, sempre son teco.   57
    Se 'l tuo crudo voler fussi piú pio,
s'io ti vedessi qui, s'io ti toccassi
le bianche mani e 'l tuo bel viso, o Dio!   60
    se meco sopra l'erba ti posassi,
† della scorza faria d'un lento salcio
una zampogna, e vorrei tu cantassi.   63
†   L'errante chiome poi strette in un tralcio,
vedrei per l'erba il candido piè movere
ballando e dare al vento qualche calcio.   66
    Poi stanca giaceresti sotto un rovere:
io pel prato côrrei diversi fiori,
† e sopra il viso tuo li farei piovere;   69

di color mille e mille vari odori
tu ridendo faresti, dove fôro
i primi còlti, uscir degli altri fuori.   72

    Quante ghirlande sopra i bei crin d'oro
farei, miste di fronde e di fioretti!
Tu vinceresti ogni bellezza loro.   75

    Il mormorio di chiari ruscelletti
risponderebbe alla nostra dolcezza
e 'l canto di amorosi augelletti.   78

    Fugga, ninfa, da te tanta durezza:
questo acerbo pensier del tuo cor caccia:
deh, non far micidial la tua bellezza!   81

    Se delle fiere vuoi seguir la traccia,
non c'è pastor o piú robusto o dotto
a seguir fère fuggitive in caccia.   84

    Tu nascosta starai sanza far motto
con l'arco in mano: io con lo spiedo acuto
†   il fèr cignale aspetterò di sotto.   87

    Lasso! quanto dolor io aggio avuto,
quando fuggi dagli occhi col piè scalzo!
e con quanti sospiri ho già temuto   90

†   che spine o fère venenose o il balzo
non offenda i tua piè! quanto n'ho sdegno!
†   per te fuggo i piè invano e per te gli alzo;   93

       come chi drizza stral veloce al segno,
poi che tratto ha, torcendo il capo, crede
†   drizzarlo: egli è già fuor del curvo legno.   96

    Ma tu se' sí leggiera, ch'io ho fede
che la tua levità porria per l'acque
†   liquide correr sanza intigner piede.   99

    Ma che paura drento al cor mi nacque,
che non facessi come fe' Narciso,
a cui la sua bellezza troppo piacque;   102

       quando al bel fonte ti lavasti il viso,
†   poi, queta la tempesta da te mossa,
miravi nel tranquillo specchio fiso!   105

    Ah mente degli amanti stolta e grossa!
Partita tu, là corsi, non credendo
†   la bella effigie fussi indi remossa.   108

Guardai nell'acqua, e, te non vi vedendo,
viddi me stesso; e parvemi esser tale
† da non esser ripreso, te chiedendo.   111
    S'io non son bianco, è il sol, né mi sta male,
sendo io pastor cosí forte e robusto:
ma dimmi: un uom, che non sia brun, che vale? 114
    Se pien di peli ho io le spalle e il busto,
questo non ti dovrebbe dispiacere,
se hai, quanto bellezza, ingegno e gusto.   117
    Tu non sai forse quanto è il mio potere:
s'io piglio per le corna un toro bravo,
a suo dispetto in terra il fo cadere.   120
    L'altrieri in uno speco oscuro e cavo
fui per cavare una coppia d'orsatti,
† ove appiccando con le man m'andavo.   123
    Giunsi alla tana; e, poi ch'io gli ebbi tratti,
† sentími l'orsa rabida e superba,
e cominciommi a far di cattivi atti.   126
    Io colsi un duro ramo, e sopra l'erba
la lasciai morta, e reca'ne la preda;
la qual, se tu vorrai, per te si serba.   129
†   Alle braccia convien che ognun mi ceda:
† vinsi l'altrier, per la festa di Pana,
† una vacca, che avea drieto la reda.   132
    Con l'arco in man certar voglio con Diana:
per premio ebbi un monton di quattro corna
† col vello bianco insino a terra piana: 135
    tuo fia, benché Neifil se ne scorna,
† a cui son per tuo amor pur troppo ingrato:
lei per piacermi intorno ognor s'adorna.   138
†   S'io son ricco, tu 'l sai; ché in ogni lato
sonar senti le valle del muggito
de' buoi, e delle pecore il belato.   141
    Latte ho fresco ad ognor, e nel fiorito
prato fragole còlte, belle e rosse,
pallide ov' è il tuo viso colorito;   144
    frutte ad ogni stagion mature e grosse;
nutrisco d'ape molte e molte milia,
né crederesti al mondo piú ne fosse;   147

che fanno un mèl sí dolce, ch'assimilia
l'ambrosia ch'alcun dice pascer Giove;
† né sol vince le canne di Sicilia.   150
   O ninfa, se 'l mio canto non ti move,
muovati almen quello d'augei diversi
† che canton con pietose voci e nòve.   153
   Non odi tu d'amor meco dolersi
† misera Filomena, che si lagna
d'altrui, com' io di te, ne' dolci versi?   156
   Questo sol sanza sonno m'accompagna.
Ma io ti credo movere a pietate;
tu ridi, se 'l mio pianto il terren bagna.   159
   Dov' è somma bellezza e crudeltate,
† è viva morte; pur mi riconforto:
non dée sempre durar la tua beltate.   162
   L'altra mattina in un mio piccolo orto
andavo, e 'l sol surgente co' sua rai
† apparia già, non ch'io 'l vedessi scorto.   165
   Sonvi piantati drento alcun' rosai,
† a' quai rivolsi le mie vaghe ciglie,
per quel che visto non avevo mai.   168
   Eranvi rose candide e vermiglie:
alcuna a foglia a foglia al sol si spiega,
stretta prima, poi par s'apra e scompiglie;   171
   altra piú giovanetta si dislega
a pena dalla boccia; eravi ancora
chi le sue chiuse foglie all'aer niega;   174
   altra, cadendo, a piè il terreno infiora.
Cosí le vidi nascere e morire
e passar lor vaghezza in men d'un'ora.   177
   Quando languenti e pallide vidi ire
le foglie a terra, allor mi venne a mente
che vana cosa è il giovenil fiorire: 180
   nostro solo è quel poco che è presente,
né 'l passato o il futuro è nostro tempo:
l'un non è piú, e l'altro è ancor niente.   183
   Cogli la rosa, o ninfa, or ch'è bel tempo."

THE ENDING ACCORDING TO EARLIER EDITIONS:

"Quando languenti e pallide vidi ire
le foglie a terra, allor mi venne a mente
che vana cosa è il giovenil fiorire.   180
  Ogni arbore ha i sua fior: e immantenente
poi le tenere fronde al sol si spiegano,
quando rinnovellar l'aere si sente.   183
† I picciol frutti ancor informi allegano,
che a poco a poco talor tanto ingrossano,
che pel gran peso i forti rami piegano   186
  né sanza gran periglio portar possano
il proprio peso; a pena regger sogliono
† crescendo, ad or ad ora se l'addossano.   189
  Viene l'autunno, e maturi si cogliono
i dolci pomi: e, passato il bel tempo,
di fior, di frutti e fronde alfin si spogliono.   192
  Cogli la rosa, o ninfa, or che è il bel tempo."

AMBRA

1   Fuggita è la stagion, che avea conversi
       i fiori in pomi già maturi e còlti;
       in ramo non può piú foglia tenersi,
       ma sparte per li boschi assai men folti
       si fan sentir, se avvien che gli attraversi
       il cacciator, e i pochi paion molti;
       la fera, se ben l'orme vaghe asconde,
       non va segreta per le secche fronde.

2   Tra gli arbor secchi stassi il lauro lieto
       e di Ciprigna l'odorato arbusto;
       verdeggia nelle bianche alpe l'abeto
       e piega i rami già di neve onusto;
       tiene il cipresso qualche uccel secreto,
       e con venti combatte il pin robusto;
       l'umil ginepro colle acute foglie
       la man non punge altrui, chi ben le coglie;

3   l'uliva in qualche dolce piaggia aprica
       secondo il vento par or verde, or bianca:
       natura in questi tal serba e nutrica
       quel verde che nell'altre fronde manca.
       Già i pellegrini uccei con gran fatica
       hanno condotto la famiglia stanca
       di là dal mare, e pel cammin lor mostri
       nereidi, tritoni ed altri mostri.

4   Ha combattuto dell'imperio e vinto
       la notte, e prigion mena il brieve giorno:
       nel ciel seren d'eterne fiamme cinto
       lieta il carro stellato mena intorno;

né prima surge, che in oceano tinto
si vede l'altro aurato carro adorno;
Orion freddo col coltel minaccia
Febo, se mostra a noi la bella faccia.

5   Seguon questo notturno carro ardente
vigilie, escubie e sollecite cure,
il sonno (e, bench' e' sia molto potente,
queste importune il vincon talor pure),
e ' dolci sogni, che ingannan la mente,
quando è oppressa da fortune dure:
di sanità, d'assai tesor fa festa
alcun, che infermo e povero si desta.

6   Oh miser quel che in notte cosí lunga
non dorme, e il disiato giorno aspetta,
se avvien che molto e dolce disio il punga,
quale il futuro giorno gli prometta!
E, benché ambo le ciglia insieme aggiunga,
e' pensier tristi escluda e ' dolci ammetta,
dormendo o desto, acciò che il tempo inganni,
gli par la notte un secol di cento anni.

7   Oh miser chi tra l'onde trova fuora
sí lunga notte, assai lontan dal lito!
E 'l cammin rompe della cieca prora
il vento, e freme il mare un fèr muggito;
con molti prieghi e voti l'Aurora
chiamata, sta col suo vecchio marito.
Numera tristo e disioso guarda
i passi lenti dalla notte tarda.

8   Quanto è diversa, anzi contraria sorte
de' lieti amanti nell'algente bruma,
a cui le notte sono e chiare e corte,
il giorno oscuro e tardo si consuma.
Nella stagion cosí gelida e forte,
già rivestiti di novella piuma,
hanno deposto gli uccelletti alquanto
non so s'io dica o i lieti versi o 'l pianto.

9   Stridendo in cielo i gru veggonsi a lunge
l'aere stampar di varie e belle forme,
e l'ultima, col collo steso, aggiunge
ov' è quella dinanzi, alle vane orme;
e, poi che negli aprichi lochi giunge,
vigile un guarda, e l'altra schiera dorme.
Cuoprono i prati e van leggier pe' laghi
mille spezie d'uccei dipinti e vaghi.

10   L'aquila spesso col volato lento
minaccia tutti, e sopra il stagno vola:
levonsi insieme e caccionla col vento
delle penne stridenti; e, se pur sola
una fuor resta del pennuto armento,
l'uccel di Giove subito la invola:
resta ingannata, misera, se crede
andarne a Giove come Ganimede.

11   Zeffiro s'è fuggito in Cipri, e balla
con Flora, oziosi per l'erbetta lieta;
l'aria, non piú serena, bella e gialla,
Borea ed Aquilon rompe ed inqueta.
L'acqua corrente e querula incristalla
il ghiaccio, e stracca or si riposa cheta.
Preso il pesce nell'onda dura e chiara,
resta come in ambra aurea zanzara.

12   Quel monte che s'oppone a Cauro fero,
che non molesti il gentil fior, cresciuto
nel suo grembo d'onor, ricchezze e impero,
cigne di nebbie il capo già canuto;
gli omer, candenti giú dal capo altero,
cuoprono i bianchi crini, e 'l petto irsuto
l'orribil barba, ch'è pel ghiaccio rigida:
fan gli occhi e 'l naso un fonte, e 'l gel lo infrigida.

13   La nebulosa ghirlanda, che cigne
l'alte tempie, gli mette Noto in testa;
Borea dall'alpe poi la caccia e spigne,
e nudo e bianco il vecchio capo resta;

Noto sopra l'ale umide e maligne
le nebbie porta, e par di nuovo il vesta.
Cosí Morello irato, or carco or lieve,
minaccia al pian suggetto or acqua or neve.

14   Partesi d'Etiopia caldo e tinto
Austro, e sazia le assetate spugne
nell'onde salse di Tirreno intinto:
appena a' destinati luoghi giugne,
gravido d'acqua e da nugoli cinto
e stanco, stringe poi ambo le pugne:
i fiumi lieti contro all'acque amiche
escon allor delle caverne antiche.

15   Rendon grazie ad Oceano padre, adorni
d'ulva e di fronde fluvial le tempie;
suonan per festa i rochi e torti corni;
tumido il ventre già superbo s'empie;
lo sdegno, conceputo molti giorni
contro alle ripe timide, s'adempie;
spumoso ha rotto già l'inimico argine,
né serva il corso dell'antico margine.

16   Non per vie lunghe o per cammino oblico,
a guisa di serpenti, a gran volumi,
sollecitan la via al padre antico:
congiungon l'onde insieme i lontan fiumi,
e dice l'uno all'altro, come amico,
nuove del suo paese e de' costumi:
cosí insieme, in una strana voce,
cercon, né trovon, la smarrita foce.

17   Quando gonfiato e largo si ristrigne
tra gli alti monti d'una chiusa valle,
stridon frenate, turbide e maligne
l'onde, e miste con terra paion gialle;
e grave pietre sopra pietre pigne,
irato a' sassi dell'angusto calle;
l'onde spumose gira, orribil freme:
vede il pastor dall'alto e, sicur, teme.

18   Tal fremito piangendo rende trista
la terra dentro al cavo ventre adusta:
caccia col fumo fuor fiamma acqua mista
gridando, ch'esce per la bocca angusta,
terribile agli orecchi ed alla vista:
teme, vicina, il suon alta e robusta
Volterra, e i lagon torbidi che spumano;
e piove aspetta se piú alto fumano.

19   Cosí crucciato il fèr torrente frende
superbo, e le contrarie ripe rode;
ma, poi che nel pian largo si distende,
quasi contento allora a pena s'ode:
incerto, se in su torna o se pur scende,
ha de' monti distanti fatto prode;
già vincitor, il cheto lago incede,
di rami e tronchi pien, montane prede.

20   A pena è suta a tempo la villana
pavida aprire alle bestie la stalla;
porta il figlio, che piange, nella zana;
segue la figlia grande, ed ha la spalla
grave di panni vili, lini e lana;
va l'altra vecchia masserizia a galla,
nuotono i porci e spaventati i buoi,
le pecorelle, e non si toson poi.

21   Alcun della famiglia s'è ridotto
in cima della casa; e su dal tetto
la povera ricchezza vede ir sotto,
la fatica, la speme; e per sospetto
di sé stesso non duolsi e non fa motto;
teme alla vita il cor nel tristo petto,
né delle cose car par conto faccia:
cosí la maggior cura ogni altra caccia.

22   La nota e verde ripa allor non frena
i pesci lieti, che han piú ampli spazi;
l'antica e giusta voglia alquanto è piena
di veder nuovi liti; e, non ben sazi,

questo nuovo piacer vaghi gli mena
a veder le ruine e ' grandi strazi
degli edifizi, e sotto l'acqua i muri
veggon lieti ed ancor non ben sicuri.

23   In guisa allor di piccola isoletta,
Ombrone amante superbo Ambra cigne;
Ambra non men da Lauro diletta,
geloso se 'l rival la tocca e strigne;
Ambra driade, a Delia sua accetta
quanto alcuna che stral fuor d'arco pigne;
tanto bella e gentil, ch'alfin li nuoce;
leggier di piedi e piú ch'altra veloce.

24   Fu da' primi anni questa ninfa amata
dal suo Lauro gentil, pastore alpino,
d'un casto amor: né era penetrata
lasciva fiamma al petto peregrino.
Fuggendo il caldo, un dí nuda era entrata
nell'onde fredde d'Ombron, d'Appennino
figlio, superbo in vista e ne' costumi,
pel padre antico e cento frati fiumi.

25   Come le membra verginali entrorno
nella acqua bruna e gelida sentío,
e mosso dal leggiadro corpo adorno,
della spelonca uscí l'altero iddio;
dalla sinistra prese il torto corno,
e nudo il resto, acceso di disio,
difende il capo inculto a' febei raggi,
coronato d'abeti e montàn faggi.

26   E verso il loco ove la ninfa stassi,
giva, pian pian, coperto dalle fronde;
né era visto, né sentire i passi
lasciava il mormorio delle chiare onde.
Cosí vicin tanto alla ninfa fassi,
che giugner crede le suo trecce bionde,
e quella bella ninfa in braccio avere,
e, nudo, il nudo e bel corpo tenere.

27   Sí come pesce, allor, che incauto cuopra
       il pescator con rara e sottil maglia,
       fugge la rete, qual sente di sopra,
       lasciando, per fuggir, alcuna scaglia;
       cosí la ninfa, quando par si scuopra,
       fugge lo dio, che addosso si li scaglia:
       né fu sí presta, anzi fu sí presto elli,
       che in man lasciolli alcun de' sua capelli.

28   E, saltando dell'onde, strigne il passo;
       di timor piena, fugge nuda e scalza;
       lascia i panni e li stral, l'arco e 'l turcasso;
       non cura i pruni acuti o l'aspra balza;
       resta lo dio dolente, afflitto e lasso:
       pel dolor le man stringe, al ciel gli occhi alza,
       maladice la man crudele e tarda,
       quando i biondi capelli svèlti guarda.

29   E, seguendola allor, diceva: "O mano,
       a svellere i bei crin presta e feroce,
       ma a tener quel corpo piú che umano
       e farmi lieto, oimè! poco veloce."
       Cosí piangendo il primo errore invano,
       credendo almeno aggiugner con la voce
       dove arrivar non puote il passo tardo,
       gridava: "O ninfa, un fiume sono, ed ardo.

30   "Tu m'accendesti in mezzo alle fredd' acque
       il petto d'un ardente disir cieco:
       perché come nell'onda il corpo giacque,
       non giace, ché staria me' assai, con meco?
       Se l'ombra e l'acqua mia chiara ti piacque,
       piú bell' ombra, piú bella acqua ha il mio speco.
       Piaccionti le mie cose, e non piaccio io:
       e son pur d'Apennin figliuolo, e dio."

31   La ninfa fugge, e sorda a' prieghi fassi:
       a' bianchi piè aggiugne ale il timore.
       Sollecita lo dio, correndo, i passi,
       fatti a seguir veloci dall'amore;

vede da pruni e da taglienti sassi
i bianchi piè ferir con gran dolore;
cresce il disio, pel quale e ghiaccia e suda,
vedendola fuggir sí bella e nuda.

32   Timida e vergognosa Ambra pur corre;
nel corso a' venti rapidi non cede;
le leggier piante sulle spighe porre
potria, e sosterrieno il gentil piede;
vedesi Ombrone ognor piú campo tôrre,
la ninfa ad ogni passo manco vede:
già nel pian largo tanto il corso avanza,
che di giugnerla perde ogni speranza.

33   Già pria per gli alti monti aspri e repenti
venía tra ' sassi con rapido corso;
i passi a lei manco spediti e lenti
faceano a lui sperar qualche soccorso;
ma giunto, lasso, giú ne' pian patenti,
fu messo quasi al fiume stanco un morso:
poi che non può col piè, per la campagna
col disio e cogli occhi l'accompagna.

34   Che debbe far l'innamorato dio,
poiché la bella ninfa piú non giugne?
Quanto gli è piú negata, piú disio
lo innamorato core accende e pugne.
La ninfa era già presso ove Arno mio
riceve Ombrone e l'onde si congiugne:
Ombrone, Arno veggendo, si conforta,
e surge alquanto la speranza morta.

35   Grida da lungi: "O Arno, a cui rifugge
la maggior parte di noi fiumi tòschi,
la bella ninfa, che come uccel fugge,
da me seguita in tanti monti e boschi,
sanza alcuna pietate il cor mi strugge,
né par che amore il duro cor conoschi:
rendimi lei e la speranza persa,
e il leggier corso suo rompi e intraversa.

36   "Io sono Ombron, che le mia cerule onde
per te raccoglio; a te tutte le serbo,
e fatte tue diventon sí profonde,
che sprezzi e ripe e ponti, alto e superbo;
questa è mia preda, e queste trecce bionde,
quale in man porto con dolore acerbo,
ne fan chiar segno; in te mia speme è sola:
soccorri presto, ché la ninfa vola."

37   Arno, vedendo Ombron, da pietà mosso,
perché il tempo non basta a far risposta,
ritenne l'acqua; e, già gonfiato e grosso,
da lungi al corso della bell' Ambra osta.
Fu da nuovo timor freddo e percosso
il vergin petto, quanto piú s'accosta:
drieto Ombron sente, e innanzi vede un lago,
né sa che farsi, il cor gelato e vago.

38   Come fera cacciata e già difesa
da' can, fuggendo la bocca bramosa,
fuor del periglio già, la rete tesa
veggendo innanzi agli occhi, paurosa,
quasi già certa dover esser presa,
né fugge innanzi o indrieto tornar osa,
teme i can, alla rete non si fida,
non sa che farsi, e spaventata grida;

39   tal della bella ninfa era la sorte:
da ogni parte da paura oppressa,
non sa che farsi se non desiar morte;
vede l'un fiume e l'altro che s'appressa,
e disperata allor gridava forte:
"O casta dea, a cui io fui concessa
dal caro padre e dalla madre antica,
unica aiuta all'ultima fatica!

40   "Diana bella, questo petto casto
non maculò giammai folle disio:
guardalo or tu, perch' io, ninfa, non basto
a dua nimici; e l'uno e l'altro è dio.

Col disio del morir m'è sol rimasto
al core il casto amor di Lauro mio:
portate, o venti, questa voce estrema
a Lauro mio, che la mia morte gema!"

41   Né eron quasi della bocca fòre
queste parole, che i candidi piedi
fûrno occupati da novel rigore;
crescerli poi e farsi un sasso vedi,
mutar le membra e 'l bel corpo colore,
ma pur, che donna fussi ancor tu credi:
le membra mostran, come suol figura
bozzata e non finita in pietra dura.

42   Ombron, pel corso faticato e lasso,
per la speranza della cara preda
prende nuovo vigor e strigne il passo,
e par che quasi in braccio aver la creda:
crescer veggendo innanzi agli occhi il sasso,
ignaro ancor, non sa donde proceda;
ma poi, veggendo vana ogni sua voglia,
si ferma pien di maraviglia e doglia.

43   Come in un parco cervia o altra fera,
ch'è di materia o picciol muro chiuso,
sopraffatta da' can, campar non spera
vicina al muro, e per timor là suso
salta e si lieva innanzi al can leggiera,
resta il can dentro misero e deluso;
non potendo seguir dov' è salita,
fermasi, e guarda il loco onde è fuggita;

44   cosí lo dio ferma la veloce orma;
guarda pietoso il bel sasso crescente,
il sasso, che ancor serba qualche forma
di bella donna, e qualche poco sente;
e come amore e la pietà lo informa,
di pianto bagna il sasso amaramente,
dicendo: "O Ambra mia, queste son l'acque,
ove bagnar già il bel corpo ti piacque.

45   "Io non aria creduto, in dolor tanto,
       che la propria pietà, vinta da quella
       della mia ninfa, si fuggissi alquanto:
       per la maggior pietà d'Ambra mia bella,
       questa, non già la mia, move in me il pianto.
       E pur la vita triste e meschinella,
       ancor che eterna, quando meco penso,
       è peggio in me che in lei non aver senso.

46   "Lasso! ne' monti miei paterni eccelsi
       son tante ninfe, e sicura è ciascuna;
       fra mille belle la piú bella scelsi,
       non so come; ed amando sol quest' una,
       primo segno d'amore i crini svelsi,
       e caccia'la dell'acqua fresca e bruna;
       tenera e nuda poi, fuggendo esangue,
       tinse le spine e i sassi il sacro sangue.

47   "E finalmente in un sasso conversa
       per colpa sol del mio crudel disio,
       non so, non sendo mia, come l'ho persa,
       né posso perder questo viver mio:
       in questo è troppo la mia sorte avversa,
       misero essendo ed immortale dio;
       ché, s'io potessi pure almen morire,
       potria il giusto immortal dolor finire.

48   "Io ho imparato come si compiacci
       a donna amata ed il suo amor guadagni,
       che a quella che piú ami piú dispiacci.
       O Borea algente, che gelato stagni,
       l'acque correnti fa' s'induri e ghiacci,
       che pietra fatto, la ninfa accompagni:
       Né 'l sol giamai co' raggi chiari e gialli
       risolva in acqua i rigidi cristalli."

FROM THE *CANZONI A BALLO*

1

    Donna, vano è il pensier che mai non crede
che venga il tempo della sua vecchiezza,
e che la giovinezza   3
† abbi sempre a star ferma in una tempre.
    Vola l'etate e fugge;
presto di nostra vita manca il fiore: 6
† e però dee pensar il gentil core
ch'ogni cosa ne porta il tempo e strugge.
    Dunque dee gentil donna aver merzede   9
e non di sua bellezza essere altèra:
† perché folle è chi spera
viver in giovinezza e bella sempre.   12

2

†   Chi tempo aspetta, assai tempo si strugge:
e 'l tempo non aspetta, ma via fugge.

    La bella gioventú giamai non torna,   3
né 'l tempo perso giamai riede indrieto;
†   però chi ha 'l bel tempo e pur soggiorna,
non arà mai al mondo tempo lieto;   6
†   ma l'animo gentile e ben discreto
† dispensa il tempo, mentre che via fugge.

    Oh quante cose in gioventú si prezza!   9
Quanto son belli i fiori in primavera!

Ma, quando vien la disutil vecchiezza
e che altro che mal piú non si spera,   12
   conosce il perso dí quando è già sera
quel che 'l tempo aspettando pur si strugge.

   Io credo che non sia maggior dolore   15
† che del tempo perduto a sua cagione:
   questo è quel mal che affligge e passa il core,
questo è quel mal che si piange a ragione;   18
   questo a ciascun debbe essere uno sprone
di usare il tempo ben, che vola e fugge.

   Però, donne gentil, giovani adorni,   21
che vi state a cantare in questo loco,
   spendete lietamente i vostri giorni,
ché giovinezza passa a poco a poco: 24
   io ve ne priego per quel dolce foco
† che ciascun cor gentile incende e strugge.

3

   Chi non è innamorato
esca di questo ballo,
ché faria fallo a stare in sí bel lato.   3

   Se alcuno è qui, che non conosca Amore,
parta di questo loco;
   perch' esser non potria mai gentil core   6
† chi non sente quel foco.
   Se alcun ne sente poco,
sí le sue fiamme accenda,   9
che ognun lo intenda; e non sarà iscacciato.

   Amor in mezzo a questo ballo stia,
e chi gli è servo, intorno.   12
   E, se alcuno ha sospetto o gelosia,
non facci qui soggiorno;

se non, che arebbe scorno. 15
Ognun ci s'innamori,
o esca fuori del loco tanto ornato.

Se alcuna per vergogna si ritiene 18
di non s'innamorare
vergognerassi, s'ella pensa bene,
piú tosto a non lo fare: 21
non è vergogna amare
chi di servirti agogna;
saria vergogna chi gli fussi ingrato. 24

Se alcuna ce ne fussi tanto vile,
che lasci per paura,
pensi bene che un core alto e gentile 27
queste cose non cura.
Non ha dato Natura
tanta bellezza a voi 30
acciò che poi sia il tempo male usato.

4

† Ragionavasi di sodo
un marito con la moglie:
† "Stu non muti viso o voglie, 3
io non muterò mai modo."

La sua moglie si dolea
che faceva un certo giuoco, 6
che veder non lo potea;
† e dicea: "Pur muta loco."
Il marito disse poco: 9
"Seguir vo' l'usanza mia;
nol vo' far per altra via,
se miglior ragion non odo." 12

"Tu ti se' male allevato;
hai apparato cattiva arte:
   non è buono alcun mercato,   15
che non fa per ogni parte."
   Il marito a questa parte:
† "Tu ne se' cagion tu stessi,   18
† ché, se miglior viso avessi,
non commetterei tal frodo."

   La si dolse co' parenti;   21
ma doluto prima gli era:
   co' vicin fe' gran lamenti,
e dicea mattina e sera: 24
†   "Fàllo il tuo in tal maniera?
Non par mai che vi s'assetti,
che le lacrime non getti: 27
pensi ognun com' io ne godo."

   Disse: "Porta in sofferenza"
il marito; "e se t'avvezzi   30
   aver meco pazienzia,
non vorrai che 'l modo sprezzi;
   e dirai ti faccia vezzi,   33
se tu gusti il giuoco mio,
tu dirai quel che dico io:
† che sia questo il proprio modo."   36

FROM THE *CANTI CARNASCIALESCHI* AND *TRIONFI*

Canzona de' confortini

†   Berricuocoli, donne, e confortini!
Se ne volete, i nostri son de' fini.

    Non bisogna insegnar come si fanno,   3
ch'è tempo perso, e 'l tempo è pur gran danno;
e chi lo perde, come molte fanno,
†   convien che facci poi de' pentolini.   6

    Quando gli è 'l tempo vostro, fate fatti,
†   e non pensate a impedimenti o imbratti:
    chi non ha il modo, dal vicin l'accatti: 9
†   e' preston l'un all'altro i buon vicini.

†   Il far quest' arte è cosa da garzoni:
basta che i nostri confortin' son buoni.   12
Non aspettate ch'altri ve li doni:
convien giuocare e spender bei quattrini.

    No' abbiam carte, e fassi alla "bassetta",   15
e convien che l'un alzi e l'altro metta;
e poi di qua e di là spesso si getta
†   le carte; e tira a te, se tu indovini.   18

    O a "sanz' uomo", o "sotto" o "sopra" chiedi,
e ti struggi dal capo infino a' piedi,
infin che viene; e, quando vien poi, vedi   21
†   stran' visi, e mugolar come mucini.

Chi si truova al di sotto, allor si cruccia,
scontorcesi e fa viso di bertuccia,   24
ché 'l suo ne va; straluna gli occhi e succia,
e piangon anche i miseri meschini.

Chi vince, per dolcezza si gavazza,   27
† dileggia e ghigna, e tutto si diguazza;
credere alla Fortuna è cosa pazza:
† aspetta pur che poi si pieghi e 'nchini.   30

† Questa "bassetta" è spacciativo giuoco,
† e ritto ritto fassi, e in ogni loco;
e solo ha questo mal, che dura poco;   33
† ma spesso bea chi ha bicchier' piccini.

Il flusso c'è, ch'è giuoco maladetto:
† ma chi volessi pure uscirne netto,   36
metta pian piano, e inviti poco e stretto:
† ma lo fanno oggi infino a' contadini.

Chi mette tutto il suo in un invito,   39
† se vien flusso, si truova a mal partito,
se lo vedessi, e' pare un uom ferito:
† che maladetto sie Sforzo Bettini!   42

"Trai" è mal giuoco, e 'l "pizzico" si suole
usare e la "dritta" a nessun duole:
chi ha le carte in man, fa quel che vuole,   45
† s'è ben fornito di grossi e fiorini.

Se volete giucar, come abbiam mòstro,
noi siam contenti metter tutto il nostro   48
in una posta, or qui per mezzo il vostro:
† sino alle casse, non che i confortini.

Canzona di Bacco

Quant' è bella giovinezza
che si fugge tuttavia:
chi vuol esser lieto, sia,   3
di doman non c'è certezza.

† Quest' è Bacco e Arianna,
belli, e l'un dell'altro ardenti: 6
  perché 'l tempo fugge e inganna,
sempre insieme stan contenti.
† Queste ninfe ed altre genti   9
sono allegre tuttavia.
Chi vuol esser lieto, sia,
di doman non c'è certezza.   12

† Questi lieti satiretti,
delle ninfe innamorati,
  per caverne e per boschetti   15
han lor posto cento agguati;
† or da Bacco riscaldati,
ballon, salton tuttavia.   18
Chi vuol esser lieto, sia,
di doman non c'è certezza.

Queste ninfe anche hanno caro   21
† da lor esser ingannate:
  non può fare a Amor riparo,
† se non gente rozze e ingrate;   24
  ora insieme mescolate
suonon, canton tuttavia.
Chi vuol esser lieto, sia,   27
di doman non c'è certezza.

Questa soma, che vien drieto
† sopra l'asino, è Sileno: 30
  cosí vecchio è ebbro e lieto,
già di carne e d'anni pieno;

se non può star ritto, almeno   33
ride e gode tuttavia.
Chi vuol esser lieto, sia,
di doman non c'è certezza.   36

†   Mida vien drieto a costoro:
ciò che tocca, oro diventa.
    E che giova aver tesoro,   39
†   s'altri poi non si contenta?
    Che dolcezza vuoi che senta
chi ha sete tuttavia?   42
Chi vuol esser lieto, sia,
di doman non c'è certezza.

    Ciascun apra ben gli orecchi,   45
†   di doman nessun si paschi;
    oggi sian, giovani e vecchi,
lieti ognun, femmine e maschi.   48
    Ogni tristo pensier caschi:
facciam festa tuttavia.
Chi vuol esser lieto, sia,   51
di doman non c'è certezza.

    Donne e giovinetti amanti,
viva Bacco e viva Amore!   54
    Ciascun suoni, balli e canti,
arda di dolcezza il core,
    non fatica, non dolore!   57
† Ciò c'ha a esser, convien sia.
Chi vuol esser lieto, sia,
di doman non c'è certezza.   60

Canzona de' sette pianeti

Sette pianeti siam, che l'alte sede
† lasciam per far del cielo in terra fede.

† Da noi son tutti i beni e tutti i mali,   3
quel che v'affligge miseri, e giova;
   ciò ch'agli uomini avviene, agli animali
e piante e pietre, convien da noi muova;   6
   sforziam chi tenta contro a noi far pruova;
† conduciam dolcemente chi ci crede.

† Maninconici, miseri e sottili;   9
ricchi, onorati, buon prelati e gravi;
   súbiti, impazienti, fèr', virili;
pomposi re, musici illustri, e savi;   12
   astuti parlator', bugiardi e pravi;
† ogni vil opra alfin da noi procede.

† Venere graziosa, chiara e bella   15
muove nel core amore e gentilezza:
   chi tocca il foco della dolce stella,
† convien sempre arda dell'altrui bellezza: 18
   fère, uccelli e pesci hanno dolcezza:
† per questa il mondo rinnovar si vede.

Orsú seguiam questa stella benigna,   21
o donne vaghe, o giovinetti adorni:
   tutti vi chiama la bella Ciprigna
† a spender lietamente i vostri giorni,   24
   sanz' aspettar che 'l dolce tempo torni,
ché, come fugge un tratto, mai non riede.

Il dolce tempo ancor tutti c'invita   27
† lasciare i pensier' tristi e van dolori.
   Mentre che dura questa brieve vita,
ciascun s'allegri, ciascun s'innamori;   30
   contentisi chi può: ricchezze e onori
per chi non si contenta, invan si chiede.

FROM THE *LAUDE*

O Dio, o sommo Bene, or come fai,
che te sol cerco e non ti truovo mai?

    Lasso! s'io cerco questa cosa o quella,   3
te cerco in esse, o dolce Signor mio:
    ogni cosa per te è buona e bella
e muove, come buona, il mio disio;   6
    tu se' pur tutto in ogni luogo, o Dio,
e in alcun luogo non ti truovo mai.

    Per trovar te la trista alma si strugge;   9
il dí m'affliggo e la notte non poso;
    lasso! quanto piú cerco, piú si fugge
il dolce e disïato mio riposo.   12
    Deh! dimmi, Signor mio, ove se' ascoso:
stanco già son, Signor, dimmelo omai.

    Se a cercar di te, Signor, mi muovo   15
in ricchezze, in onore o in diletto,
    quanto piú di te cerco, men ne truovo,
onde stanco mai posa il vano affetto.   18
    Tu m'hai del tuo amore acceso il petto;
poi se' fuggito, e non ti veggo mai.

    La vista, in mille varie cose vòlta,   21
ti guarda e non ti vede, e sei lucente;
    l'orecchio ancor diverse voci ascolta:
il tuo suono è per tutto, e non ti sente;   24
    la dolcezza comune a ogni gente
cerca ogni senso, e non la truova mai.

Deh! perché cerchi, anima trista, ancora   27
beata vita in tanti affanni e pene?
†   Cerca quel cerchi pur, ma non dimora,
nel luogo ove tu cerchi, questo bene: 30
   beata vita onde la morte viene
† cerchi, e vita ove vita non fu mai.

   Muoia in me questa mia misera vita,   33
† acciò che io viva, o vera vita, in te;
   la morte in multitudine infinita
† in te sol vita sia, che vita se';   36
   muoio quando te lascio e guardo me:
† converso a te, io non morrò già mai.

†   Degli occhi vani ogni luce sia spenta,   39
perché vegga te, vera luce amica:
   assorda i miei orecchi, acciò che io senta
la disïata voce che mi dica: 42
   "Venite a me, chi ha peso o fatica,
† ch'io vi ristori: egli è ben tempo omai."

   Allor l'occhio vedrà luce invisibile,   45
l'orecchio udirà suon ch'è senza voce:
   luce e suon che alla mente è sol sensibile,
né il troppo offende o a tal senso nuoce: 48
   stando i piè fermi, correrà veloce
l'alma a quel ben che è seco sempre mai.

   Allor vedrò, o Signor dolce e bello,   51
che questo bene o quel non mi contenta,
   ma levando dal bene e questo e quello,
† quel ben che resta il dolce Dio diventa;   54
   questa vera dolcezza e sola senta
chi cerca il ben: questo non manca mai.

La nostra eterna sete mai non spegne   57
l'acqua corrente di questo o quel rivo,
    ma giugne al tristo foco ognor piú legne:
sol ne contenta il fonte eterno e vivo.   60
    O acqua santa, se al tuo fonte arrivo,
berrò, e sete non arò piú mai.

Tanto disio non dovria esser vano;   63
a te si muove pure il nostro ardore.
    Porgi benigno l'una e l'altra mano,
o Iesú mio: tu se' infinito amore.   66
    Poiché hai piagato dolcemente il core,
sana tu quella piaga che tu fai.

LA RAPRESENTATIONE DI SAN GIOVANNI ET PAVLO COM POSTA PEL MAGNIFICO LAVRENTIO DE MEDICI

OLTI amici fitibundi dileggere com
pofitori che fcriuono, parole di Dio
benedicto, effendo di Dio: Si come, e fcri pto,
Chi, e, di Dio nõ inuito ode lefue parole. Cõ
ogni dũche ftudio, diligétia, & gratia orãdo
mi che dia loro oportunita di fruire quello
chel noftro Magnifico Laurentio de Medici
in rima egregia ha catholicamente fcripto ab

RAPPRESENTAZIONE DI SAN GIOVANNI E PAOLO[1]

INTERLOCUTORI

ANGELO *annunziatore*
PRIMO PARENTE *di sant' Agnesa*
SECONDO PARENTE *di sant' Agnesa*
TERZO PARENTE *di sant' Agnesa*
COSTANZA[2]
UN SERVO *di Costanza*
SANT' AGNESA[3]
COSTANTINO,[4] *padre di Costanza*
GALLICANO[5]
ATTICA, *una delle figliuole di Gallicano*
ARTEMIA, *altra figliuola di Gallicano*
GIOVANNI
PAULO
UN ANGELO *che apparisce*
TROMBETTO
RE
PRINCIPE
MESSO *a Costantino*
COSTANTINO, *figliuolo di Costantino imperatore*
COSTANTE, *uno de' fratelli*
COSTANZIO, *altro fratello*
IMPERADORE, *il nuovo*[6]

UN SERVO	UN FANTE
UN CONFORTATORE	UN ACCUSATORE
TERENZIANO	SAN BASILIO,[7] *vescovo*
MARIA VERGINE	
TESORIERE	ASTROLOGI

THE MARTYRDOM OF
SAINTS JOHN AND PAUL[1]

DRAMATIS PERSONÆ

An ANGEL, *the Presenter*
FIRST RELATIVE *of St Agnes*
SECOND RELATIVE *of St Agnes*
THIRD RELATIVE *of St Agnes*
CONSTANCE[2]
A MANSERVANT *to Constance*
SAINT AGNES[3]
CONSTANTINE,[4] *father to Constance*
GALLICAN[5]
ATTICA, *daughter to Gallican*
ARTEMIA, *daughter to Gallican*
JOHN
PAUL
An ANGEL, *who appears*
A HERALD
A KING
A PRINCE
A MESSENGER *to Constantine*
CONSTANTINE, *son to Emperor Constantine*
CONSTANS, *one of his brothers*
CONSTANTIUS, *another brother*
The new EMPEROR[6]

A SERVANT	*A* SOLDIER
A COMFORTER	*An* ACCUSER
TERENCE	ST BASIL,[7] *bishop*
The VIRGIN MARY	
A TREASURER	ASTROLOGERS

L'ANGELO ANNUNZIA E DICE:

1   Silenzio, o voi che ragunati siete:
       voi vedrete una istoria nuova e santa;
       diverse cose e devote vedrete,
       esempli di fortuna varia tanta.
       Sanza alcun motto stien le voci chete,
       massimamente poi quando si canta.
       A noi fatica, a voi il piacer resta:
       però non ci guastate questa festa.

2   Santa Costanza, dalla lebbra monda,
       con devozion vedrete convertire;
       nella battaglia molto furibonda
       gente vedrete prendere e morire;
       mutar lo imperio la volta seconda;
       e di Giovanni e Paulo il martíre;
       e poi morir l'apostata Giuliano
       per la vendetta del sangue cristiano.

3   La Compagnia del nostro san Giovanni
       fa questa festa, e siam pur giovanetti:
       però scusate i nostri teneri anni,
       se i versi non son buoni o ver ben detti;
       né sanno de' signor vestire i panni,
       o vecchi o donne esprimer, fanciulletti:
       puramente faremo e con amore;
       sopportate l'età di qualche errore.

* * *

PRIMO PARENTE DI SANTA AGNESA:

4   Forse, tacendo il ver, sarei piú saggio,
       che, dicendolo a voi, parer bugiardo:
       ma, essendo parenti e d'un legnaggio,

THE ANGEL INTRODUCES THE PLAY:

1   Silence, all you who are assembled here!
A story new and holy you will see.
Strange deeds and sacred marvels will appear,
Fortune's effects in great variety.
Without a word, no murmuring let us hear,
And when we sing, listen attentively.
To you the pleasure and to us the toil:
And so our celebration do not spoil.

2   Of leprosy fair Constance will be cured,
By prayer converted to our holy faith.
In furious battles much will be endured,
Captives in chains, men gasping their last breath.
Of two new emperors we shall bring you word,
And John and Paul will meet a martyr's death.
At last the apostate Julian will be killed,
In vengeance for the blood of Christians spilled.

3   The Company of our St John will play
These festive scenes, but we are still quite young;
So let our tender years excuse us, pray,
If verses are ill wrought or not well sung,
If boys look strange in noblemen's array,
And clad as women or old men seem wrong.
With love we shall perform and with pure hearts,
So pardon any errors in our parts.

*   *   *

FIRST RELATIVE OF ST AGNES:

4   It may yet prove a wiser thing for me
To hold my tongue, else liar I may seem;
But of one lineage kinsfolk all are we,

non arò nel parlar questo riguardo;
perché, se pur parlando in error caggio,
non erro, quando in viso ben riguardo:
questa coniunzion di sangue stretta
fa che tra noi ogni cosa è ben detta.

5   Il caso, che narrar vi voglio, è questo.
In quest' ultima notte ch'è fuggita,
io non dormivo e non ero ben desto:
la santa vergin morta m'è apparita,
Agnesa, che morí, oggi è il dí sesto;
lieta, divota e di bianco vestita:
con lei era un umil candido agnello,
e di molte altre vergini un drappello.

6   E, consolando con dolce parole
il dolor nostro di sua morte santa,
diceva: "Il torto avete, se vi duole
ch'io sia venuta a gloria tale e tanta:
fuor dell'ombra del mondo or veggo il sole
e sento il coro angelico che canta:
però ponete fin, cari parenti,
se ancor me amate, al dolore e ' lamenti."

SECONDO PARENTE:

7   Non dir piú là: tu m'hai tratto di bocca
quel che volevo dir, ma con paura,
temendo di non dir qualcosa sciocca.
Ancor a me, sendo alla sepoltura
per guardar che da altri non sia tócca,
apparve questa vergin santa e pura:
con l'agnel, con le vergini veniva.
Cosí la vidi come fussi viva.

TERZO PARENTE:

8   E' non si crederrà, e pur è vero.
Io la vidi anche, e senti' quel che disse;

And to be open counts for much, I deem.
To talk to you needs no apology:
Your faces will soon tell me if I dream.
Our common blood between us is a token
That nothing need or should remain unspoken.

5   The event of which I want to speak took place
Precisely this last all too fleeting night:
As half-asleep I lay there in my space,
I saw our Agnes, holy virgin bright,
Now dead six days, and yet with joyful face,
And mien devout, apparelled all in white;
A lamb, snow-white, all meek and mild she held,
And other virgins with her I beheld.

6   With kindness, sweet consoling words she spoke,
To help us see how foolish is our grief:
"Dare not regret," she said, "like mindless folk,
That I'm reborn, for such is our belief.
After life's darkness in God's sun I woke,
To glory and choirs eternal, nay not brief.
So please, I beg you, end your lamentation,
If you still love me, as your dear relation."

SECOND RELATIVE OF ST AGNES:

7   Stop, stop! No more! Your words are but the speech
That I myself held back, afraid to incur
Your ridicule. Believe me, I beseech:
As I kept watch beside her sepulchre
The virgin Agnes came, within my reach,
Holy and pure, as we remember her.
With other virgins and the lamb she came;
As if still with us, she looked quite the same.

THIRD RELATIVE:

8   You'll not believe me, but I swear it's true:
I also saw and what she said did hear;

i' non dico dormendo o col pensiero,
ma tenendo le luci aperte e fisse.
I' cominciai, e non forni' l'intero.[8]
"O vergin santa e bella..." Allor si misse
in via per ritornarsi al Regno santo:
io restai solo e lieto in dolce pianto.

IL PRIMO PARENTE UN'ALTRA VOLTA:

9   Benché a simil fallaci visione
chi non è molto santo non dé' credere
(ché spesso son del diavol tentazione),
questa potrebbe pur da Dio procedere,
essendo ella apparita a piú persone.
Dobbiam Dio ringraziare, e merzé chiedere,
e rallegrarci di questa beata;
ché abbiamo in paradiso un'avvocata.

*   *   *

COSTANZA:

10   Misera a me! che mi giova esser figlia
di chi regge e governa il mondo tutto?
aver d'ancille e servi assai famiglia,
ricchezza e gioventú? Non mi fa frutto
l'onor, l'esser amata a maraviglia,
se 'l corpo giovenil di lebbra è brutto.
Non darò al padre mio nipoti o genero,
sendo tutto ulcerato il corpo tenero.

11   Meglio era che quest' anima dolente
nel corpo mio non fussi mai nutrita;
e, se pur v'è venuta, prestamente
nella mia prima età fussi fuggita:
piú dolce è una morte veramente
che morire ad ogn' ora in questa vita,
e dare al vecchio padre un sol tormento,
che, vivendo cosí, dargliene cento.

Mine was no dream: I was awake, I knew;
With open eyes I stared at what was clear.
To address her I began: "Good Virgin, you,
So beautiful and whom we hold so dear..."
But then she turned to go back to her Lord.
Sweet tears I shed, alone but much restored.

FIRST RELATIVE AGAIN:

9   Although belief in such beguiling dreams
      All but the very saintly should withhold
      (For often they are devilish, evil schemes),
      Yet frequent was this vision, as is told;
      So that it came from God it surely seems.
      Ask Him for mercy, and your thanks unfold.
      Let us rejoice! Our Agnes now is blest:
      In heaven she can plead at our request.

* * *

CONSTANCE:

10   Oh grief! What benefit is it to be
      An emperor's child, quite happy, they presume,
      Because so many servants wait on me?
      What is the use of love, and in the bloom
      Of youth to have great wealth and dignity,
      When my fresh body leprosy does doom?
      No grandson for my father I'll engender,
      And barren leave my body sick and tender.

11   How better truly for my sorrowing soul
      If my weak flesh had never nurtured it;
      And better too if death had rung my toll
      While still in early infancy. More fit
      And sweeter far to die while we are whole
      Than hourly fade away just bit by bit.
      Then my old father one sharp pain would know;
      My living death brings him unending woe.

UN SERVO DI COSTANZA:

12   Bench' io presuma troppo o sia importuno,
     madonna, pur dirò quel che m'occorre:
     quando un mal è sanza rimedio alcuno,
     a cose nuove e strane altri ricorre:
     medicina, fatica o uom nessuno
     poiché non può da te questo mal tôrre,
     tentar nuovi rimedi è 'l parer mio,
     ché, dove l'arte manca, abbonda Dio.

13   Io ho sentito dir da piú persone
     che Agnesa, la qual fu martirizzata,
     a' parenti è venuta in visione,
     e credesi per questo sia beata:
     io proverrei ad ir con devozione
     là dove questa santa è sotterrata:
     raccomàndati a lei con umil voce:
     e' non è mal tentar quel che non nuoce.

COSTANZA:

14   I' ho già fatte tante cose invano,
     che questi pochi passi ancor vo' spendere;
     se 'l corpo mio debbe diventar sano,
     questa è poca fatica: io la vo' prendere;
     e forse l'andar mio non sarà vano.
     Già sento in devozione il cuore accendere,
     già mi predice la salute mia:
     orsú, andiam con poca compagnia.

*   *   *

COSTANZA, POICH' È GIUNTA ALLA SEPOLTURA DI SANT' AGNESA, DICE:

15   O Vergin santa, d'ogni pompa e fasto
     nemica e piena dell'amor di Dio,

A MANSERVANT OF CONSTANCE:

12   I beg forgiveness, Madam, for presuming
And trespassing beyond what is my place:
But your disease is painful and consuming,
And one must try new ways to help your case.
No cure has yet been found, so I'm assuming
That all that has been tried has left no trace.
If human skill can bring no remedy,
Then turn to God to heal your malady.

13   I hear reports and rumours spreading fast,
That Agnes, who in death did end her quest,
In vision came to kinsfolk some nights past,
And all, because of this, believe her blest.
I'd go to where she lies, with eyes downcast,
And pray devoutly, and her help request.
With humble voice commit yourself to her;
Nothing is lost if you in this should err.

CONSTANCE:

14   I've tried so many methods, all in vain;
A few more steps may lead me to my rest.
But if my limbs are to be whole again,
Then this is little trouble; I will test
My fortune, hoping my good health to gain—
I feel devotion swelling in my breast.
Let some of you set out along with me;
My heart has faith: of illness I'll be free.

*   *   *

CONSTANCE, AT THE GRAVE OF ST AGNES, SAYS:

15   Oh virgin, who for love of God rejected
Vain glory, casting luxury aside,

pe' merti dello sparso sangue casto
ti prego vòlti gli occhi al mio desio:
abbi pietà del téner corpo guasto,
abbi pietà del vecchio padre mio:
bench' io nol merti, o Vergin benedetta,
rendimi al vecchio padre sana e netta.

ADDORMENTASI; E SANT' AGNESA LE VIENE IN VISIONE, DICENDO:

16   Rallégrati, figliuola benedetta.
Dio ha udito la tua orazione
ed esaudita, ed ègli suta accetta,[9]
perch' ella vien da vera devozione,
e se' libera fatta, monda e netta.
Rendi a Dio grazie, ché tu n'hai cagione;
e per questo mirabil benefizio
ama Dio sempre ed abbi in odio il vizio.

COSTANZA SI DESTA E DICE:

17   Egli è pur vero. Appena creder posso,
e vedo e tocco il mio corpo esser mondo:
fuggito è tutto il mal che aveva addosso;
son netta come il dí ch'io venni al mondo.
O mirabile Dio, onde se' mosso
a farmi grazia? ed io con che rispondo?
Non mia bontà o merti mia preteriti,
ma mosso han tua pietà d'Agnesa i meriti.

18   L'odor suave di sua vita casta,
come incenso salí nel tuo cospetto;
ond' io, che son cosí sana rimasta,
fo voto a te, o Gesú benedetto,
che, mentre questa brieve vita basta,
casto e mondo ti serbo questo petto:
e 'l corpo, che di fuor or mondo sento,
con la tua grazia anco sia mondo drento.

Let not, I pray, your pure eyes be deflected
From my sad plight, but remedy provide.
That my old father be from pain protected,
Show mercy on my body putrified.
Oh virgin blest, though I deserve it not,
Return me whole to him who me begot.

SHE FALLS ASLEEP; ST AGNES APPEARS TO HER IN A VISION AND SAYS:

16   Most blessèd daughter, in the Lord rejoice!
       For He has heard your humble, heartfelt plea;
       He heard sincere devotion in your voice,
       So what you asked He grants in majesty.
       Go, give Him thanks, as it is now His choice
       That you be cleansed and purified and free.
       And for this wondrous benefit and grace
       Love God, and from your life all sin efface.[9]

CONSTANCE AWAKES AND SAYS:

17   I scarcely can believe it, but it's true;
       I see, I touch my body: it is clean!
       No plague, no sickness anywhere I view;
       I am as sound as I have ever been.
       Oh wondrous God, I cannot say why you
       Bestow on me the grace which I now glean.
       Our martyr's merits caused your grace to flow;
       'Twas not my goodness, nor my deeds, I know.

18   Like incense rich and strong, so upward ran
       Her saintly scent all heaven to invade,
       Hence I, reborn to health and strength, now can
       Vouchsafe, my Jesus, to remain your maid.
       While my brief life completes its portioned span
       My chastity I never shall degrade.
       From outward plague my body is secure:
       From plague of sin your grace will keep it pure.

E, VOLTASI A QUELLI CHE SONO SECO, DICE:

19   Diletti miei, queste membra vedete,
che ha monde la suprema medicina.
Insieme meco grazie a Dio rendete
dell'ammirabil sua pietà divina.
Simili frutti con dolcezza miete
colui che nel timor di Dio cammina.
Torniamo a casa, pur laudando Dio,
a dar quest' allegrezza al padre mio.

MENTRE NE VA A CASA:

20   O Dio, il qual non lasci destituto
della tua grazia ancor gli umani eccessi,[10]
e chi arebbe però mai creduto
che d'una lebbra tanti ben nascessi?
Cosí utile e sano è 'l mio mal suto;
convien che i miei dolor dolci or confessi.
O santa infermità per mio ben nata,
c'hai mondo il corpo e l'anima purgata!

*   *   *

E, GIUNTA AL PADRE, DICE:

21   Ecco la figlia tua, che lebbrosa era,
che torna a te col corpo bello e netto;
sana di sanità perfetta e vera,
però che ha sano e il corpo e l'intelletto.
Troppo son lieta, e la letizia intera,
o dolce padre, vien per tuo rispetto;[11]
però che Dio mirabilmente spoglia
me dalla lebbra e te da tanta doglia.

COSTANTINO, IL PADRE, RISPONDE:

22   Io sento, figlia mia, tanta dolcezza,
che pare il gaudio quasi fuor trabocchi;

AND, TURNING TO THOSE WHO ARE WITH HER, SHE SAYS:

19   My body, cherished people, now behold
Renewed and healed through medicine divine.
Together let us thank, out loud and bold,
Our gracious God, who has been so benign.
Such sweet, rich fruits are gathered hundredfold
By those who place their faith in God's design.
Exultantly let's sing our Saviour's worth,
Then share our joy with him who gave me birth.

AS SHE GOES HOME:

20   Oh God of mercy, never known to fail
Those sinners who most humbly seek Your grace,
How dare one loudly 'gainst one's illness rail,
When from it good abounds? I prove the case.
Gone is my sorrow, I must change my tale,
For sweet is now that pain that left no trace.
Oh holy illness, for my welfare sent!
My body is healed, my soul on heaven bent.

*   *   *

AND, HAVING RETURNED TO HER FATHER, SHE SAYS:

21   Behold your daughter, leper once outcast;
Behold her limbs now beautiful and healed,
Restored to health that will forever last
In body healthy, with true faith her shield.
Your joy will add to hers, quite unsurpassed,
When of all this the cause will be revealed;
The power of God has cleansed me of disease,
And all your anguish turns to joyful ease.

CONSTANTINE HER FATHER ANSWERS:

22   I feel, my dearest daughter, such delight
That joy but half-controlled now takes its course;

né posso far che per la tenerezza
non versi un dolce pianto giú dagli occhi.
Dolce speranza della mia vecchiezza,
creder nol posso infin ch'io non ti tocchi.

E, DICENDO COSÍ, GLI TOCCA LA MANO:

Egli è pur vero. Oh gran cosa inaudita!
Ma dimmi, figlia mia: chi t'ha guarita?

RISPONDE COSTANZA:

23   Non m'ha di questa infermità guarita
medico alcun, ma la divina cura:
io me n'andai e devota e contrita
d'Agnesa a quella santa sepoltura;
feci orazion, la qual fu in cielo udita;
poi dormi'; poi desta'mi netta e pura;
feci allor voto, o caro padre mio,
che 'l mio sposo e 'l tuo genero sia Dio.

COSTANTINO RISPONDE:

24   Grande e mirabil cosa certo è questa:
chi l'ha fatta non so, né 'l saper giova.
Basta: se sana la mia figlia resta,
sia chi si vuol: questa è suta gran pruova.
Su, rallegriamci tutti e facciam festa.
O scalco, su, da far colezion truova.
Fate che presto qui mi vengh' innanzi
buffoni e cantator, chi suoni e danzi.

TORNA IN QUEST' ALLEGREZZA GALLICANO DI PERSIA CON VITTORIA,
E DICE:

25   Io son tornato a te, divo Augusto,[12]
e non so come, tra tanti perigli.
Ho soggiogato il fèr popol robusto,
né credo contra te piú arme pigli.

The tenderness that moves me with its might
Is of these sweet and copious tears the source.
Sweet hope that will to my old age bring light,
Do let me touch and my belief enforce.

AND WITH THESE WORDS HE TOUCHES HER HAND:

Unheard-of wonder! Yes! It's true! It's real!
Tell me, my child, what power has made you heal?

CONSTANCE ANSWERS:

23　No doctor treated my infirmity;
　　God's intervention was the healing cure.
　　I went, contrite for my iniquity,
　　Where saintly Agnes lies, and prayed demure
　　That heaven grant my health's entirety;
　　I slept, and I awoke, all cleansed and pure.
　　I vowed, dear father, with firm will and free,
　　To wed the Lord, who then your son would be.

CONSTANTINE ANSWERS:

24　What an amazing portent here is seen!
　　Whose deed this be, I neither know nor care.
　　Enough: if Constance is of illness clean,
　　To question further is not our affair.
　　Come servants, lay a banquet for a queen;
　　Let us have song and banish all despair.
　　Singers and dancers bring before my sight,
　　Jugglers and clowns, to celebrate aright!

IN THE MIDST OF THE MERRYMAKING
GALLICAN RETURNS VICTORIOUS FROM PERSIA AND SAYS:

25　Divine Augustus,[12] conqueror here I stand—
　　I marvel how, so savage was the fray.
　　The once proud foes are under my command;
　　Armies against you they'll no more array.

Per tutta Persia[13] il tuo scettro alto e giusto
or è tenuto; e di sangue vermigli
fe' con la spada i fiumi correr tinti:
e' son per sempremai domati e vinti.

26   Tra ferro e fuoco, tra feriti e morti
con la spada abbiam cerco la vittoria
io e' tuoi cavalieri audaci e forti:
di noi nel mondo fia sempre memoria.
Io so ben che tu sai quanto t'importi
questa cosa al tuo stato ed alla gloria:
che s'ella andava per un altro verso,
era il nome romano e 'l regno perso.

27   Benché la gloria e 'l servir signor degno
al cor gentil debb' esser gran merzede,[14]
pur la fatica, l'animo e l'ingegno,
ancor ch'io mi tacessi, premio chiede.
Se mi dài la metà di questo regno,
non credo mi pagassi, per mia fede;
ma minor cosa mi paga abbastanza,
se arò per sposa tua figlia Costanza.

RISPONDE AUGUSTO, CIOÈ COSTANTINO:

28   Ben sia venuto il mio gran capitano,
ben venga la baldanza del mio impero,
ben venga il degno e fido Gallicano,
domator del superbo popol fero;
ben sia tornata la mia destra mano,
e quel, nella cui forza e virtú spero;
ben venga quel che, mentre in vita dura,
l'imperio nostro e la gloria è sicura.

29   Ogni opera e fatica aspetta merto,
e' tuoi meriti meco sono assai:
e, se aspettavi il merto fusse offerto,
io non t'arei potuto pagar mai.
Darti mia figlia gran cosa è per certo,

I have set up for ever, sword in hand,
Your mace and arms; and justice will hold sway.
The Persian rivers ran with crimson gore;[13]
Our foe is vanquished now for evermore.

26   'Midst fire and steel they died, the warriors fell:
'Twas bloody victory, most dearly bought.
How your brave knights slew those who dared rebel
Will last for years to come in living thought.
The outcome of all this, I know full well,
Both strength and glory to your state has brought.
Without it Rome's proud name would now be lost,
And with your kingdom you would pay the cost.

27   Great the reward, if noble be his heart,
A man will find in service of his king;[14]
Yet labour, courage, skill, too, played their part,
And all of this a handsome prize should bring.
But if with half your realm you were to part,
'Twould not repay my loyal soldiering.
By something less I will be satisfied:
Give me your daughter Constance as my bride.

AUGUSTUS, THAT IS, CONSTANTINE REPLIES:

28   Welcome, great captain! Conqueror brave and strong,
Praised be the boldness that has saved my state;
Praised be your worthy service loyal and long,
My Gallican who's quenched the foe's proud hate.
I welcome back the man who's righted wrong,
Whose strength and valour I so highly rate.
As long as he shall in this life endure,
Our empire and our glory are secure.

29   Labour and toil deserve a high reward
And much your excellence deserves from me;
But any gesture I might make toward
Your just deserts would insufficient be.
To give my treasured daughter as award

e quanto io l'amo, Gallican, tu il sai:
gran cosa è certo un pio paterno amore,
ma il tuo merito vince ed è maggiore.

30   Se tu non fussi, lei non saria figlia
d'imperadore, il qual comanda al mondo:
però, s'altri n'avessi maraviglia
e mi biasma, con questo gli rispondo.
Credo che lei e tutta mia famiglia
e 'l popol tutto ne sarà giocondo,
ed io di questo arò letizia e gloria,
non men ch'io abbi della gran vittoria.

31   In questo punto ir voglio, o Gallicano,
a dir qualcosa a mia figlia Costanza:
tornerò resoluto a mano a mano.
Intanto non t'incresca qui la stanza.

MENTRE CHE VA, DICE:

Oh ignorante capo! oh ingegno vano!
O superbia inaudita! oh arroganza!
E cosí l'aver vinto m'è molesto,
se la vittoria arreca seco questo.

32   Che far? Darò io ad un suggetto
la bella figlia mia, che m'è sí cara?
S'io non la do, in gran pericol metto
lo Stato. E chi è quel che ci ripara?
Misero a me! Non c'è boccon del netto:[15]
tanto Fortuna è de' suoi beni avara.
Spesso chi chiama Costantin felice,
sta meglio assai di me, e 'l ver non dice.

POICHÉ È GIUNTO A COSTANZA, DICE:

33   Io ti vengo a veder, diletta figlia,
con gli occhi, come ti veggo col cuore.

Were prize indeed, as my life's blood is she!
Though great and holy is a father's love,
What you deserve is over and above.

30 Without your triumph, Constance would not stand
As heiress to a king whose mighty voice
Is heard with fear and trembling through the land.
So let there be no carping at my choice.
My daughter will not question my command,
And all my kin and people will rejoice.
From this I'll gain in happiness and glory
No less than when I heard your martial story.

31 Dear, worthy Gallican, I must make haste
To Constance now, to tell her this glad news.
Please give me time, with patience and good grace,
To ascertain that she will not refuse.

AS HE GOES HE SAYS:

What arrant ignorance upon his face!
Unheard-of pride that no one could excuse!
If conquest such a bitter price demand,
Too great a cost it were to rule my land.

32 Oh never to a subject will I give
My cherished daughter full of grace and charm.
If I refuse, in danger we shall live;
Our unprotected state will come to harm.
Mean Fortune takes her toll, and fugitive
Her gifts; against her blows men vainly arm.
For many men who envy Constantine
Are wrong; their lives are better far than mine.

WHEN HE HAS REACHED CONSTANCE HE SAYS:

33 Sweet child, I come to see with my own eyes
The image which is ever in my heart.

COSTANZA:

O padre, io veggo in mezzo alle tue ciglia
un segno che mi dice c'hai dolore,
che mi dà dispiacere e maraviglia.
O padre dolce, se mi porti amore,
dimmi ch'è la cagion di questo tedio;
e s'io ci posso fare alcun rimedio.

34   Dimmelo, padre, sanz' alcun riguardo.
Io son tua figlia per darti dolcezza;
e però dopo Dio a te sol guardo,
pur ch'io ti possa dar qualche allegrezza.

COSTANTINO:

Io sono a dirti questa cosa tardo.
Pietà mi muove della mia vecchiezza
e del tuo corpo giovenil, che sano
è fatto acciò che il chiegga Gallicano.

COSTANZA:

35   O padre, deh pon' freno al tuo dolore!
Intendo quel che tu vuoi dire a punto.
Il magno Dio, ch'è liberal signore,
non stringerà la grazia a questo punto.
Io veggo onde ti vien tal pena al core:
se dài a Gallican quel c'ha presunto,
offendi te e me; e s'io nol piglio
per mio marito, il regno è in gran periglio.

36   Quando il partito d'ogni parte punga,
né sia la cosa ben secura e netta,
io ho sentito dir che il savio allunga
e dà buone parole, e tempo aspetta.
Benché il mio ingegno molto in su non giunga,
padre, io direi che tu me gli prometta:

CONSTANCE:

Father, the frown upon your brow implies
That once again you suffer sorrow's smart.
Within my breast dismay and grief arise:
Belovèd father, let your pain depart;
Tell me the reason of your present grief,
And let me see if I can bring relief.

34   Without ado, please tell me, I beseech:
I ask as your dear daughter, who will give
You all the joy that is within her reach,
Since, after God, for you alone I live.

CONSTANTINE:

Regretful and reluctant is my speech:
I mourn that I am old and can't forgive
That your young body, now made whole and sound,
To Gallican, in wedlock, must be bound.

CONSTANCE:

35   Dear father, to your grief some comfort take,
For well I understand what is involved;
Almighty God, who miracles can make,
Will not leave our dilemma unresolved.
I see precisely why you feel such ache:
We've made a vow and cannot be absolved.
But if I now refuse to be his wife,
The empire runs the risk of deadly strife.

36   When one is harried, badgered every way,
And no escape is seen both safe and straight,
Wise men, I've heard, judiciously must play
For time, and cautiously prevaricate.
Take my advice: to him go now and say
That I will marry him, but he must wait.

d'assicurarlo ben fa' ogni pruova,
e poi lo manda in questa impresa nuova.

37   Benché forse io parrò presuntuosa,
fanciulla, donna e tua figlia, se io
ti consigliassi in questa ch'è mia cosa,
prudente, esperto e vecchio, padre mio;
tu gli puo' dir quant' è pericolosa
la guerra in Dacia,[16] e che ogni suo disio
vuoi fare; e, perché creda non lo inganni,
per sicurtà dà Paulo e Giovanni.

38   Questi statichi meni, acciò che intenda
ch'io sarò donna sua, da poi ch'e' vuole;
e d'altra parte indietro lui ti renda
Attica, Artemia, sue care figliuole.
In questa guerra vi sarà faccenda,
e 'l tempo molte cose acconciar suole.[17]

COSTANTINO:

Figlia, e' mi piace assai quel che m'hai detto:
son lieto, e presto il metterò ad effetto.

DA SÉ, MENTRE CHE RITORNA DA GALLICANO:

39   Laudato sia Colui che in te spira
bontà, prudenzia, amor, figliuola mia.
Io ho giú posto la paura e l'ira,
e cosí Gallican contento fia;
l'onor fia salvo, il qual drieto si tira
ogni altra cosa, sebben cara sia.
Passato questo tempo e quel periglio,
vedrem poi quel che fia miglior consiglio.

E, GIUNTO A GALLICANO:

40   Io torno a te con piú letizia indrieto
ch'io non andai: e Costanza consente

Slight though my wisdom be, it does suggest
That some new feat of arms you now request.

37   Perhaps in this I am presumptuous:
I am a girl, your daughter, and unwed;
Advice from me must seem gratuitous,
Since you have years of wisdom in your head.
Tell him the Dacians have set out to crush us:
Our armies into battle must be led;[16]
And lest of your good faith he doubtful be,
Let John and Paul be our security.

38   Give him these pledges of our firm intent
To grant his wish that I his bride should be;
And in exchange his daughters must be sent—
Artemia and Attica—to stay with me.
For often time our troubles will prevent;
It may take long to gain new victory.[17]

CONSTANTINE:

Well spoken, dear, you have restored my joy:
Away he goes, the Dacians to destroy.

SPEAKING TO HIMSELF, AS HE RETURNS TO GALLICAN:

39   Blessèd be He who gave you so much sense,
Goodness and wisdom—daughter, I am pleased.
Gone have my fear and wrath, though both immense,
As Gallican for now will be appeased.
My honour has been saved without offence;
Had it not been, all joys would soon have ceased.
This time will pass, we've wriggled from the snare;
We may yet see how better we may fare.

AND, HAVING REACHED GALLICAN:

40   My friend, I'm back to you with joy and pride;
Doubtful I left, but certain I return,

esser tua donna. Io son tanto piú lieto,
quanto piú dubbio avevo nella mente.
Pareva volta ad un viver quieto,
sanza marito o pratica di gente.
Mirabilmente di quel suo mal monda,
bella consente in te, sana e gioconda.

41   Direi: facciam le nozze questo giorno
e rallegriam con esse questa terra;
ma, se ti par, facciam qualche soggiorno;
ché tu sai ben quanto ci stringe e serra
Dacia rebelle, qual ci cigne intorno;
e non è ben accozzar nozze e guerra:
ma dopo la vittoria, se ti piace,
farem le nozze piú contenti in pace.

42   So ben c'hai di Costanza desidèro,
ma piú del tuo onore e del mio Stato,
anzi del tuo, ché tuo è questo impero,
perché la tua virtú l'ha conservato.
Per fede, Gallican, ch'io dica il vero,
Giovanni caro a me, Paulo amato
teco merrai; e sicurtà sien questi.
Artemia, Attica tua, qui meco resti.

43   Tu sarai padre a' dua diletti miei;
Costanza madre alle figliuole tue
e non matrigna; e sia certo che lei
le tratterà siccome fussin sue.
Io spero nell'aiuto degli dèi,
ma molto piú nella tua gran virtue,
che contro a' Daci arem vittoria presta.
Costanza è tua: allor farem la festa.

GALLICANO:

44   Nessuna cosa, o divo imperadore,
brama il mio cuor, quanto farti contento,
conservare il tuo Stato e 'l mio onore:

For Constance has agreed to be your bride
Although I feared your offer she might spurn—
So fond she seemed of living by my side,
For company and husband she'd no yearn.
Her malady miraculously went:
Now well and beautiful, she gives consent.

41   I'd give the word to start the celebration
And with great merrymaking fill our land;
But we must needs postpone our jubilation
For in revolt the Dacian people stand.
Weddings fit ill with war's contamination,
So let us first the enemy disband.
When victory is ours, then, as you please,
Your nuptials we shall celebrate at ease.

42   I know full well how much you long to wed,
But more you prize your honour and my state—
Indeed, not mine, but yours, for you have led
My men to war and sealed the Persians' fate.
The guarantors of all that I have said
Are John and Paul, whom you away will take;
While in exchange, I formally decree,
Artemia and Attica you leave with me.

43   In you my loved ones will a father find,
And Constance to your girls will mother be:
With deepest bond of true love she will bind
Your daughters to her heart eternally.
I trust our gods to us will be most kind,
But more I trust in you for victory.
Your prowess will the Dacian foe destroy,
And then your wedding we shall toast with joy!

GALLICAN:

44   Naught matters more, my emperor divine,
Than your glad heart; your state I must preserve,
My honour too, ere Constance can be mine,

Costanza sanza questo m'è tormento.
Io spero tornar presto vincitore;
so che fia presto questo fuoco spento:
proverrà con suo danno il popol strano
la forza e la virtú di questa mano.

45   Quando un'impresa ha in sé grave periglio,
non metter tempo nella espedizione:
pensata con maturo e buon consiglio,
vuole aver presta poi l'esecuzione.
Però sanza piú indugio il cammin piglio:
arò Paulo e Giovanni in dilezione
come fratelli o figli tuttavia;
e raccomando a te Costanza mia.

46   O fidato Alessandro,[18] presto andrai:
Attica, Artemia, fa' sien qui presenti.
E tu, Anton, trova danari assai,
e presto spaccia[19] tutte le mie genti.
O forti cavalier, che meco mai
non fuste vinti, o cavalier potenti
nutriti nella ruggine del ferro,
noi vinceremo ancor: so ch'io non erro.

GALLICANO, POICHÉ SONO GIUNTE LE FIGLIUOLE, DICE A COSTANTINO:

47   Non posso dirti con asciutte ciglie
quel ch'io vorrei delle dolci figliuole.
Io te le lascio acciò che sien tue figlie.
Fortuna nella guerra poter suole;
io vo di lungi molte e molte miglie
fra gente che ancor ella vincer vuole:
bench' io speri tornar vittorioso,
l'andare è certo, e 'l tornar è dubbioso.

VOLTOSI ALLE FIGLIUOLE, DICE:

48   E voi figliuole mie (da poi ch'e' piace
ch'io vada in questa impresa al mio signore),

Or else to claim her hand I'd not deserve.
I hope of victory soon to bear the sign,
And fiercely, soon, our angry foe unnerve.
It will be seen in that barbaric land,
What strength, what valour lie in my right hand.

45   When serious risks a venture may present,
The wise make haste, once all has been agreed,
And thoughtful counsel gives mature assent
That matters may advance with all due speed.
So I set forth and go with your consent;
Your John and Paul will be my friends indeed:
As brothers or as sons they come with me.
Look after Constance, my dear bride to be.

46   My faithful Alexander,[18] quickly, go:
Fetch Attica, Artemia, here desired.
You, Anthony, get money, be not slow,
Marshal as many troops as are required.
Strong valiant knights, well used to overthrow,
To rout, to win, and to pursue untired,
Nurtured amid the clash and rust of swords,
We'll triumph once again, you mark my words.

HIS DAUGHTERS HAVING ARRIVED, GALLICAN SAYS TO CONSTANTINE:

47   My eyes are moist, I brush away a tear,
As of these girls I speak with love and pride;
As daughters I entrust them—keep them near—,
For only Fortune knows the winning side.
Long is my journey, and I have no fear;
Determined 'gainst a direful foe I ride;
Though victory, I hope, will be my lot,
To go is easy, to return is not.

TURNING TO HIS DAUGHTERS HE SAYS:

48   I undertake this arduous task to please
My lord, and leave you in his tender care.

pregate Giove che vittoria o pace
riporti sano, e torni con onore:
se là resta il mio corpo e morto giace,
il padre vostro fia lo imperadore;
per lui i' metto volentier la vita:
Costanza mia da voi sia riverita.

UNA DELLE FIGLIUOLE DI GALLICANO:

49   Quando pensiam, padre nostro diletto,
che forse non ti rivedrem mai piue,
copron gli occhi di pianto il tristo petto.
E dove lasci le figliuole tue?
Già mille e mille volte ho maladetto
l'arme e la guerra e chi cagion ne fue.
Benché un buon padre e degno ci abbi mostro,
pur noi vorremmo il dolce padre nostro.

L'ALTRA FIGLIUOLA, A COSTANTINO:

50   Alto e degno signor, deh, perché vuoi
che noi restiam quasi orfane e pupille?
Risparmia in questa impresa, se tu puoi,
il padre nostro: de' suoi par c'è mille,
ma altro padre piú non abbiam noi;
contentaci, ché puoi; facci tranquille.

COSTANTINO:

Su, non piangete: il vostro Gallicano
tornerà presto con vittoria e sano.

GALLICANO SI VOLTA A COSTANTINO, E DICE:

51   Io vo' baciarti il piè, signor sovrano,
prima ch'io parta, ed a mie figlie il volto.
E credi che 'l fedel tuo Gallicano
Giovanni e Paul tuo osserva molto:
l'uno alla destra, alla sinistra mano

Success or peace of Jove ask on your knees;
Plead for my health and honour in your prayer.
Yet have no fear; the Emperor agrees
To be your father, should I perish there.
For him most willingly I risk my life,
And you respect dear Constance as my wife.

ONE OF GALLICAN'S DAUGHTERS:

49   When we but think, belovèd father dear,
That we may never see your face again,
Our tearful hearts are pierced as by a spear.
And, so bereft, oh how shall we live then?
A thousand times all those who engineer
These wars I've cursed, for they divide all men.
The king's a kindly father, you've well shown,
Both good and worthy, but we want our own.

THE OTHER DAUGHTER, TO CONSTANTINE:

50   Most high and worthy lord, is it your will
That wards and almost orphans we become?
Oh, free our father! Let him not fulfil
This pledge. A thousand men to you will come
To fight your war, for many have the skill,
But fatherless we'll be, should he succumb.

CONSTANTINE:

Come, dry your eyes: your father will return
Successful, safe, for victory he'll earn.

GALLICAN TURNS TO CONSTANTINE AND SAYS:

51   I bow and kiss your foot, my sovereign king,
And both my daughters lovingly embrace.
Your John and Paul to battle I will bring
And keep them close to me in every place;
To my left arm I want you, Paul, to cling,

l'altro terrò, perché non mi sia tolto;
se senti alcuna loro ingiuria o torto,
tu puoi dir certo: "Gallicano è morto."

E, VOLTATOSI A' CAVALIERI, DICE:

52   Su cavalier, cotti e neri dal sole,
dal sol di Persia, ch'è cosí fervente!
Il nostro imperador provar ci vuole
tra ' ghiacci e neve di Dacia al presente:
la virtú il caldo e il freddo vincer suole;
periglio, morte alfin stima niente.
Ma facciam prima sacrifizio a Marte,[20]
ché sanza Dio val poco o forza o arte.[21]

DETTO QUESTO, FA SACRIFICIO IN QUALCHE LUOGO
DOVE NON SIA VEDUTO ALTRIMENTI; DI POI SI PARTE CON LO ESERCITO,
E NE VA ALLA IMPRESA DI DACIA.

*   *   *

COSTANZA AD ATTICA ED ARTEMIA, QUALE LEI CONVERTE:

53   O care mie sorelle in Dio dilette,
o cara Artemia, o dolce Attica mia;
io credo il vostro padre mi vi dette
non sol per fede o per mia compagnia,
ma acciò che sane, liete e benedette
vi renda a lui quando tornato fia;
né so come ben far possa quest' io,
se prima sane non vi rendo a Dio.

54   O care, o dolci sorelle, sappiate
che questo corpo di lebbra era brutto;
e queste membra son monde e purgate
dall'autore de' ben, Dio, che fa il tutto:
a lui botai la mia verginitate,
finché sia il corpo da morte destrutto;

John at the right hand, as the foe we face.
If you should hear that captive they are led,
Then rest assured that Gallican is dead.

AND TURNING TO HIS KNIGHTS HE SAYS:

52   My swarthy knights all blackened by the sun—
      The scorching sun of Persia—, let us go,
      For so our Emperor bids. The war, begun
      In Dacia with its wastes of ice and snow,
      Must, through our prowess, be advanced and won.
      Come heat, come cold, our courage we will show.
      But first to Mars let's offer sacrifice:[20]
      Without God's help no valour will suffice.[21]

      HAVING SAID THIS, HE OFFERS SACRIFICE IN SOME PLACE
      WHERE HE IS NOT SEEN. HE THEN SETS OUT WITH HIS ARMY
      TO EMBARK ON THE DACIAN CAMPAIGN.

                    *   *   *

CONSTANCE TO ATTICA AND ARTEMIA, WHOM SHE CONVERTS:

53   Artemia, Attica, my sisters dear,
      Beloved of God: your father, it is plain,
      Pledged you to stay as my companions here,
      And I in turn my promise must maintain,
      To give you back, in health and free from care,
      When from his battles he comes home again.
      But how can I this sacred trust fulfil
      If first I do not bring you to God's will?

54   My dear, sweet sisters, know that once disease
      Destroyed most foully all my body's beauty.
      My limbs are clean, for mighty God did please
      To heal what leprosy had robbed as booty.
      And until death this body shall release,
      To Him as virgin I am pledged in duty.

e servir voglio a lui con tutto il core:
né par fatica a chi ha vero amore.

55   E voi conforto con lo esemplo mio
che questa vita, ch'è brieve e fallace,[22]
doniate liete di buon core a Dio,
fuggendo quel che al mondo cieco piace:
se volterete a lui ogni disio,
arete in questa vita vera pace,
grazia d'aver contra 'l demòn vittoria;
e poi nell'altra vita eterna gloria.

ARTEMIA:

56   Madonna mia, io non so come hai fatto:
per le parole sante, quali hai detto,
io sento il cuor già tutto liquefatto,[23]
arder d'amor di Dio il vergin petto:
e mi senti' commuovere ad un tratto,
come, parlando, apristi l'intelletto:[24]
di Dio innamorata, son disposta
seguir la santa via che m'hai proposta.

ATTICA:

57   Ed io, madonna, ho posto un odio al mondo,
già come fussi un capital nemico;
prometto a Dio servare il corpo mondo:
con la bocca e col cuor questo ti dico.

COSTANZA:

Sia benedetto l'alto Dio fecondo,
ed io in nome suo vi benedico.
Or siam vere sorelle, al parer mio:
orsú, laudiamo il nostro padre Dio.

I want to serve Him now with all my heart;
This is no hardship if with love you start.

55   Let my example comfort and sustain
You both, as life is treacherous and brief.[22]
For our true God, with joyful hearts disdain
All worldly joys, which lead the blind to grief.
Turn your desires to God, and you will gain
True peace, and from all sorrows find relief.
You will defeat the Prince of Darkness here,
And glory will be yours in heaven's sphere.

ARTEMIA:

56   Lady, I know not how you this achieved:
The holy words by your sweet lips just spoken
Melted my heart and in it is conceived
A burning love that ne'er before was woken.
My virgin breast was suddenly upheaved;
My darkness, by your words of light, was broken.
I long to take the holy path you trace:
It leads to God, Whom I with love embrace.

ATTICA:

57   My lady, I have changed: the world I hate
As if it were a mortal foe to shun.
My chastity to God I consecrate;
In pledging this my heart and words are one.

CONSTANCE:

Blessèd be God, whose power is ever great.
I bless you in His name: His will be done.
We are made sisters by our common vow,
So praise we God, Who is our father now.

COSTANZA, ARTEMIA ED ATTICA CANTANO TUTTE E TRE INSIEME:

58   A te sia laude, o Carità perfetta
       c'hai pien di caritate il nostro cuore;
       l'amor, che questi dolci prieghi getta,[25]
       pervenga a' tuoi orecchi, o pio Signore:
       questi tre corpi verginali accetta
       e gli conserva sempre nel tuo amore.
       Della Vergine già t'innamorasti:
       ricevi, o Sposo nostro, i petti casti.

*   *   *

CONCIONE DI GALLICANO A' SOLDATI:

59   O forti cavalier, nel padiglione
       il capitan debb' esser grave e tardo;
       ma, quando è del combatter la stagione,
       sanza paura sia forte e gagliardo.
       Colui che la vittoria si propone,
       non stima spade, sassi, lance o dardo.
       Là è il nimico, e già paura mostra:
       su, diamci drento: la vittoria è nostra.

AFFRONTASI CON GLI NIMICI, E GLI È ROTTO TUTTO L'ESERCITO;
       E, RESTATO SOLO CON GIOVANNI E PAULO, DICE:

60   Or ecco la vittoria ch'io riporto!
       Ecco lo Stato dello imperadore!
       Lasso! meglio era a me ch'io fussi morto
       in Persia, ché morivo con onore!
       Ma la Fortuna m'ha campato a torto,
       acciò ch'io vegga tanto mio dolore.
       Almanco fuss' io morto questo giorno!
       ché non so come a Costantin ritorno.

58   Oh perfect Love, to You our hearts we raise,
      Which You have won by mercies manifold;
      You, righteous Lord, for ever more we praise,
      As we sing loud, with charity untold.
      These three chaste bodies keep with love ablaze
      And ever in Your loving arms enfold.
      As You the Virgin Mary chose in love,
      Be now our Bridegroom in the realm above.[25]

*   *   *

59   Brave soldiers, hear: a captain in his tent
      Should slow and thoughtful be in his decision;
      But when the time comes on the foe to vent
      His ire, then boldly let him seek collision;
      He fears not swords nor stones, on victory bent;
      All spears and darts he scorns with much derision.
      Behold our foes, already showing fear;
      Up and attack them! Victory is near.

HE MEETS THE ENEMY IN BATTLE, AND HIS ENTIRE ARMY IS DEFEATED.
LEFT ALONE WITH JOHN AND PAUL HE SAYS:

60   Now see what noble victory I have won!
      See how my Emperor's power has turned to dust!
      Oh would, a thousand times, I'd been undone
      On Persia's fields, with honour full and just!
      To suffer all this pain I have lived on:
      So willed by Fortune, whom we should not trust.
      Would that I too had met my death today!
      To my lord Constantine what can I say?

GIOVANNI:

61   Quando Fortuna le cose attraversa,
si vuol reputar sempre che sia bene.
Se tu hai oggi la tua gente persa,
ringrazia Dio, ché questo da lui viene.
Non vincerà giamai la gente avversa
chi contra sé vittoria non ottiene;
né vincer altri ad alcuno è concesso,
se questo tal non sa vincer sé stesso.

62   Forse t'ha Dio a questo oggi condotto,
perché te stesso riconoscer voglia.
E se l'altrui esercito hai già rotto,
sanza Dio non si volge in ramo foglia.
Quel che può l'uom da sé, mortal, corrotto,
altro non è se non peccato e doglia.
Riconosciti adunque, ed abbi fede
in Dio, dal qual ciaschedun ben procede.

PAULO:

63   Non creder che la tua virtute e gloria,
la tua fortezza e ingegno, o Gallicano,
t'abbia con tanto onor dato vittoria:
Dio ha messo il poter nella tua mano.
Perché n'avevi troppo fumo e boria,[26]
Dio t'ha tolto l'onore a mano a mano,
per mostrare alle tue gonfiate voglie
che lui è quel che 'l vincer dà e toglie.

64   Ma, se tu vuoi far util questa rotta,
ritorna a Dio, al dolce Dio Gesue:
l'idol di Marte ch'è cosa corrotta,
(ferma il pensier)[27] non adorar mai piue;
poi vedrai nuova gente qui condotta,
in numer grande e di maggior virtue.
Umilia te a Gesú alto e forte,
ché lui sé umiliò fino alla morte.

JOHN:

61   When Fortune turns a deaf ear to our pleas,
We should believe that she is ever wise.
For this reverse, thank God upon your knees:
It may well be a blessing in disguise.
Man cannot hope to win great victories
Until his inner self he mortifies.
No battles over others you will win
Unless you vanquish first the foe within.

62   To make you know yourself God may intend:
For this, perhaps, He's made you suffer so.
There's a divinity that shapes our end:
No leaf without it to a branch will grow.
Without God's aid our deeds to sorrow tend;
From our corruption only sin can flow.
First know yourself, then turn to God above,
As all the good we get comes from His love.

PAUL:

63   Victorious once you were, that much is true,
And for your strength and genius you had fame;
Esteem and glory seemed to be your due:
But praise of one's own prowess leads to blame.
For God it was who gave success to you.
When full of pride and boasting you became,
He stopped you in your tracks to make you see
That He it is who gives the victory.

64   If you want gain to come out of defeat,
Return to God, to Jesus our sweet Lord.
Cast Mars away and with him your conceit:
Henceforth let pagan idols be abhorred.
Then you will see, in armour all complete,
A valiant host with courage beyond word.
Humble yourself to Jesus great and strong,
For He died humbly to redeem our wrong.

GALLICANO:

65 Io non so come a Gesú fia accetto,
se a lui me umilio, come m'è proposto;
ché da necessità paio costretto
in questo miser stato che m'ha posto.
Io ho sentito alcun cristian, c'ha detto
che Dio ama colui, quale è disposto
dargli il cuor lietamente e voluntario:
la mia miseria in me mostra il contrario.

GIOVANNI:

66 In ogni luogo e tempo accetta Dio
nella sua vigna ciascun operaio;
e 'l padre di famiglia dolce e pio
a chi vien tardi ancor dà 'l suo danaio.[28]
Dà' pur intero a lui il tuo disio,
poi cento ricorrai per uno staio:
inginòcchiati a Dio col corpo e core;
e lui ti renderà gente ed onore.

GALLICANO S'INGINOCCHIA E DICE:

67 O magno Dio, omai la tua potenzia
adoro, e me un vil vermin confesso.[29]
Se piace alla tua gran magnificenzia,
fa' che vincer mi sia oggi concesso:
se non ti piace, io arò pazienzia.
Nel tuo arbitrio, Dio, mi son rimesso:
disposto e fermo non adorar piue
altro che te, dolce signor Gesue.

GIOVANNI, INGINOCCHIATI CHE SONO TUTTI A TRE:

68 O Dio che desti a Giosuè l'ardire
e grazia ancor che 'l sol fermato sia,
e che facesti mille un sol fuggire,
e diecimila due cacciassin via,

GALLICAN:

65   I cannot see how Jesus now will find
Acceptable to Him my humbled pride;
Necessity it is that has consigned
Me to this wretched state and holds me tied.
Some Christians tell us, as I call to mind,
God loves whoever will in Him confide,
Surrendering to Him with joyful heart.
But why should He to me His grace impart?

JOHN:

66   God to His vineyard, any time and place,
Welcomes all labourers, however late.
Landowner kind, whatever be the case,
He gives to first and last the one same rate.[28]
Into His hands your heartfelt wish emplace;
From one, a hundred bushels He'll create.
Kneel down and pray: an army will arise
And history will praise you to the skies.

GALLICAN KNEELS AND SAYS:

67   Almighty God, Your power I extol;
Myself a lowly worm I do confess.[29]
If I am now to play the victor's role
I leave to You and Your divine largesse.
If not, I'll still be true to You, the sole
Dispenser of my failure or success.
Resolved I am henceforth and ever more
You only, sweet Lord Jesus, to adore.

JOHN SAYS, AS ALL THREE KNEEL:

68   Oh God, Who emboldened Joshua that day
And stopped the sun from moving down the sky,
Who willed that one a thousand men dismay,
While two alone ten thousand should defy,

e che facesti della fromba uscire
il fatal sasso che ammazzò Golia,[30]
concedi or forza e grazia a questa mano
del tuo umiliato Gallicano.

UN ANGELO APPARISCE A GALLICANO CON UNA CROCE IN COLLO,
E DICE:

69   O umil Gallicano, il cor contrito
a Dio è sacrifizio accetto molto;
e però ha li umil tuo' prieghi udito
ed è pietoso al tuo disio or vòlto:
va' di buon core in questa impresa ardito,
ché 'l regno fia al re nimico tolto;
daratti grande esercito e gagliardo:
la croce fia per sempre il tuo stendardo.

GALLICANO COLLE GINOCCHIA IN TERRA:

70   Questo non meritava il cuor superbo
di Gallicano e la mia vanagloria:
tu m'hai dato speranza nel tuo verbo,
ond' io veggo già certa la vittoria.
O Dio, la mia sincera fé ti serbo,
sanza far piú de' falsi dèi memoria.
Ma questa nuova gente onde ora viene?
Solo da Dio, autor d'ogni mio bene.

E, VOLTATOSI A QUELLI SOLDATI VENUTI MIRABILMENTE,
DICE:

71   O gente ferocissime e gagliarde,
presto mettiamo alla città l'assedio.
Presto portate sien qui le bombarde
(Dio è con noi: e' non aran rimedio),
passavolante, archibusi e spingarde,
acciò che non ci tenghin troppo a tedio;
fascine e guastator: la terra è vinta,
né può soccorso aver dal campo cinta.

Who made the stone Your guiding hand obey
That brought Goliath in the dust to lie;[30]
Grant of Your strength and grace unto this man,
Your humbled and believing Gallican.

AN ANGEL CARRYING A CROSS APPEARS TO GALLICAN
AND SAYS:

69   Oh contrite, humbled, broken Gallican,
Our God is pleased with this your sacrifice;
He's heard your humble cries, and now His plan
Is mercy to dispense from paradise.
With dauntless heart go forth, for now you can;
The rival king will lose: let that suffice.
A large and mighty army you'll command,
The cross of Christ you'll raise with your right hand.

GALLICAN, KNEELING:

70   My heart so proud and filled with vain conceit
Such generosity did not deserve;
Your word gives hope that God today will mete
Assured success to one who's pledged to serve.
For ever lie forgotten, obsolete,
False gods! From steadfast faith I shall not swerve.
But whence come these new soldiers that I see?
God, source of all my good, sends them to me.

AND, TURNING TO THE SOLDIERS WHO HAVE MIRACULOUSLY ARRIVED,
HE SAYS:

71   Soldiers ferocious, vigorous and bold,
Let's haste and to the city now lay siege.
Bring bombards quickly, your positions hold—
They cannot win, with us is God our liege—;
Bring culverin, springal, arquebus, as told:
No long-drawn, tedious battle need we wage.
Have sappers lay their mines: the city's won,
We ring them round; relief there will be none.

72   Fate i graticci, e' ripari ordinate
       per le bombarde; e ponti sien ben forti;
       i bombardier securi conservate,
       che dalle artiglierie non vi sien morti.
       E voi, o cavalieri, armati state
       a far la scorta, vigilanti, accorti;
       ché 'l pensier venga agli assediati meno,
       e le bombarde inchiodate non sièno.[31]

73   Tu, Giovanni, provvedi a strame e paglia,
       sí che 'l campo non abbi carestia;
       venga pan fatto ed ogni vettovaglia;
       e Paulo sarà teco in compagnia.
       Fate far scale onde la gente saglia.
       Quando della battaglia tempo fia,
       ciascun sia pronto a far la sua faccenda.
       Sol Gallican tutte le cose intenda.

74   Fate tutti i trombetti ragunare
       súbito; fate il consueto bando:
       ché la battaglia io vorrò presto dare.
       L'esercito sia in punto al mio comando:
       chi sarà il primo alle mure a montare,
       mille ducati per premio gli mando,
       cinquecento e poi cento all'altra coppia;
       e la condotta a tutti si raddoppia.

                    TROMBETTO:

75   Da parte dello invitto capitano
       si fa intendere a que' che intorno stanno,
       se non si dà la terra a mano a mano
       al campo, sarà data a saccomanno;
       né fia pietoso poi piú Gallicano;
       e chi arà poi il male, abbiasi il danno.
       A' primi montator dare è contento,
       per gradi, mille, cinquecento e cento.

           FASSI LA BATTAGLIA, E PIGLIANO IL RE.

72   Prepare and mend the hurdles, to protect
       From injury our valiant bombardiers;
       Strong bridges also you must needs erect;
       Ensure that every shot our own line clears.
       Alert, you cavalry! Do not neglect
       To escort the infantry as danger nears.
       Let the besieged of victory have no thought,
       Nor shelter from our bombardiers be sought.[31]

73   You, John, look to the fodder and the hay;
       See that our camp is stocked with good supplies;
       Ensure that bread is baked fresh every day;
       And Paul will come to help and to advise.
       We'll need strong ladders for the final fray;
       And when the noise of battle shakes the skies,
       His task perform let each and every man—
       While overseeing all stands Gallican.

74   Summon the heralds hither, one and all:
       Our customary ban let them proclaim.
       Time's short: for battle soon I'll sound the call;
       To obey me then must be the army's aim.
       The man who is the first to scale the wall
       A thousand ducats as a prize may claim;
       Five hundred to the next, one to the third,
       And double pay to all, I give my word.

HERALD:

75   My formidable captain bids me cry
       The news. Lend ear to what I have to tell.
       You must surrender or prepare to die,
       For all resistance he will surely quell.
       Nothing our Gallican will satisfy
       Till he has put to death those who rebel.
       The men first on the walls will get a gift
       Of coins in plenty—'tis no time for thrift.

THE BATTLE TAKES PLACE AND THE KING IS CAPTURED.

IL RE PRESO DICE:

76   Chi confida ne' regni e negli Stati
      e sprezza con superbia gli alti dèi,
      la città in preda e me legato or guati,
      e prenda esempio da' miei casi rei.
      O figli, ecco i reami ch'io v'ho dati,
      ecco l'eredità de' padri miei!
      Voi e me, lassi! avvolge una catena;
      con l'altra preda il vincitor ci mena.

E, VOLTATOSI A GALLICANO, DICE:

77   E tu, nelle cui man Fortuna ha dato
      la vita nostra ed ogni nostra sorte,
      bastiti avermi vinto e subiugato,
      arsa la terra, ucciso il popol forte:
      e non voler che vecchio io sia campato,
      per veder poi de' miei figliuol la morte.
      Per vincer si vuol fare ogni potenzia,
      ma dopo la vittoria usar clemenzia.

78   Io so che se' magnanimo e gentile,
      e in cor gentil so pur pietà si genera:[32]
      se non ti muove l'età mia senile,
      muovati l'innocenzia e l'età tenera:
      uccidere un legato è cosa vile,
      e la clemenzia ciascun lauda e venera.
      Il regno è tuo; la vita a noi sol resti,
      la qual a me per brieve tempo presti.

IL PRINCIPE, UNO DE' FIGLIUOLI DEL DETTO RE, DICE:

79   Noi, innocenti e miser figli suoi
      (poiché Fortuna ci ha cosí percossi),
      preghiam salvi la vita a tutti noi,
      piacendoti; e, se ciò impetrar non puossi,
      il nostro vecchio padre viva, e poi
      non ci curiam da vita esser rimossi.[33]

THE CAPTURED KING SAYS:

76   Those who in state and kingship put their trust,
Disdaining in their pride the gods on high,
Look now upon my city razed to dust
And learn from me as captive I may die.
My sons, the realm I gave you is now lost;
Our heritage is gone, while you and I
Are captives bound together in one chain,
Trundled as booty in a victor's train.

AND TURNING TO GALLICAN HE SAYS:

77   You, now that Fortune places in your hand
Our lives and full control of our sad fate;
Be satisfied that, humbled, here I stand,
My people slaughtered and destroyed my state.
For my old age was this the ending planned—
To lose my sons to appease the victor's hate?
To conquer, every force may be excused;
In victory, forbearance should be used.

78   You are magnanimous and just, I hold,
And noble hearts engender clemency.[32]
But if your ear is deaf to one so old,
My children's tender years may speak for me.
To kill a prisoner is cowardly, not bold,
While mercy is a manly quality.
The realm is yours, leave us our life intact;
This ripe old age will soon its toll exact.

THE PRINCE, ONE OF THE SONS OF THE ABOVE KING, SAYS:

79   Fortune has dealt a most unkindly blow
To us poor innocent and woeful princes.
We beg you, clemency on us bestow.
We humbly pray that our poor plea convinces;
If not, to our old father mercy show:
Kill us, not him—we offer no defences.

Se pur d'uccider tutti noi fai stima,
fa' grazia almeno a noi di morir prima.

GALLICANO:

80   La pietà vostra m'ha sí tócco il core,
che d'aver vinto ho quasi pentimento:
ad ogni giuoco un solo è vincitore,
e l'altro vinto dé' restar contento.
Dell'una e l'altra età, pietà, dolore;
lo esemplo ancor della Fortuna sento:
però la vita volentier vi dono,
insin che a Costantin condotto sono.

*   *   *

IL MESSO, CHE PORTA LE NUOVE DELLA VITTORIA A COSTANTINO,
DICE COSÍ:

81   O imperador, buone novelle porto.
Gallican tuo ha quella città presa;
e credo che 'l re sia o preso o morto:
vidi la terra tutta in fiamma accesa.
Per esser primo a darti tal conforto,
non so i particolar di questa impresa.
Basta, la terra è nostra; e questo è certo.
Dammi un buon beveraggio, ch'io lo merto.

COSTANTINO:

82   Io non vorrei però error commettere,
credendo tai novelle vere sièno.
Costui di Gallican non porta lettere;
la bugia in bocca e 'l ver portano in seno.
Orsú, fatelo presto in prigion mettere:
fioriranno, se queste rose fièno:
se sarà vero, arai buon beveraggio;
se no, ti pentirai di tal viaggio.

But if to slay us all it be your will,
Ensure that us his children first you kill.

GALLICAN:

80　　My heart is touched so by your piteous plight
That having triumphed almost I regret;
In contests only one can win the fight:
The loser must his former hopes forget.
I still can feel the wound of Fortune's spite,
Now old and young her fickleness have met.
I can at least your death decree repeal
Until before my emperor I kneel.

*　*　*

THE MESSENGER WHO BRINGS NEWS OF THE VICTORY TO CONSTANTINE
SPEAKS AS FOLLOWS:

81　　Rejoice, my Lord! Good news in haste I bring:
Brave Gallican has won these latter frays.
It seems that dead or taken is the king;
With my own eyes I saw the city blaze.
The details I know not: the pressing thing
For me was first your doubting heart to raise.
Enough of this: the city now is ours.
Give me a drink. Good health, my Lord, be yours!

CONSTANTINE:

82　　I must be cautious, and with care react,
Be slow ere I accept this news as true.
He brings no script to prove this is a fact;
Men often lie and hide the truth from view.
Imprison him, this may be but an act!
If these be roses you have brought with you,
We'll know their blooms, and you shall have your drink;
If not, prepare to pay more than you think.

TORNA IN QUESTO GALLICANO, E DICE A COSTANTINO:

83   Ecco, il tuo capitan vittorioso
      ritorna a te dalla terribil guerra,
      d'onor, di preda e di prigion copioso;
      ecco il re già signor di quella terra.
      Ma sappi ch'ella andò prima a ritroso,
      ché chi fa cose assai, spesso ancor erra:
      pur, con l'aiuto che Dio ci ha concesso,
      abbiam la terra e 'l regno sottomesso.

IL RE PRESO A COSTANTINO DICE:

84   O imperadore, io fui signore anch' io;
      or servo e prigion son io e ' miei figli.
      Se la Fortuna, ministra di Dio,
      questo ha voluto, ognuno esemplo pigli;
      ed ammonito dallo stato mio,
      de' casi avversi non si maravigli.
      Il vincer è di Dio dono eccellente,
      ma piú nella vittoria esser clemente.

COSTANTINO RISPONDE:

85   L'animo che alle cose degne aspira,
      quanto può cerca simigliare Dio:
      vincer si sforza e superar desira
      finché contenta il suo alto desio;
      ma poi lo sdegno conceputo e l'ira,
      l'offesa mette subito in oblio.
      Io ti perdono, e posto ho giú lo sdegno:
      non voglio il sangue, ma la gloria e 'l regno.

E, VOLTOSI A GALLICANO:

86   O Gallican, quando tu torni a me,
      sempre t'ho caro ancor sanza vittoria:
      or pensa adunque quanto car mi se',
      tornando vincitor con tanta gloria.

GALLICAN RETURNS AND SAYS TO CONSTANTINE :

83   Behold your captain comes with slaves in tow;
        Among them, chained, the captive king is led.
        With honour I have crushed our fiercest foe;
        Those lands of all their riches I have bled,
        Though first it seemed that it would turn to woe,
        That I had erred, and trouble was ahead.
        But with great help from God who is so glorious,
        The state is in our power: we are victorious.

THE CAPTURED KING SAYS TO CONSTANTINE:

84   Oh Emperor, long years I too did rule,
        But now, bound with my sons, I am a slave.
        So Fortune wills, and she is but God's tool.
        Take heed, all men, as you for triumph crave:
        Be not amazed if throne be changed to stool;
        Remembering me, have courage and be brave.
        Great is God's gift should He success ordain,
        But greater gift it is to be humane.

CONSTANTINE ANSWERS:

85   The man who to the highest deeds aspires
        Boldly all hurdles aims to overcome;
        This man to be in all like God requires:
        He does not rest until that work is done.
        But when he has achieved what he desires,
        His anger and his deep offence go numb.
        I pardon you and put aside all blame;
        Glory and kingdom, not your blood, I claim.

AND, TURNING TO GALLICAN:

86   Whether success or just yourself you bring,
        To see you here to happiness gives rise.
        But think what joy from my sore heart will spring
        Now that I know you come with such a prize.

Veder legato innanzi agli occhi un re!
cosa che sempre arò nella memoria.
Ma dimmi: questa croce onde procede,
che porti teco? hai tu mutato fede?

RISPONDE GALLICANO A COSTANTINO:

87   Io non ti posso negar cosa alcuna:
or pensa se negar ti posso 'l vero;
il ver, che mai a persona nessuna
di negarlo uom gentil dé' far pensiero.
Di questa gloriosa mia fortuna
rendute ho grazie a Dio, or in San Piero.[34]
Perché 'l vincer da Cristo è sol venuto,
porto il suo segno, e l'ho da Cristo avuto.

88   Io t'accennai nelle prime parole:
in effetto fui rotto e fracassato.
Campò di tanti tre persone sole:
io e questi duo cari qui dallato;
facemmo tutt' a tre come far suole
ciascun che viene in vile e basso stato:
chi non sa e non può, tardi (s'occorre)
per ultimo rimedio a Dio ricorre.

89   Tu intenderai da Paulo e Giovanni,
per grazia e per miraculo abbiam vinto.
Conosciuto ho de' falsi dèi gl'inganni,
della fede di Cristo armato e cinto;
disposto ho dare a lui tutti i miei anni,
quieto e fuor del mondan labirinto.[35]
e di Costanza, sutami concessa,
t'assolvo, imperador, della promessa.

COSTANTINO:

90   Tu non mi porti una vittoria sola,
né sola un'allegrezza in questa guerra;
tu m'hai renduto un regno e la figliuola,

To see before me bound a once great king
Will keep this scene for years before my eyes.
But tell me now, that cross you bear erected
What does it mean? Have our gods been rejected?

GALLICAN ANSWERS CONSTANTINE:

87   Never could I deny your just request,
Especially as truth you want laid bare;
We have no right to hide this in our breast,
And truth is something noble men should share.
For Fortune's rich miraculous bequest,
In church I thanked my God with heartfelt prayer.
For Christ it was, not I, who won this war;
So Christ's my standard is, for ever more.

88   To be defeated, broken, as I said,
Was my initial lot; with ravaged pride
We stood, three men alive, all others dead:
Myself, and these our dear ones by my side.
As is the wont of all who know the dread
Of life's disasters and with fate collide,
When no way out of trouble we discerned,
To God, as to a last recourse, we turned.

89   What we shall tell our listeners will amaze:
We speak of aid divine and intervention;
For I have seen our false gods' lying ways,
And placed my faith and trust in Christ's redemption.
Now to withdraw from this confusing maze
And give my life to Him is my intention.
Your Constance, Emperor, whom I wished to wed,
Is yours, and you are free from all we said.

CONSTANTINE:

90   This is no question of one victory:
A double joy from war is seen to spring;
My daughter you are giving back to me,

piú cara a me che l'acquistata terra.
E, poi che se' della cristiana scuola[36]
ed adori uno Dio che mai non erra,
puoi dir d'aver te renduto a te stesso:
Dio tutte queste palme t'ha concesso.

91   E, per crescer la tua letizia tanta,
intenderai altre miglior novelle:
perché Costanza, la mia figlia santa,
ha convertite le tue figlie belle:
e tutti siate rami or d'una pianta,[37]
e in ciel sarete ancor lucenti stelle:[38]
per suoi vuol Gallican, Attica, Artemia
Dio, che per grazia e non per merto premia.[39]

GALLICANO:

92   Miglior novelle, alto signore e degno,
ch'io non ti porto, or tu mi rendi indrieto:
ché, s'io ho preso e vinto un re e 'l regno,
son delle mie figliuole assai piú lieto;
che, convertite a Dio, han certo pegno
di vita eterna, che fa 'l cor quieto:
chi sottomette i re e le province
non ha vittoria, ma chi 'l mondo vince.[40]

93   Chi vince il mondo e 'l diavol sottomette
è di vera vittoria certo erede;
e 'l mondo è piú che le province dette,
e 'l diavol re che tutto lo possiede:
sol contra lui vittoria ci promette
e vince il mondo sol la nostra fede:
adunque questa par vera vittoria,
che ha per premio poi eterna gloria.

94   Però, alto signor, se m'è permesso
da te, io vorrei starmi[41] in solitudine,
lasciare il mondo, e viver da me stesso,
la corte e ogni ria consuetudine.

Worth more than land, than conquered state and king.
New born a Christian, from our bondage free,
Firmly to One who never errs you cling.
God, now that victor o'er yourself you stand,
Placed all these palms of triumph in your hand.

91   Let me now add more joy to your delight!
I will impart to you this news of mine:
My daughter Constance with true faith alight
Now shares with your fair ones the Christian sign.
In heaven you will all be stars most bright,
As now you all are branches of Christ's vine;[37]
God chose you three among the human race
Not for your deeds but solely by His grace.[39]

GALLICAN:

92   Oh worthy Lord and sovereign mine, your news
Outstrips by far the deeds in my account;
To take both kings and lands is little use:
The joy of finding God is paramount.
My daughters certainly will never lose
Belief in God, of inner peace the fount;
He ends all strife and gives us quietude,
If from our hearts the world we can exclude.[40]

93   For one who routs the world and Satan too,
Heaven's eternal kingdom is the prize;
The world extends beyond these lands we view,
And Satan is its king, in shrewd disguise.
Only our faith can fight and beat anew
This guileful one, and all his ways excise.
That is the war that you must wage with sin,
And then eternal glory you will win.

94   My worthy lord, I pray you grant me leave
To be alone, in peace to make my way,
To leave the world and court. Pray do not grieve:
Let me depart from all that leads astray.

Per te piú volte ho già la vita messo,
pericoli e fatiche in multitudine;
per te sparto ho piú volte il sangue mio:
lascia me in pace servire ora a Dio.

COSTANTINO:

95   Quand' io penso al mio stato e all'onore,
par duro a licenziarti, o Gallicano;
ché, sanza capitan, lo imperadore
si può dir quasi un uom sanza la mano;
ma, quand' io penso poi al grande amore,
ogni pensier di me diventa vano:
stimo piú te che alcuno mio periglio,
e laudo molto questo tuo consiglio.

96   Benché mi dolga assai la tua partita,
per tua consolazion te la permetto.
Ma, poiché Dio al vero ben t'invita,
séguita ben, sí come hai bene eletto;
ché brieve e traditora è questa vita,
né altro al fin che fatica e dispetto.
Metti ad effetto i pensier santi e magni,
ché arai ben presto teco altri compagni.

GALLICANO SI PARTE, E DI LUI NON SI FA PIÚ MENZIONE.

* * *

COSTANTINO LASCIA LO IMPERIO A' FIGLIUOLI, E DICE:

97   O Costantino, o Costanzio, o Costante,
o figliuoli miei, del mio gran regno eredi,[42]
voi vedete le membra mie tremante
e 'l capo bianco e non ben fermi i piedi:
questa età, dopo mie fatiche tante,
vuol che qualche riposo io li concedi;
né puote un vecchio bene, a dire il vero,
reggere alle fatiche d'un impero.

Many a time, your victories to achieve,
I risked my life, faced dangers in the fray.
For you I shed much blood, and bore much pain;
Now let me go in peace, our God to gain.[41]

CONSTANTINE:

95   With state and honour foremost in my mind,
Oh Gallican, how hard to let you go!
If my commander goes, he leaves behind
A king who lacks a hand to strike the foe.
But when I think what love has seized your mind,
My thoughts of loss recede and cease to flow.
To your intent I bow and give full praise:
It matters more than troubles foes may raise.

96   Though your departure causes me much grief,
'Twill bring you solace; therefore go with leave.
God calls you to embrace the true belief,
So stray not from that path, but to it cleave.
What's life? A journey treacherous and brief:
We labour and are scorned, and nought achieve.
Among the chosen go to take your place,
For many soon will follow you in grace.

GALLICAN TAKES HIS LEAVE AND IS HEARD OF NO MORE.

*   *   *

CONSTANTINE LEAVES HIS EMPIRE TO HIS SONS AND SAYS:

97   Oh Constantine, and you my other sons,
The rightful heirs of all I have acquired,
My limbs now tremble, which was not so once;
My head is hoary and my feet are tired.
My strength is ebbing as the hourglass runs,
And rest, after life's labours, is required.
To rule the state I know my strength is gone,
And time has come to say old age has won.

98   Però, s'io stessi in questa regal sede,
       saria disagio a me, al popol danno;
       l'età riposo, e 'l popol signor chiede:
       di me medesmo troppo non m'inganno.
       E chi sarà di voi del regno erede,
       sappi che 'l regno altro non è che affanno,
       fatica assai di corpo e di pensiero;
       né, come par di fuor, dolce è l'impero.

99   Sappiate che chi vuole il popol reggere,
       debbe pensare al bene universale;
       e chi vuol altri dagli error correggere,
       sforzisi prima lui di non far male:
       però conviensi giusta vita eleggere,
       perché lo esemplo al popol molto vale,
       e quel che fa il signor, fanno poi molti,
       ché nel signor son tutti gli occhi vòlti.[43]

100   Non pensi a util proprio o a piacere,
       ma al bene universale di ciascuno:
       bisogna sempre gli occhi aperti avere
       (gli altri dormon con gli occhi di quest' uno)[44]
       e pari la bilancia ben tenere;
       d'avarizia[45] e lussuria esser digiuno;
       affabil, dolce e grato si conservi:
       il signor dée esser servo de' servi.[46]

101   Con molti affanni ho questo imperio retto,
       accadendo ogni dí qualcosa nuova:
       vittoriosa la spada rimetto,
       per non far piú della fortuna pruova,
       ché non sta troppo ferma in un concetto;
       chi cerca assai, diverse cose truova.
       Voi proverete quanto affanno e doglia
       dà il regno, di che avete tanta voglia.

COSTANTIN PADRE, DETTO CHE HA QUESTE PAROLE, SI PARTE
E SE NE VA COPERTAMENTE, E DI LUI NON SI RAGIONA PIÚ.[47]

98   If I persist on this imperial seat,
       I cause my subjects harm, and pain to me;
       I need repose—myself I cannot cheat—;
       The people's need is that good rule there be.
       To rule is wearisome, a bitter feat,
       As he will learn, whom emperor you decree.
       Men see the outer sweetness, and are blind
       To kingship's strain of body and of mind.

99   The good of the community must guide
       The acts of him who rules and takes the throne.
       Before he dare the wrongs of others chide,
       Let him first look at errors of his own;
       A way of life most just and dignified
       His people need at all times to be shown.
       Their eyes are ever fixed upon their king,
       And many follow him in everything.[43]

100   The ruler to his pleasure gives no thought;
       Self-interest too comes after public good.
       His people's sleep with his concern is bought,
       As, watchful, he safeguards their livelihood.
       He metes out justice, and is swayed by nought,
       As lure of greed and lust he has withstood.
       To gentle thoughts and mild he is inclined,
       The servant of all servants of mankind.[46]

101   With endless tribulation I have reigned
       And met the dangers offered by each day.
       Rest there, my sword with victories ingrained;
       No more I'll challenge Fortune in the fray.
       Fickle is she: men lose what they have gained,
       And those who seek too much will go astray.
       The pain of rule, its anguish, sons, you'll learn
       When you control the state for which you yearn.

CONSTANTINE THE ELDER, HAVING UTTERED THESE WORDS,
LEAVES UNOBTRUSIVELY, AND IS HEARD OF NO MORE.[47]

COSTANTINO FIGLIUOLO ALLI DUE ALTRI FRATELLI DICE COSÍ:

102   Cari fratei, voi avete sentito
       di nostro padre le savie parole:
       di non governar piú preso ha partito.
       Succeder uno in questo imperio vuole;
       ché, se non fussi in un sol fermo e unito,
       saria diviso, onde mancar poi suole:[48]
       io sono il primo; a me dà la natura
       e la ragion, ch'io prenda questa cura.

COSTANTE, UNO DE' FRATELLI, DICE:

103   Io, per me, molto volontier consento
       che tu governi, come prima nato:
       e, se di te, o fratel, servo divento,
       questo ha voluto Dio e 'l nostro fato.

COSTANZIO, L'ALTRO FRATELLO:

       Ed io ancor di questo son contento,
       perché credo sarai benigno e grato:
       io minor cedo, poiché 'l maggior cede.
       Or siedi ormai nella paterna sede.

IL NUOVO IMPERADORE:

104   O dolci frati, poiché v'è piaciuto
       che, di fratel, signor vostro diventi,
       e che dal mondo tutto abbi tributo
       e signoreggi tante varie genti,
       l'amor fraterno sempre fra noi suto
       sempre cosí sarà, non altrimenti:
       se Fortuna mi dà piú alti stati,
       siam pur d'un padre e d'una madre nati.

CONSTANTINE THE YOUNGER SPEAKS THUS TO HIS TWO BROTHERS:

102   Brothers, you heard the words our father dear
      Has uttered in the wisdom of old age:
      He wants to rule no more, and, it is clear,
      That one of us succeed him at this stage.
      It must be one, and he must have no peer,
      Unless we wish that civil strife should rage.
      I am the eldest: willed by nature's law,
      By reason's too, I take this charge with awe.

CONSTANS, ONE OF HIS BROTHERS, SAYS:

103   My claim I here renounce for ever more,
      Accepting you among us as firstborn.
      So God and fate decree; I shall ignore
      My rank and to a subject's life be sworn.

CONSTANTIUS, THE OTHER BROTHER:

      I too assent, and comment, for this chore,
      That you have kindness and goodwill inborn.
      As youngest son, my elder's wish I meet,
      And call on you to take our father's seat.

THE NEW EMPEROR:

104   My brothers dear and kind, as it did please
      You both to choose that I become your king,
      The rights the world now owes to me I seize,
      And many nations take beneath my wing.
      Fraternal love that bound us will not cease,
      But from my heart for ever it will spring.
      Whatever Fortune give me on this earth,
      One father and one mother gave us birth.

UN SERVO:

105   O imperadore, e' convien ch'io ti dica
       quel che tener vorrei piú presto occulto.
       Una parte del regno t'è nimica,
       e rebellata è mossa in gran tumulto,
       perché tuo padre piú non vuol fatica:
       contra a' tuoi officiali han fatto insulto,
       né stimon piú i tuoi imperi e bandi:
       convien che grande esercito vi mandi.

IMPERADORE:

106   Ecco la profezia del padre mio,
       che disse che 'l regnare era un affanno.
       A pena in questa sede son post' io,
       ch'io lo conosco con mio grave danno:
       in questo primo caso spero in Dio
       che questi tristi puniti saranno.
       O Costanzio, o Costante, presto andate
       con le mie genti, e i tristi gastigate.

107   Io non ho piú fidati capitani;
       sapete ben che questo imperio è vostro:
       poiché 'l metteste voi nelle mie mani
       potete dir veramente: "Egli è nostro."

COSTANTE E COSTANZIO RISPONDONO, DICENDO:

       I tuoi comandamenti non fien vani:
       andrem per quel cammin, il qual ci hai mostro,
       e perché presto tal fuoco si spenga,
       noi ci avviamo, e 'l campo drieto venga.

IMPERADORE:

108   In ogni luogo aver si vuol de' suoi,
       che son di piú amore e miglior fede.
       Andate presto o uno o due di voi

A SERVANT:

105   My liege, it is my duty to relate
      What I would wish within my heart to keep.
      Rebels have seized a portion of your state,
      With tumult, riot, passion running deep.
      Hearing your father's will to abdicate,
      Vile insults on your officers they heap;
      Their orders too they mock and laugh to scorn.
      Your army send before of lands you're shorn.

EMPEROR:

106   Alas, a father's prophecy comes true!
      Did he not say that rulers have much woe?
      But, barely crowned, my kingship I now rue,
      As I feel sharply smitten by this blow.
      May God make haste, give us support anew,
      And vengeance wreak upon the wicked foe.
      My brothers, with my men go forth in haste:
      Punish the rebels, lay their lands to waste.

107   No captains have I whom like you I trust;
      Dear kinsmen, we are partners in this state:
      To me you gave the crown as right and just,
      Yet your own rights remain inviolate.

CONSTANS AND CONSTANTIUS ANSWER, SAYING:

      Accepted be your orders, as they must;
      We'll promptly take the path you indicate.
      It is our plan this fire at once to quench;
      The troops will follow, ready to entrench.

EMPEROR:

108   'Tis good to have one's own in every place,
      As loyally they serve and love us best.
      Attendants, hear: run at a smarting pace

al tempio dove lo dio Marte siede,
e farete ammazzar pecore e buoi;
ché gran tumulto mosso esser si vede;
pregando Dio che tanto mal non faccia,
quanto in questo principio ci minaccia.

UN FANTE DICE:

109   O imperador, io vorrei esser messo
di cose liete e non di pianti e morte:
pur tu hai a saper questo processo
da me o da altri: a me tocca la sorte.
Sappi che 'l campo tuo in rotta è messo,
e morto o preso ogni guerrier piú forte;
e' tuo' fratelli ancora in questa guerra
morti reston con gli altri su la terra.

IMPERADORE:

110   O padre Costantin, tu mi lasciasti
a tempo questo imperio e la corona.
A tanto mal non so qual cor si basti
o qual fortezza sia costante e buona.
Ecco or l'imperio, ecco le pompe e ' fasti,
ecco la fama e 'l nome mio che suona!
Non basta tutto il mondo si ribelli;
c'ho perso ancora i miei cari fratelli.

UNO LO CONFORTA E DICE:

111   O signor nostro, quando il capo duole,
ogn' altro membro ancor del corpo pate.
Perdere il cor sí presto non si vuole:
piglia del mal, se v'è, niuna bontate.
Chi sa quel che sia meglio? Nascer suole
discordia tra fratei molte fiate:
forse che la fortuna te gli ha tolti,
acciò che in te sol sia quel ch'era in molti.

To Mars, our god, within his temple blest;
Go slaughter sheep and oxen, beg his grace,
As clearly there is danger and unrest.
Let us pray God to shield us from such evil,
For great's the threat I see in this upheaval.

A SOLDIER SAYS:

109   My lord, good tidings I would wish to bear,
    And not assail your ears with news of woe,
    But soon from me or others you must hear
    What I now say: fate has decreed it so.
    Your camp is routed, funeral torches flare,
    Your champions captured, slaughtered or laid low.
    Amid these deeds of horror and of death
    Your own two brothers gasped their dying breath.

EMPEROR:

110   Oh dearest father Constantine, your crown
    To me, and empire, timely did you leave.
    What fortress can prevent it falling down?
    Events like these my stalwart heart will cleave.
    Gone is our empire with its great renown;
    O'er my disgrace and hollow name I grieve.
    While this rebellion sweeps away our state,
    My keenest sorrow is my brothers' fate.

SOMEONE COMFORTS HIM AND SAYS:

111   Oh king, when pain first springs into one's head,
    To other organs it will quickly leap.
    Do not lose heart, have courage now instead:
    What good there be in evil try to reap.
    For who knows best? Sometimes discord can spread
    Even in brothers bound by love most deep.
    And Fortune may have willed with sleight of hand
    That you should be sole ruler of this land.

112 Ritorna in sedia e lo scettro ripiglia,
  ed accomoda il core a questo caso,
  e prendi dello imperio in man la briglia,
  e Dio ringrazia che se' sol rimaso.

LO IMPERADORE DICE:

  Io vo' far quel che 'l mio fedel consiglia
  e quel che la ragion m'ha persuaso,
  tornar in sedia, come mi conforti:
  co' vivi i vivi, i morti sien co' morti.

113 Io so che questa mia persecuzione
  da un error che io fo, tutto procede:
  perch' io sopporto in mia iurisdizione
  questa vil gente, quale a Cristo crede:
  io vo' levar, se questa è la cagione,
  perseguitando, questa vana fede;
  uccidere e pigliar sia chi si voglia.
  Oimè, il cor! quest' è l'ultima doglia.

DETTE QUESTE PAROLE, SI MUORE, E QUELLI CHE RESTONO SI CONSIGLIANO,
ED UNO DI LORO PARLA:

114 Noi siam restati sanza capo o guida:
  l'imperio a questo modo non sta bene:
  il popol rugghia, e tutto 'l mondo grida.
  Far nuovo successor presto conviene.
  Se c'è tra noi alcun che si confida
  trovare a chi lo imperio s'appartiene,
  presto lo dica: ed in sedia sia messo.
  Quant' io per me, non so già qual sia desso.

UN ALTRO:

115 E' c'è Giulian, di Costantin nipote,
  ché, benché mago e monaco sia stato,
  è di gran cuore, e d'ingegno assai puote,
  ed è del sangue dello imperio nato:

112   Regain your seat, your sceptre grasp with mettle,
       Adjust your heart to this most sad event,
       Hold firm the reins of empire in full fettle,
       And thank the Lord all rivalry is spent.

THE EMPEROR SAYS:

       My faithful man is right, so I shall settle;
       Reason persuades me also to assent.
       Back on my throne of empire, as you said,
       We must live on: let dead bury their dead.

113   An error on my part is the sole root
       Of these misfortunes, which must surely spring
       From tolerating people whose repute
       Is that to faith in Jesus Christ they cling.
       This vain belief I shall now persecute;
       Its devotees are vile: they'll feel my sting;
       Prison and death await those whom I catch.
       What pain, my heart! No more can I dispatch.

HAVING SAID THESE WORDS, HE DIES.
THOSE PRESENT CONSULT EACH OTHER AND ONE OF THEM SAYS:

114   We have no guide or king, for he lies dead;
       This is no way for government to thrive:
       The people shout, we need to choose a head
       Without delay, if we are to survive.
       To whom the state should go now in his stead
       Among us, it is clear, we must contrive.
       Come forward with suggestions, if you can,
       As I have no idea who is this man.

ANOTHER MAN SAYS:

115   Of Constantine a nephew, Julian named:
       Though necromancer, sometime monk he's been;
       Brilliant of mind, for courage he is famed,
       Of royal birth, in regal ways not green.

bench' egli stia in parte assai remote,
verrà, sentendo il regno gli sia dato.

UN TERZO:

Questo a me piace.

UN QUARTO DICE:

Ed a me molto aggrada.

PRIMO:

Orsú! presto, per lui un di noi vada.

* * *

GIULIANO, NUOVO IMPERADORE:

116   Quand' io penso chi stato è in questa sede,
non so s'io mi rallegri o s'io mi doglia
d'esser di Giulio e d'Augusto erede,[49]
né so se imperadore esser mi voglia.
Allor, dove quest' aquila si vede,
tremava il mondo, come al vento foglia:
ora in quel poco imperio che ci resta
ogni vil terra vuol rizzar la cresta.

117   Da quella parte là, donde il sol muove,
infin dove poi stracco si ripone,
eron temute le romane pruove:
or siam del mondo una derisione.
Poi che fûr tolti i sacrifizi a Giove,
a Marte, a Febo, a Minerva, a Giunone,
e tolto è 'l simulacro alla Vittoria,[50]
non ebbe questo imperio alcuna gloria.

118   E però son fermamente disposto,
ammonito da questi certi esempli,

He lives quite distant, but if king proclaimed,
To sit on this famed throne he will be keen.

A THIRD:

This pleases me.

A FOURTH SAYS:

None better do I know.

FIRST ONE:

Then bring him quickly; one of us must go.

*   *   *

JULIAN, THE NEW EMPEROR:

116   The thought of those before me on this seat
Stirs me with joy, yet troubles me as well.
Heir of Augustus, Julius—what a feat![49]
But do I wish to rule? I cannot tell.
This eagle forced all armies to retreat,
Trembling like leaves as their proud standards fell;
Throughout this shred of empire there's unrest,
As every hamlet seeks to raise its crest.

117   From where our sun appears in furthest east,
To where, quite jaded, it lies down to rest,
The fear of Roman exploits never ceased;
But now of other rulers we're the jest.
To Jove, and Mars, and Juno, there's no priest
To offer sacrifice and call them blest;
Since Victory's statue is no more revered,[50]
All glory and success have disappeared.

118   So I resolve to undo our mistake,
Warned by these signs, as clear as they could be.

che 'l simulacro alla Vittoria posto
sia al suo luogo, e tutti aperti i templi;
e ad ogni cristian sia tolta tosto
la roba, acciò che libero contempli:
ché Cristo disse a chi vuol la sua fede:
"Renunzi a ogni cosa ch'e' possiede."

119   Questo si truova ne' Vangeli scritto:
io fui cristiano, allor lo intesi appunto.
E però fate far pubblico editto:
"Chi è cristian, roba non abbi punto
—né di questo debb' esser molto afflitto
chi veramente con Cristo è congiunto—;
la roba di colui che a Cristo creda,
sia di chi se la truova giusta preda."[51]

UNO, CHE ACCUSA GIOVANNI E PAULO:

120   O imperador, in Ostia,[52] già molti anni,
posseggon roba e possession assai
due cristiani, cioè Paulo e Giovanni,
né il tuo editto obbedito hanno mai.

GIULIANO IMPERADORE:

Costor son lupi, e di pecore han panni;[53]
ma noi gli toserem, come vedrai.
Va' tu medesmo; usa ogni diligenzia,
acciò che sian condotti in mia presenzia.

121   Che val signor, che obbedito non sia
da' suoi soggetti, e massime allo inizio?
Perché un rettor d'una podesteria
ne' primi quattro dí fa il suo offizio.[54]
Bisogna conservar la signoria[55]
reputata, con pena e con supplizio.
Intendo, poi ch'io son quassú salito,
ad ogni modo d'essere obbedito.

I'll open temples, and no more forsake
But rather raise again our Victory.
To help the Christians with their prayers, I'll take
Their worldly goods and set their spirits free.
For Christ bids those who would His faith profess:
"Give up your wealth and all that you possess."

119   For that is what one finds in Holy Writ:
I was a Christian once, and so I read.
Proclaim an edict and let this be it:
"Promptly must Christians all their riches shed;
No pain or woe this order will inflict
Since poverty for Christ you freely wed.
The goods of those who in this Christ believe
All men are fully authorized to thieve."[51]

SOMEONE WHO ACCUSES JOHN AND PAUL:

120   For many years, nearby, in Ostia town[52]
Have lived two Christians, Paul and John by name,
Who have ignored the edict of your crown,
Though they as men of property have fame.

EMPEROR JULIAN:

These wolves who dress like sheep we will bring down,[53]
And fleece them well: you'll see them shorn and tame.
Be off and lead them here with diligence,
To get a taste of my intransigence.

121   What use the lord whom subjects fail to obey
Right from the start, behaving as they please?
Foundations of strong rule one has to lay
At once, or lawlessness spreads like disease.
Respect for government men will display
When forced, and if in fear of torture's squeeze.
At all events, most fully I intend,
No rule of mine shall any subject bend.

A GIOVANNI E PAULO, CONDOTTI DINANZI ALL'IMPERADORE,
ESSO IMPERADORE GIULIANO DICE:

122   Molto mi duol di voi, dappoi ch'io sento
       che siate cristian veri e battezzati;
       ché, benché assai fanciullo, io mi rammento
       quanto eri[56] a Costantin, mio avol, grati:
       pure stimo piú il mio comandamento;
       ché la reputazion mantien gli Stati.
       Ora, in poche parole: o voi lasciate
       la roba tutta, ovver Giove adorate.

GIOVANNI E PAULO:

123   Come a te piace, signor, puoi disporre
       della roba, e la vita anche è in tua mano:
       questa ci puoi, quando ti piace, tôrre;
       ma della fede ogni tua pruova è invano.
       E chi a Giove, vano dio, ricorre,
       erra; e ben crede ogni fedel cristiano:
       vogliamo ir per la via che Gesú mostra:
       fa' quel che vuoi; questa è la voglia nostra.

GIULIANO IMPERADORE DICE:

124   S'io guardassi alla vostra ostinazione,
       io farei far di voi crudele strazio:
       pietà di voi mi fa compassione;
       se non, del vostro mal mai sare' sazio.
       Ma il tempo spesse volte l'uom dispone:[57]
       però vi do di dieci giorni spazio
       a lasciar questa vostra fede stolta;
       e se no, poi vi sia la vita tolta.

125   Or va', Terenziano,[58] e teco porta
       di Giove quella bella statuetta;
       e in questi dieci dí costor conforta
       che adorin questa, e Cristo si dimetta:[59]
       se stanno forti a ir per la via torta,

JOHN AND PAUL ARE LED BEFORE EMPEROR JULIAN,
WHO SAYS TO THEM:

122   Saddened I am by what I hear of you,
       That you are Christians, faithful and baptized,
       For I recall that as a child I knew
       By Constantine you were much loved and prized.
       But fame for firmness I must now pursue,
       So that the state may not be jeopardized.
       In brief: your goods and all your wealth hand o'er,
       Or otherwise our Jove you must adore.

JOHN AND PAUL:

123   Just as you wish, oh king: you may dispose
       Of all our goods; our lives are in your hand.
       You cannot win against the faith we chose;
       But take the rest, as freely you command.
       Our faith is right, as every Christian knows,
       And wrong are those who by vain Jove will stand.
       Our Jesus points the way that we shall take:
       Do as you please; we will not Him forsake.

EMPEROR JULIAN SAYS:

124   Your stubbornness I would not tolerate,
       But cruelly would I torture and torment;
       Yet some compassion I feel operate,
       That checks what I intend to implement.
       Oft, time intransigence will moderate:
       Ten days you have in which to give assent,
       Your foolish faith reject and laugh to scorn,
       Or else of earthly life you will be shorn.

125   Terence,[58] pay heed—my words I do not mince—:
       Go fetch Jove's lovely statuette of gold.
       You have ten days in which you must convince
       These men to worship it and faith withhold
       From Christ. A pledge they must evince,

il capo lor giú dalle spalle getta.
Pensate ben, se la vita v'è tolta,
che non ci si ritorna un'altra volta.

GIOVANNI E PAULO:

126 O imperadore, invan ci dài tal termine,
però che sempre buon cristian saremo:
il zel di Dio e questo dolce vermine
ci mangia e mangerà fino allo estremo:
il gran, che muore in terra, sol par germine;[60]
per morte adunque non ci pentiremo:
e, se pur noi ci potessim pentire,
per non potere abbiam caro il morire.

127 Dunque fa' pur di noi quel che tu vuoi:
paura non ci fa la morte atroce.
Ecco! giú 'l collo lieti porrem noi
per Quel che pose tutto 'l corpo in croce.
Tu fusti, pur ancor tu, già de' suoi;
or sordo non piú odi la sua voce.
Fa' conto questo termin sia passato:
il corpo è tuo, lo spirito a Dio è dato.

GIULIANO IMPERADORE:

128 E' si può bene a forza a un far male,
ma non già bene a forza è far permesso:
nella legge di Cristo un detto è tale:
che "Dio non salva te sanza te stesso":[61]
e questo detto è vero e naturale
(benché tal fede vera non confesso).
Da poi che il mio pregar con voi è vano,
va', fa' l'officio tuo, Terenziano.

TERENZIANO A GIOVANNI E PAULO DICE:

129 E' m'incresce di voi, che, giovinetti,[62]
andate come pecore al macello.

Or else chop off their heads, so proud and bold.
You two, think well; for if your lives you lose,
To come back to this world you cannot choose.

JOHN AND PAUL:

126　Oh king, there is no need to bide this time,
　　　As faithful Christians we shall always be;
　　　Our zeal for God is like a worm sublime
　　　That eats us to the core eternally.
　　　As soil renews the seed through change of clime,[60]
　　　So death will life renew and set us free.
　　　There is no way that death we shall regret;
　　　Its coming, therefore, does not pose a threat.

127　So do with us whatever be your will;
　　　The most atrocious death evokes no fear.
　　　With joy we bare our necks, our spirits still
　　　In Him Who for the cross did volunteer.
　　　You know, as once you followed Him; until,
　　　Now deaf become, His call you do not hear.
　　　Let us not wait: for us the bell now tolls,
　　　Here are our bodies, God will have our souls.

EMPEROR JULIAN:

128　'Tis easy enough by force a man to hurt,
　　　Less easy though by force to do him good;
　　　That "God helps those who help themselves" is curt;
　　　The laws of Christ Himself this text include—
　　　A maxim that makes sense and is quite pert
　　　(But to accept His faith I'm far too shrewd).
　　　Since useless seem all efforts I have made,
　　　Terence, perform your duty unafraid.

TERENCE SAYS TO JOHN AND PAUL:

129　So young,[62] you go to slaughter just like sheep,
　　　A sight that hurts me greatly to behold.

Deh! pentitevi ancor, o poveretti,
prima che al collo sentiate il coltello.

GIOVANNI:

Se a questa morte noi saremo eletti,
fu morto ancor lo immaculato Agnello.[63]
Non ti curar de' nostri teneri anni:
la morte è uno uscir di molti affanni.

TERENZIANO:

130   Questa figura d'oro che in man porto
l'onnipotente Giove rappresenta:
non è meglio adorarla ch'esser morto,
poiché lo imperador se ne contenta?

PAULO:

Tu se', Terenzian, pur poco accorto:
chi dice: "Giove è Dio", convien che menta:
Giove è pianeta, che il suo ciel sol muove;
ma piú alta potenzia muove Giove.[64]

GIOVANNI:

131   Ma ben faresti tu, Terenziano,
se adorassi il dolce Dio Gesue.

TERENZIANO:

Quest' è appunto quel che vuol Giuliano;
e meglio fia non se ne parli piue.
Qua venga il boia: e voi di mano in mano,
per esser morti, vi porrete giue.
Su, mastro Pier, gli occhi a costor due lega,
ch'i' veggo il ciambellotto ha fatto piega.[65]

Oh, pray repent and o'er your errors weep
Ere on your necks the knife falls sharp and cold.

JOHN:

If called to such a death, reward we reap:
So died the unblemished Lamb,[63] as Scripture told.
Be not dismayed because our lives were brief,
For death to many troubles brings relief.

TERENCE:

130   This golden effigy of mighty Jove,
     Which here I hold before you in my hand,
     That you accept as god it will behove,
     For then the king will cancel his command.

PAUL:

To state that Jove is not true god we strove,
But, Terence, you have failed to understand:
A planet, Jove, that only moves its sphere,
Is subject to the power that we revere.[64]

JOHN:

131   Oh Terence, better would it be for you
     To adore that Jesus who is God most sweet.

TERENCE:

I shall now act as Julian bade me to,
Once and for all these arguments defeat.
Call Peter hangman here. Lie down, you two;
Taking your lives will make our task complete.
Come master, bind their eyes: they will not blink;
Though at the trough, too stubborn they to drink![65]

POSTI GINOCCHIONI CON GLI OCCHI LEGATI, INSIEME DICONO COSÍ:

132   O Gesú dolce misericordioso,
 che insanguinasti il sacrosanto legno
 del tuo sangue innocente e prezioso
 per purgar l'uomo e farlo del ciel degno;
 volgi gli occhi a due giovani, pietoso,
 che speran rivederti nel tuo regno.
 Sangue spargesti e sangue ti rendiamo:
 ricevilo, ché lieti te lo diamo.

GIULIANO IMPERADORE:

133   Chi regge imperio e in capo tien corona,
 sanza reputazion, non par che imperi,
 né puossi dir sia privata persona:
 rappresentano il tutto i signor veri.
 Non è signor chi le cure abbandona
 e dassi a far tesoro o a' piaceri:
 di quel raguna, e le cure lasciate,
 e del suo ozio tutto il popol pate.

134   Se ha grande entrata, per distribuire
 liberalmente e con ragion, gli è data:
 faccia che 'l popol non possa patire
 dall'inimici, e tenga gente armata.
 Se 'l grano è caro, debbe suvvenire
 ché non muoia di fame la brigata;
 a' poveretti ancor supplir conviene.
 E cosí 'l cumular[66] mai non è bene.

135   La signoria, la roba dello impero,
 già non è sua, anzi del popol tutto:
 e, benché del signor paia lo 'ntero,
 non è né 'l posseder, né l'usufrutto;
 ma distribuitore è 'l signor vero:
 l'onore ha sol di tal fatica frutto:
 l'onor, che fa ogn' altra cosa vile,
 ch'è ben gran premio al core alto e gentile.

ON THEIR KNEES, BLINDFOLD, BOTH SAY TOGETHER:

132   With mercy look towards us, Jesus kind,
Whose precious blood upon the cross was shed;
That man might be redeemed and heaven find,
Though innocent for him to death You bled.
Two youths we are, both firm and of one mind,
In hope that heavenward we will be led.
You gave Your blood and blood to You we give
With gladdened heart because in You we live.

EMPEROR JULIAN:

133   The majesty of our imperial throne
Is built upon the emperor's good name.
He is no private person on his own,
But stands for all his subjects by acclaim.
He is not lord if duty he disown
To make pursuit of luxuries his aim.
Duty neglected, greed and sloth will bring
To all his subjects pain and suffering.

134   If large his income, then arrange he must
To give with sense and liberality.
His people need an army he can trust
To fight the foe in all adversity.
If corn is dear because the crop is lost,
No one should starve in such perversity.
Essential also that he help the poor,
And thus of wealth he will resist the lure.

135   The lordship and the coffers of the state
Are not his own but for the public weal:
The lord may think he can appropriate
The wealth; but shunned will be all private deal!
His task is to dispense and mediate.
Great honour comes to him for his ordeal,
And honour makes all else fade into naught,
As it alone by noble men is sought.

136   Lo stimol dell'onor sempre mi punge,
      la fiamma della gloria è sempre accesa:
      questa sproni al caval, che corre, aggiunge,
      e vuol ch'io tenti nuova e grande impresa
      contr' a' Parti,[67] che stanno sí da lunge,
      da' quai fu Roma molte volte offesa:
      e di molti romani il sangue aspetta,
      sparso da lor, ch'io faccia la vendetta.

137   Però sien tutte le mie gente in punto
      a compagnarmi a questa somma gloria.
      Su, volentier! non dubitate punto:
      a guerra non andiamo, anzi a vittoria:
      con la vostra virtú so ch'io li spunto.
      Le ingiurie antiche ho ancor nella memoria:
      il sangue di que' buon vecchion romani
      fia vendicato per le vostre mani.

138   E' fûrno i padri, di che siam discesi;
      onde conviensi la vendetta al filio.
      Mettete in punto tutt' i vostri arnesi;
      fate ogni sforzo: questo è il mio consilio:
      a una fava due colombi presi
      saranno; ché in Cesàrea è 'l gran Basilio,
      nimico mio, amico di Gesue:
      s'io 'l truovo là, non scriverà mai piue.

139   Su, tesorier, tutte le gente spaccia:
      quattro paghe in danar, due in panni e drappi;
      e fa' che lor buon pagamenti faccia:
      convien far fatti, e non che ciarli o frappi.
      Fate venire innanzi alla mia faccia
      gli astrologi, ché 'l punto buon si sappi:
      Marte sia ben disposto e ben congiunto.
      Ditemi poi quando ogni cosa è in punto.

*   *   *

136   Now honour goads me on from deed to deed;
      The torch of glory ever burns alight.
      'Tis this allurement drives and spurs my steed,
      And calls me to a new and glorious fight
      Against the hated Parthians,[67] far-off breed
      That many times has dared great Rome to slight.
      The blood of Romans slain by them awaits:
      In me the call to vengeance resonates.

137   Let therefore all my armies to a man
      Serve me in this most glorious enterprise.
      Be eager, men, and cowardice firmly ban;
      This is no war; we go to fetch the prize—
      We'll win—; your prowess will ensure we can.
      Old injuries die hard, and hate likewise:
      "Avenge our ancient Romans" is the call,
      And by your hands their enemies will fall.

138   They were our fathers—straight is our descent—;
      And sons are bound to avenge ancestral wrong.
      Sharpen your arms, for Cæsarea we are bent,
      And I suggest you keep your purpose strong.
      One stone will kill two birds: and my intent
      Is that great Basil there will not live long:
      An enemy of mine, of Jesus friend,
      To all his writing I will put an end.

139   Come, treasurer, give all my soldiers pay:
      Four parts in wages and two more in cloth.
      Pay liberally, skimp not in any way:
      Less talk from you, produce the goods, not froth.
      Astrologers be called and let them say
      If stars are now propitious or in wrath.
      The house of Mars must needs be well disposed.
      When ready, call; our business is now closed.

*   *   *

IL VESCOVO SANTO BASILIO DICE COSÍ:

140   O Padre eterno, apri le labbra mia,
      e la mia bocca poi t'arà laudato:[68]
      donami grazia che 'l mio orare sia
      sincero e puro e sanza alcun peccato:
      la Chiesa tua, la nostra madre pia,
      perseguitata veggio d'ogni lato;
      la Chiesa tua, da te per sposa eletta:
      fa' ch'io ne vegga almen qualche vendetta.

LA VERGINE MARIA APPARISCE SOPRA LA SEPULTURA DI SANTO MERCURIO,
E DICE:

141   Esci, Mercurio,[69] della oscura tomba;
      piglia la spada e l'arme già lasciate,
      sanza aspettar del Giudizio la tromba;[70]
      da te sien le mie ingiurie vendicate.
      Il nome tristo di Giulian rimbomba
      nel cielo e le sue opre scellerate.
      Il cristian sangue vendicato sia;
      sappi ch'io son la Vergine Maria.

142   Giuliano imperador per questa strada
      debbe passare, o martir benedetto:
      dàgli, Mercurio, con la giusta spada,
      sanza compassione, a mezzo al petto:
      non voglio tanto error piú innanzi vada,
      per pietà del mio popol poveretto:
      uccidi questo rio venenoso angue,
      il qual si pasce sol del cristian sangue.

* * *

IL TESORIERE TORNA ALLO IMPERADORE, E DICE:

143   Invitto imperador, tutta tua gente
      in punto sta al tuo comandamento,
      coperta d'arme belle e rilucente,

BISHOP ST BASIL SPEAKS THUS:

140   Open my lips, oh everlasting Lord,
      And then my mouth shall well show forth Your praise;[68]
      My pure and sinless plea be not ignored,
      Nor be the words that from my mouth I raise.
      Against our mother Church is drawn the sword
      Of persecution with its evil ways.
      This is the Church You chose to be Your bride.
      I pray to see that You avenge our side.

THE VIRGIN MARY APPEARS OVER THE GRAVE OF ST MERCURY
AND SAYS:

141   Mercury,[69] come from darkness underground;
      Put on your cast-off armour, take your spear,
      Await not Judgement Day with trumpet sound:[70]
      I want you to avenge me without fear.
      The name of wicked Julian is renowned
      For dire iniquity, in heaven's sphere.
      The blood that Christians shed avenged must be;
      This is the Virgin Mary whom you see.

142   The Emperor Julian soon will pass this way.
      My blessèd martyr Mercury I bid
      You show no mercy and all skill display:
      Strike through his chest wherein his heart is hid.
      I hear my suffering faithful people pray;
      Forthwith of this great scourge they must be rid.
      This poisonous serpent kill in all his greed;
      On Christian blood alone he fain would feed.

*   *   *

THE TREASURER RETURNS TO THE EMPEROR AND SAYS:

143   Unconquered Emperor, all the tasks are done
      Just as you said, your orders carried out:
      With armour shining bright as midday sun,

e pargli d'appiccarsi ogn' ora cento:[71]
danari ho dati lor copiosamente:
se gli vedrai, so ne sarai contento:
mai non vedesti gente piú fiorita,
armata bene, obbediente, ardita.

GLI ASTROLOGI, CHE FECE CHIAMARE LO IMPERADORE, DICONO:

144   O imperador, noi ti facciam rapporto.
Secondo il cielo, e' c'è un sol periglio,
il qual procede da un uom ch'è morto.
Forse ti riderai di tal consiglio.

LO IMPERADORE DICE:

S'io non ho altro male, io mi conforto:
se un morto nuoce, io me ne maraviglio:
guardimi Marte pur da spade e lance;
ché queste astrologie son tutte ciance.[72]

145   Il re e 'l savio son sopra le stelle:[73]
ond' io son fuor di questa vana legge:
i buon punti e le buone ore son quelle
che l'uom felice da sé stesso elegge.
Fate avviar le forti gente e belle:
io seguirò, pastor di questa gregge.
O valenti soldati, o popol forte,
con voi starò, alla vita, alla morte.

GIULIANO PARTESI CON L'ESERCITO.
E, NEL CAMMINO FERITO MORTALMENTE DA SANTO MERCURIO, DICE:

146   Mirabil cosa! in mezzo a tanti armati
stata non è la mia vita secura.
Questi non son de' Parti fèr gli agguati;
la morte ho avuta innanzi alla paura.[74]
Un solo ha tanti cristian vendicati.
Fallace vita! oh nostra vana cura!
Lo spirto è già fuor del mio petto spinto.
O Cristo Galileo, tu hai pur vinto.

Your men can't wait to strike and thrash about.
I've paid them richly, each and every one,
And when you see them, you will have no doubt.
You never saw such troops in splendid form:
Courageous, daring, trained and armed to storm.

THE ASTROLOGERS WHOM THE EMPEROR SENT FOR SAY:

144   Oh King, hear our report, which is not long.
Among the heavens' signs, one gives alarm:
Beware a man now dead, for he is strong.
That's our advice; scoff not, it is no charm.

THE EMPEROR SAYS:

How reassuring if no more is wrong:
It baffles me how one now dead can harm.
Protect me, Mars, from swords and spears in battle;
Astrology is only tittle-tattle.[72]

145   Wise men and kings are well above such powers,[73]
And so outside these useless laws am I.
Which are the most propitious days and hours
The shrewd man will decide and not the sky.
Send forth these strong and handsome men of ours;
As shepherd of my flock I will be nigh.
Oh valiant soldiers, people strong and free,
With you in life, by you in death, I'll be.

JULIAN SETS OUT WITH HIS ARMY. DURING THE JOURNEY
HE IS MORTALLY WOUNDED BY ST MERCURY, AND SAYS:

146   Amazing wonder that among armed men
I could not be protected from a snare.
'Twas not the Parthians, waiting in their den:
Death came with guile, giving no time for scare.
One man these Christians has avenged: Amen!
Perfidious life! How pointless is our care!
My spirit leaves my breast, my life's undone,
For you, oh Christ of Galilee, have won.

LETTER TO GIOVANNI

Messer Giovanni; voi sète molto obbligato a Messer Domenedio, e tutti noi per rispetto vostro,[1] perché oltra a molti benefici e onori, che ha ricevuti la casa nostra da lui, ha fatto che nella persona vostra veggiamo la maggior dignità che fosse mai in casa; e ancora che la cosa sia per sé grande, le circostanzie la fanno assai maggiore, massime per l'età vostra e condizione nostra. E però il primo mio ricordo è che vi sforziate esser grato a M. Domenedio,[2] ricordandovi ad ogni ora che non i meriti vostri, prudenzia o sollecitudine, ma mirabilmente esso Iddio v'ha fatto cardinale, e da lui lo riconosciate, comprobando questa condizione[3] colla vita vostra santa, esemplare e onesta, a che siete tanto piú obbligato per avere voi già dato qualche opinione nella adolescenzia vostra da poterne sperare tali frutti. Saria cosa molto vituperosa, e fuor del debito vostro e aspettazione mia, quando, nel tempo che gli altri sogliono acquistare piú ragione e miglior forma di vita, voi dimenticaste il vostro buono instituto.[4] Bisogna dunque che vi sforziate alleggerire il peso della dignità che portate, vivendo costumatamente e perseverando nelli studi convenienti alla professione vostra. L'anno passato io presi grandissima consolazione, intendendo che, senza che alcuno ve lo ricordasse, da voi medesimo vi confessaste piú volte e communicaste; né credo che ci sia miglior via a conservarsi nella grazia di Dio, che lo abituarsi in simili modi, e perseverarvi. Questo mi pare il piú utile e conveniente ricordo che per lo primo vi posso dare.

Conosco che andando voi a Roma, che è sentina di tutti i mali, entrate in maggior difficultà di fare quanto vi dico di sopra, perché non solamente gli esempi muovono,[5] ma non vi mancheranno particolari incitatori e corruttori, perché, come voi potete intendere, la promozione vostra al cardinalato, per l'età vostra e per le altre condizioni sopradette, arreca seco grande invidia, e quelli che non hanno potuto impedire la perfezione di questa vostra dignità,[6] s'ingegneranno sottilmente diminuirla, con denigrare l'opinione della vita vostra e farvi sdrucciolare in quella stessa fossa dove essi sono caduti, confidandosi molto debba lor riuscire per l'età vostra.[7] Voi dovete tanto piú opporvi a queste difficultà quanto nel Collegio[8] ora si vede manco virtú: e io mi ricordo pure avere veduto in quel Collegio buon numero d'uomini dotti e buoni e di santa vita; però è meglio seguire questi esempi, perché, facendolo, sarete tanto piú conosciuto e stimato quanto l'altrui condizioni vi distingueranno dagli altri.

È necessario che fuggiate, come Scilla e Cariddi,[9] il nome della ipocrisia, e come la mala fama, e che usiate mediocrità,[10] sforzandovi in fatto fuggire tutte le cose che offendono, in dimostrazione e in conversazione non mostrando austerità o troppa severità; che sono cose le quali col tempo intenderete e farete meglio, a mia opinione, che non le posso esprimere. Voi intenderete di quanta importanza ed esempio sia la persona d'un cardinale, e che tutto il mondo starebbe bene se i cardinali fussino come dovrebbono essere; perciocché farebbono sempre un buon papa,[11] onde nasce quasi il riposo[12] di tutti i cristiani. Sforzatevi dunque di essere tale voi, che, quando gli altri fussin cosí fatti, se ne potesse aspettare questo bene universale. E perché non è maggior fatica che conversar bene con diversi uomini, in questa parte vi posso mal dar ricordo, se non che v'ingegnate che la conversazione vostra con gli cardinali e altri uomini di condizione sia caritativa e senza offensione; dico misurando ragionevolmente, e non secondo l'altrui passione, perché molti, volendo quello che non si dée, fanno della ragione ingiuria. Giustificate adunque la conscienzia vostra in questo, che la conversazione vostra con ciascuno sia senza offensione; questa mi pare la regola generale molto a proposito vostro, perché quando la passione pur fa qualche inimico, come si partono questi tali senza ragione dall'amicizia, cosí qualche volta tornano facilmente.[13] Credo per questa prima andata vostra a Roma sia bene adoperare piú gli orecchi che la lingua.[14]

Oggimai io vi ho dato del tutto a M. Domenedio e a S. Chiesa;[15] onde è necessario che diventiate un buono ecclesiastico e facciate ben capace ciascuno,[16] che amate l'onore e stato di S. Chiesa e della Sede Apostolica innanzi a tutte le cose del mondo, posponendo a questo ogni altro rispetto; né vi mancherà modo, con questo riservo, d'aiutare la città e la casa; perché per questa città fa l'unione della Chiesa, e voi dovete in ciò essere buona catena e la casa ne va colla città. E benché non si possano vedere gli accidenti che verranno, cosí in general credo che non ci abbiano a mancare modi di salvare, come si dice, la capra e i cavoli, tenendo fermo il vostro primo presupposto, che anteponiate la Chiesa ad ogni altra cosa.[17]

Voi siete il piú giovane cardinale non solo del Collegio, ma che fusse mai fatto insino a qui; e però è necessario che, dove avete a concorrere con gli altri, siate il piú sollecito, il piú umile, senza farvi aspettare o in cappella o in concistoro[18] o in deputazione. Voi conoscerete presto gli piú e gli meno accostumati. Con gli meno si vuol fuggire la conversazione molto intrinseca, non solamente per lo fatto in sé, ma per l'opinione,[19] a largo conversare con ciascheduno.[20] Nelle pompe[21] vostre loderò piú presto stare di qua dal moderato che di là; e piú presto vorrei bella stalla e famiglia ordinata e polita[22] che ricca e pomposa. Ingegnatevi di vivere accostumatamente, riducendo a poco a poco le cose al termine,[23] che, per essere ora la famiglia e il padron nuovo, non si può. Gioie e seta in poche cose stanno bene a' pari vostri. Piú presto[24] qualche gentilezza di cose antiche e belli libri, e piú presto famiglia accostumata e dotta che grande. Convitar piú spesso che andare a conviti, né però superfluamente. Usate per la persona vostra cibi grossi,[25] e fate assai esercizio, perché in cotesti panni[26] si viene presto in qualche infermità, chi non ci ha cura. Lo stato del cardinale è non manco sicuro che grande; onde nasce che gli uomini si fanno negligenti, parendo loro avere conseguito assai e poterlo mantenere con poca fatica; e questo nuoce spesso e alla condizione e alla vita, alla quale è necessario che abbiate grande avvertenza; e piú presto pendiate nel fidarvi poco che troppo. Una regola sopra l'altre vi conforto ad usare con tutta la sollecitudine vostra. E questa è di levarvi ogni mattina di buona ora, perché oltra al conferir molto alla sanità, si pensa ed espedisce tutte le faccende del giorno; e al grado che avete, avendo a dir l'ufficio,[27] studiare, dare audienza ecc., ve 'l troverete molto utile. Un'altra cosa ancora è sommamente necessaria a un pari vostro, cioè pensare sempre, e massime in questi principii, la sera dinanzi tutto quello che avete da fare il giorno seguente, acciocché non vi venga cosa alcuna immediata.[28] Quanto al parlar vostro in concistorio, credo sarà piú costumatezza e piú laudabil modo in tutte le occorrenze che vi si proporranno, riferirsi alla Santità di N. S., causando che,[29] per essere voi giovane e di poca esperienzia, sia piú officio[30] vostro rimettervi alla S. S.[31] e al sapientissimo giudizio di quella. Ragionevolmente voi sarete richiesto di parlare e intercedere appresso a N. S. per molte specialità.[32] Ingegnatevi in questi principi di richiederlo manco potete, e dargliene poca molestia,[33] che di sua natura il Papa è piú grato a chi manco gli spezza gli orecchi.[34] Questa parte mi pare da osservare per non lo infastidire; e cosí l'andargli innanzi con cose piacevoli, o, pur quando accadesse, richiederlo con umiltà e modestia doverà sodisfargli piú ed esser piú secondo la natura sua. State sano.[35]

NOTES

LA NENCIA DA BARBERINO

See Introduction pp. 27–34 and the Appendix (pp. 253–55).
In this section "Bessi" refers to her edition of *La Nencia*, while "Giustiniani" refers to his *Il testo della "Nencia"*.
The present text is taken from Lorenzo, *Scritti scelti*, with modifications derived from Bessi (A-text).

LANGUAGE: The popular register of the poem makes it linguistically rather difficult, and this is compounded by the fact that the A-text, printed here, has features of the dialect of the Mugello area, in which Barberino is situated. The following will simplify the reader's labour, but there are inconsistencies: for **-ggh-** read *-gl-* (**Figghine** = *Figline*, **migghiaio** = *migliaio*, **begghi** = *begli* etc.); for **-gli** read *-lli* (**capegli** = *capelli*, **anegli** = *anelli* etc.); for **ghi** (definite article) read *gli*. For **me/te/se/ce/ve** (pronouns) read *mi/ti/si/ci/vi*; for the nominative pronoun **la** read *ella/lei* (**la se rivolge** = *lei si rivolge*, **l'ha ghi occhi** = *lei ha gli occhi* etc.). This pleonastic use of *la* is frequently heard in colloquial Florentine, for example *la m'ha detto* for standard Italian *m'ha detto*. For **ento/into/entro/drento** read *dentro*; for **dirieto** read *dietro*; for **livi** read *lí*; for **gnuno/gnuna/ignuna** read *nessuno/nessuna*. **Nenciozza** and **Gigghiozzo** are forms of endearment of *Nencia* and *giglio* (lily). Verbal forms: **guata** = *guarda*, **guatalla** = *guardarla*; **trafiggere'** = *trafiggerebbe*, **creperre'** = *creperebbe*; **fesse** = *facesse*; **vennon** = *vennero*.

1   **1–2**: *ardere* and *struggere* are common in Italian lyric poetry from the time of the Sicilian school; in English, too, one speaks of a burning love that melts the heart; **otta** = *ora*; this is an example of the deliberate attempt to give the poem a countrified linguistic patina; **brilla**: "throbs"; **5**: "there are no women comparable to her for beauty"; **fiaccole d'amore** belongs to the elevated style of the love lyric. In this poem parody is achieved by using the context of the classical tradition, its august connotations leading the reader to certain expectations that are not then met. It contains enough of

the *aulico* to expose, by contrast, the banal; the latter can be defined as such only in terms of the former.

2   **mercato**: "fair". The listing of places recalls a similar list in Cielo d'Alcamo's *Contrasto* (written between 1231 and 1250). The places mentioned by Vallera are all quite close to Florence; Barberino is approximately twenty miles away; **Borgo** is Borgo S. Lorenzo. **Nencia** is a diminutive of Lorenza or Vincenza.

3   **saviamente rilevata**: "well reared". Bessi, (p. 55, n. 72) suggests a possible additional meaning connected with the figurative arts, in which case the expression would mean "with harmonious prominent features"; **testa**: "forehead"; **ben quadrata**: "well proportioned"; **ciglia**: *occhi*. **8**: This is a parody of a concept dear to love poetry, that the beauty of the loved one is such that only an artist of great standing could have created her. Perhaps, but hardly with a gimlet.

4   To some extent the description of Nencia follows the conventions for describing a woman (*descriptio mulieris*), though its sequence does not show the rigour of its counterparts in classical authors. There are departures from the canon that lower the tone: **filare** is normally used of rows of trees, not teeth; and the horse was certainly not a suitable term of comparison in this context. The rhyme *cavallo/cristallo* highlights the technique: the connotations of the two words are diametrically opposed in the ranges of expression they evoke; their juxtaposition is incongruous. Much of the poem's charm rests on the perfect balance achieved between the serious and the ridiculous; **liscio**: "cosmetics"; **scorticamenti**: treatments of the skin to make it smoother, possibly like the modern "peeling". **8**: a stock ending to the octave.

5   **1–2**: Bessi (p. 94) paraphrases: "ella ha lo sguardo cosí potente da esser capace, per rubare un cuore, di trafiggere, non che il petto, addirittura un muro", but the text is not quite clear; **ciottolo**: "stone rounded by the effect of water, usually cobblestone". It is traditional to compare the hard heart of the beloved to stone, enamel, diamond etc., so the author is keeping within the expected range of comparison, but chooses a low-register word not generally considered "poetic".

6   **concio** and **graticcio** echo the burlesque poems of Burchiello (1404–49), but Dante had also used *concio* in this way—a word that has moved from one tradition into a lower one. **5–8**: "I have become as thin as a rake (**graticcio**: "rush matting") and all because of what I am enduring in my heart (and without rebelling!), she has so tied me with a hundred withies"; **ritortole** here replaces the chains and yokes of traditional love poetry.

7   **1–2**: "She could favourably stand comparison with a thousand beautiful women from the city"; **l'ha ghi occhi suoi**: "her eyes are"; **biondelline**: "blonde". There appears to be, as Bessi suggests (p. 57), a link

with Cavalcanti's "In un boschetto trova' pasturella" ("Cavelli avea bion-detti e ricciutelli"), in which case the suffix *-ello* has been moved from *ricciuto*, where we would expect it, to *biondo*. The poem frequently exploits the unexpected. There may also be a link with *biondella* (*erythræa centaurium*), a herb used for bleaching hair. 7–8: "the ends of her hair are so curly that you would think a thousand rings were attached to it."

8   1: "She dances as one should"; **scarpetta**: This is not a diminutive but simply "shoe"; **duo colpi** = *due volte*; **iscambietta**: The *scambietto* is a "passo di danza con scambio dei piedi" (Bessi, p. 126); hence "she performs a couple of dance steps."

9   1: This type of statement generally concludes the conventional descriptions of women; the combination of white and red is also within the norm, as is Nencia's dimple in the middle of her chin (3), though in the latter case the use of **buco**, a far from poetic word, shifts the tone from *aulico* to *parodico*. 6: "I think nature created her as a pattern of perfection."

10   **fioraliso**: (*fiordaliso* = *centaurea cyanus*), "cornflower", a metaphor for Nencia that is very much within the canon. The meaning of the line is "the man who will enjoy Nencia naked", a pleasure that will be less coyly expressed in *Ambra*, 26. The reticence is necessary here to prevent the poem becoming a complete mockery of the lyric genre; enough parody is created by the use of **sugnaccio** (an inferior quality of lard, *sugna*), which may be an apposite simile for the softness and whiteness of the cuddly Nencia, but hardly the one we would expect. The infinitives **aver** and **veder** need to be translated as gerunds.

11   **tralucenti**: Tracing uses of this word in Petrarch, Alberti and Ficino, Bessi (p. 63) suggests that it be read as "transparent", in the philosophical context of the soul being reflected in the eyes; **te creperre' el cuore**: "your heart would burst" [with feeling for me]; **serventi** = *spasiman-ti*, an ironic reference to those who served Love in courtly poetry. **Vallera** is the name of the man speaking throughout. This entire octave bears a strong resemblance to Boccaccio, *Filostrato*, IV. 160.

12   3–5: "If without pain I could open up myself, then I would split myself open in order to show you that I have you within my heart, and I would have you touch it." 7: There are plenty of instances in both religious and secular poetry prior to this of the image of the cutting of the heart. We find something similar in Scripture (Luke 2. 35: "and thy own soul a sword shall pierce").

13   4–8: "it seems that he (**un altro**) pulls my heart out of my breast. You have so pierced through my heart, that I pour out daily a thousand sighs, full of sobs and all tear-sodden, and I send them all to you directly." The hope that the poet's sighs will reach his beloved is commonplace, but there is parody in the exaggeration and speedy dispatch; **lucciolando** is another "rusticalismo intenzionale", as Giustiniani (p. 116) calls the words

superimposed on the original text to give it "local" flavour; *lucciolone* is still used with a touch of endearment for a huge tear.

14   7–8: "and I stayed there [**livi**] more than an hour and a half, until the moon set, in the cool air [**al rezzo**]."

15   3: "my heart increased [with joy] by a whole span"; 4: This seems to describe the sudden wave of goose-flesh that can precede weeping; **vie quinentro**: "right here"; 8: The second half of the line, with its stress on **tu**, turns to comedy Vallera's strong emotion and tension as he hopes to join Nencia.

16   2: "I collapse [**abbioscio**], tossing and turning [**voltoloni**], on that grass"; the switch to the present tense in this line may arise from Vallera's recalling this detail of his experience with intensity, as if he were reliving it. 4: "until your wethers [= castrated rams] pass by"; **castroni** is to be found in burlesque verse and shifts the tone of the octave from the lovelorn to the sexual in preparation for the final line. **Vientene**: "Come"; **valiconi**: "passes". This word is unique to Text A and according to Bessi (p. 177) is probably erroneous—a confusion with the earlier **valicorno**. It is likely that it should be **saliconi** ("willows").

17   **duo somelle/de schegge**: "two loads of sticks"; a *soma* was a specific quantity for the purposes of taxation; **schegge** were strips of wood for either burning or working. **Procura**: "think carefully"; **cavelle**: "something", from the latin *quod velles*; **cartoccino**: seems to have been used at the time only in perfumery and pharmaceutics, and may have designated a specific quantity (see Bessi, p. 52, citing Volpi). 8: "a few pennyworths [**quattrino** was a Florentine copper coin] of little pins (**squilletti**) and needles (**agora**)".

18   **un collarin *to* mezzo**: "a coral necklet with a pendant in the middle". 4: Corals seem to have been sold in two specified sizes. 5-6: "If I were to pull them out from the marrow of my shin or other bones"; **gonnella**: type of overall worn by both men and women.

19   **zaccherella**: "small item of no value"; 2–8: "I know that you use a hundred different types of them: some lace for your skirt [or overall], or hooks or buckles or buttons, or do you want a satchel for your tunic, or tapes to tie your bonnets [there is doubt about **scuffioni**: they may be a type of hose], or do you want a pale blue silk belt to tie your coat?"

20   **tu te farai con Dio** = *addio*; **mona Masa**: Madonna Tommasa (feminine of Tommaso), perhaps Vallera's employer, is obviously someone he must heed; **i' me ne vo cantando**: Bessi (p. 58) sees this as "un calco vero e proprio dall'incipit di una canzone del Saviozzo"; this was the nickname of the Sienese Simone Serdini (*c*.1360–1419/20), and the poem referrred to is "Addio chi sta, ch'io me ne vo cantando." There is an interesting contrast between **baloccar** and **cantando**. The first is a trivialization of the Cyclops's behaviour in Theocritus, *Idylls*, XI.12ff, but the balance is redressed by **cantando**. This use of two contrasting linguistic registers epitomizes the

technique cultivated throughout. Moreover, the words of the close echo the poem's opening two lines.

APPENDIX: THE TEXT OF *LA NENCIA DA BARBERINO*

Giustiniani and Bessi are the two most important publications on the so-called *questione nenciale*. Four separate versions of *Nencia* exist. They are generally referred to as V, A, P and M, and Bessi offers critical editions of all of them. V, the only version known prior to our century, is generally referred to as the *vulgata*—hence V for Bessi and other editors (but H for Giustiniani). It is contained in five manuscripts, and there are some two dozen printed editions prior to Simioni's of 1913–14. It was printed as a text of 50 octaves, but the three editions which appeared before December 1515, and are closer to the text of A, P, and M than subsequent printings, contain 51. The earliest printed version is in the library of Erlangen University; it has no date, printer's name or place of publication but it can be safely assumed to have been printed in Florence *circa* 1490–91. It is the only printed text of *Nencia* before the eighteenth century to present the poem without its usual companion, Pulci's *Beca da Dicomano*, a poem that is broader in tone than *Nencia* and better defined as burlesque. (The two poems may have been written as part of a poetic contest.) It is the Erlangen text that is published by Bessi.

The controversy that made *Nencia* such a contentious work began in 1908, when Guglielmo Volpi published what is generally called the A-text. This version is in 20 octaves, all of which, except one, are contained in the *vulgata*, though in a different order. The P-text was published by Federico Patetta in 1934 from a manuscript then in his possession; it consists of 39 octaves and, as with the A-text, all except one are to be found, in a different order, in V. Patetta's manuscript is the only one to bear a date: "Finito a dí 11 d'ottobre 1476." Lastly, the M-text was discovered by Michele Messina and published in 1951. Curiously, like the others, only one octave is unique to it, as is the order of its 12 stanzas; it bears a note by the copyist to the effect that 37 more followed. The first two octaves, common to the other three versions, are here missing; were one to add these to what is given and what was not copied, the total would be 51 octaves, as in V. Bigi's edition contains texts A and V (in the post-1515 version), but generally editors have opted to print only the A-text, as this was hailed as the "real" one by scholars who did not heed the note of caution sounded by its discoverer. Volpi had merely suggested that his newly found version *might* be the original text, which, proving very popular, had subsequently been elaborated and augmented by unknown hands.

The eloquence of Fubini, above all others, convinced many that A was the original *Nencia* and also that it was the work of Lorenzo. It is not altogether surprising, then, to find Rochon asserting, "It is beyond doubt that the A redaction is the original text of the poem" (*La Jeunesse de Laurent*, p. 384). The meticulously detailed examination of the four texts carried out by Bessi shows quite clearly that none of them can be regarded as an archetype from which the others derive. There are numerous variants between the versions, of which some have the character of corrections to an extant form and drafts of possible alternatives. (Giustiniani, p. 30 will not call the versions *redazioni* but rather "*raccolte* fatte *a posteriori*".) Text A has phonetic and morphological features that differentiate it from the others, but they are not consistent, and both Bessi and Giustiniani argue convincingly that they were not originally present but incorporated later (probably rather profusely, but then reduced in number) in order to give some semblance of the speech of the country folk of the Mugello area, thereby increasing the "authenticity" of Vallera—even though other rustic compositions of the period do not attempt mimesis of country parlance. That someone in late Quattrocento Florence had an interest in reproducing the *parlata rusticale* seems to have been the case according to Bessi (p.118), but there is no evidence to indicate that that person was *Nencia*'s author. So it must be concluded that no version can claim either chronological priority or superiority over the others.

The principal argument in favour of the A-text has been an aesthetic one: the 20 octaves offer, at first sight, an interconnected sequence that is lacking in the diffuse, rambling V-text. It is clear that the 20 octaves fall into two equal sections: in the first ten Vallera speaks of Nencia in the third person, listing her attributes and generating a crescendo of emotion that breaks out after the tenth octave in a direct address to her. In Octaves 11–13 he flaunts the intensity of the suffering love causes him; in 14–16 he speaks of his anguish and sleeplessness; in 17–19 he lists the presents that he is willing to buy Nencia; and the final stanza contains his valediction. Rochon (p. 416) even finds a perfect metrical and linguistic balance between the first two lines of the poem and the final couplet (note: *cantare/cuore* and *cantando/cuor*). A closer look at the A-text, however, shows that it is less compact than it has appeared. Bessi (pp. 74–92) examines the tradition of the description of a woman, in which the poet praised his lady according to a canon that was strictly adhered to: the lady's attributes were listed from top to bottom—hair, face, throat etc. to feet—, often with exceptional detail but without the intercalation of extraneous matter. Considering Octaves 3–10 of *Nencia*, we find that 5, 6 and 8 (quite a high proportion) do not fit into this tradition; 5 and 6 describe Vallera's jealousy and suffering and are thematically much more related to 14–16. The units that form the second half of the poem are in no way interconnected, and Bessi shows that there are octaves in the V-text that could complement these sections. Alone among critics she draws attention to an inconsistency at the end: the herd is spontaneously moving homeward (as in Theocritus,*Idylls*, xi.12ff), so we suppose it to be sunset; but Vallera's outpouring of his longings has been set in the early morning (like that of the Cyclops in Theocritus). The source has been used without the appropriate adjustment of time in relation to the preceding part of the poem. So the praise lavished on the A-text as being a "poemetto unitario coerentemente costituito", while oft repeated, cannot be justified (Bessi, p. 91).

So what is an editor's effective choice? It is evidently between Texts A and V, as M is self-confessedly incomplete and V encompasses nearly all of P. There appear to be no decisive factors that would make us accept the A-text as the definitive version of a poem that may never have set out to be a cohesive unit, but it does have more balance and measure than V. The latter's only superiority is that of being two-and-a-half times as long and thereby providing commensurately more of the features that are characteristic of this poetic piece, though without enhancing them in any way. V's only distinctive feature is an element of dialogue in a few of the octaves, which leads one to link it to the rustic drama of the period. In this connection it is worth noting that Giustiniani, on the basis of the numerous Nencia-types that feature in the poetry of the area in that period, suggests— albeit with a degree of uncertainty—that "nel folklore delle campagne fiorentine, e piú particolarmente del Mugello, intorno al 1470 si fosse formata e definita una figura-tipo di contadina, chiamata appunto Nencia e dotata *in nuce* di certe sue caratteristiche: un personaggio che già in questa sua preistoria arieggia molto alla lontana i tipi della Commedia dell'Arte ancora di là da venire" (p. 42). Of all the hypotheses the most sustainable is that we have in these texts collections of *rispetti* that Poliziano was to call *continuati. Rispetti* are octaves or other rhyming stanza-forms each of which forms a unit, with love as their subject; they were sung as a serenade to one's beloved, often in the *maggiolate*, when young men went round in groups singing in celebration of love, in the month traditionally associated with its fulfilment. *Beca* (64.1)—"Io t'arrecai stanotte, Beca, un maio"— establishes a direct link with the *maggiolate*. (The *maio* was a highly decorated flowering branch left at the door of the beloved during the night before *calendimaggio*, the first of May.) *Continuati* defines compositions in which such *rispetti* are loosely grouped together on a common theme. If we approach the A-text as such a collection, it offers us more cohesion than one might expect, and enables us to enjoy an excellent specimen of the genre (if one may so call it), without the meanderings of V. It is this latter text and Pulci's *Beca* that Orvieto describes as "'opere aperte', passibili di infinite e non controllate aggiunte" (P. Orvieto, *Pulci medievale* [Rome, Salerno, 1978], p. 113). The uncontrolled additions can be repetitive, whereas, despite some looseness of structure, the A-text holds together and has a measure of compactness. This, then, is the version that has been selected for the present edition.

UCCELLAGIONE DI STARNE

See Introduction pp. 34–37.

In this section "Martelli" refers to Martelli's edition of the *Uccellagione*, the source of the text here reproduced; "ad loc." means "at the point in the commentary corresponding to the point in the text under discussion".

TITLE: "Fowling for partridges".

SYNOPSIS: (1–9) Before sunrise the poet is wakened by activity in preparation for a day's fowling for partridges. The master of the hounds is to set out first so that the hounds do not get in the way of the horses. When they have gone part of the way, four falconers follow on horseback. One of these is the reluctant Dionigi, whose mind is much more on the comfortable bed he has been forced to abandon than on his present activity, hence his fall from horseback, the injury to his hawk and his squashing it. (10–12) Three falconers are left, together with a largish group of supporters and onlookers on foot or on horseback. Strozzo degli Strozzi, master of the hunt, brings up the rear. An ideal spot for the day's sport is found. (13–19) The hounds are released with lively exhortations to frighten the birds out of hiding and into flight, so that the hawks can be sent in pursuit. Giovan Francesco releases his hawk without removing its hood, which results in quite a fiasco. (20–24) Guglielmo, who is very proud of his hawk, releases it towards a partridge that is duly brought to the ground, though the hawk only narrowly escapes capture by a hound. Giovan Francesco releases his hawk a second time towards a young partridge but the intervention of the mother partridge leaves the hawk the worse for the experience. (25–32) Foglia also comes in for disappointment as the partridge caught by his inexperienced hawk is badly injured. The ensuing scene is reminiscent of the fight between the devils at the end of *Inferno* XXII: the hawks of Foglia and Guglielmo pursue a partridge but end up in a fight with each other. Guglielmo finds it hard to hide his delight as he believes his hawk is getting the better of Foglia's, but the opposite turns out to be the case. (33–40) The heat becomes intense, the men have had enough, and they set out for home, some delighted with their catch, others silenced by their failure to fill their bags. Giovan Francesco, whose heart has not been in the exercise, enquires about three absent friends. Braccio replies that they were better off without two of them anyway as they are such hopeless fowlers, while the other (the poet Luigi Pulci) was no doubt fantasizing somewhere. (41–45) Back home, they drink, eat and greatly exaggerate the day's takings. The ill feeling between Foglia and Guglielmo impairs the atmosphere of joviality and Dionigi, the chubby, easy-going friend, tries to heal the rift. The sun sets, two of the absentees appear (the third, Giovan Simone, is too serious and has returned to work), the wine helps to drown troubles, and the friends go to bed before the next expedition, a fishing one.

LEXIS: The following terms, which occur more than once, assume a specialized meaning when related to fowling: **brigata**: flock of birds; **cappello**: the hood put over the head of a hawk to keep it quiet; **frullare**: to whirr (vibratory sound from birds' wings in movement); **getto/gittare**: the releasing of a hawk in pursuit of its prey; **levare**: to rise in flight (of birds).

The notes below respect the tense of the original text: there is frequent alternation of past and present.

1   6: "it was almost day-break", as **quel ch'amò l'alloro** is Apollo, the sun-god, who loved Daphne (to escape his pursuit, she was turned into a laurel tree); 8: "the tawny owl [*strix aluco*] and the barn owl [*tyto alba*] and the little owl [*athene noctua*]".

2   3–4: "the moon (**Diana**) had risen and set, or else [the wolf] might have been seen"; 5–6: compare *Ambra*, 20. 1–2; 8: "the morning gave hope of a good day."

3   1–2: The noises are from the bells on the collars round the necks of hawks and from the alluring of hounds; **gli è tardi**: a form still heard in Florence for *è tardi*; **canattier**: the master of the hounds (from *cane*) whose name is **Cappellaio**; **guastassin**: modern Italian would have a present subjunctive *guastino*.

4   The hounds and bitches are here listed by name.

5   1–2: "When the hounds have already gained some ground in the fields, four falconers with their hawks followed." **Guglielmo** de' Pazzi (born 1437) accompanied the young Lorenzo (his brother-in-law) on his embassies to Milan. He was exiled after the Pazzi conspiracy. **Giovan Francesco** Ventura (born 1442), known to us through his correspondence with Lorenzo, seems to have been an intimate friend. He was a merchant who did not engage in political activity. Lorenzo dedicated one of his religious *capitoli* to him. **Dionigi** Pucci (born 1442) was a convivial friend. Given civic duties by Lorenzo's father Piero, he carried out various public offices until his death in 1494. **Foglia Amieri** (born 1444) was of an impoverished noble family. Neither he nor his three brothers ever held public office. 8: Dionigi, still half-asleep, is losing his balance on horseback. The

cerimonial and religious connotations of **riverenza** and **inchina** give a humorous overtone to this act of morning worship.

6   **alia** = *ala*; **macerogli 'l fianco**: "crushed his side"; 8: "because his lady-love is [called] don't-overdo-it" (Dionigi is glad to have an excuse not to exert himself).

7   **egli** *to* **tondo**: "he rolls down the slope like a round stone". Gismondo is Sigismondo della Stufa (1445–1525), friend of Lorenzo and holder of various public offices. It was to him that Bartolomeo della Scala addressed the letter concerning *Nencia*; **'n camicia in su le pocce**: "with only his shirt on his chest"; 8: "I'll not get into such a mess again if I survive this one", meaning "I'll not go to another hunt."

8   1: "I was indeed the simpleton". **Birria**: the lazy, greedy but amiable servant in a popular humorous poem in *volgare*, *Geta e Birria*, written some hundred years earlier. It was based on a twelfth-century satirical Latin poem by Vitale de Blois which took its story-line from Plautus's *Amphitruo*, though the character Birria is from Terence's *Andria*; **sotto**: "under [the bed covers]"; 5: "I could have helped to prepare a good meal". Martelli, ad loc.: "ti fa sentire il profumo delle vivande! Come il **coperta di fiori** ti fa sentire e vedere il profumo di un candido e lindo desco di campagna!" 7–8: "better exhaust your mattress and pillow than your horse and than do damage to the bird on your arm". A delightful octave in which one can really relish the comfort of staying abed ensconced in the softness of down (in contrast with the severe **uscire per tempo**) and also the sensuous pleasure in the preparation of the meal.

9   1–2: "In the meantime he wants to grasp his hawk again, but it is so bashed that it cannot climb back to its position on his glove"; 3–4: These lines can be understood only imprecisely but their meaning seems to be that the hawk is in a bad way and lopsided. Martelli (ad loc.) comments that the image is "singolarmente felice: che cosa di più sbilenco, cui ravvicinare, con una singolare intelligenza d'associazione, quel malcapitato sparviero, di una tovaglia o di una coperta che, messe malamente sulla tavola o sul letto, pendano sgraziatamente da un lato?" Dionigi's thoughts were indeed on beds and tables in the previous octave. 6–8: "while [Dionigi] was settling his open glove (**manica**) [on which the hawk would sit] the bird seized his hand, whereupon [Dionigi] plunged it down, hopped on it and reduced it to a pie (**cofaccia** = *focaccia*)."

10   1: "Three able fowlers are left." **Bartolo** di Bartolo Tedaldi (born 1433) was a *bon viveur* who is appropriately Lorenzo's guide in the *Simposio*. **Ulivier** Sapiti (born 1430) was another member of the Brigata. **Braccio** Martelli (born 1442) belonged to a family that was very loyal to the Medici. He had an excellent knowledge of the classics and philosophy and was a close friend of Lorenzo's. **Piero Alamanni** (born 1434) was the father of the poet Luigi Alamanni. He was one of the few, according to the historian

Guicciardini, whom Lorenzo trusted totally. He held many public offices and ably negotiated, in Rome, the election as cardinal of Lorenzo's son Giovanni. The identity of 'l **Parente** and 'l **Portinar Giovanni** remains unknown. **8**: "he looks like a barn owl at 3 pm", i.e. he is a misfit in such an occasion; an owl out in the sun is like a fish out of water.

11   **Strozzo** degli Strozzi (born 1424) belonged to one of the most important Florentine families. As master of the hunt he keeps a certain distance from the group. **5**: "and so they go, some on horseback and some on foot (**pedestro**)."

12   **rimunita e netta**: "neat and tidy", i.e. cleared of undergrowth; **riprezzo**: Martelli (p. 69) suggests this means "far ritornare in pregio", which would give the general meaning that the place is so ideal for hunting that even a man with gout or one who is blind would wish to hunt, an activity that he has abandoned because of physical disability.

13   **4**: "they pause to look and to plan"; **6–7**: "and, so that the outcome will be as successful as possible, some go with the hounds [these will cause the partridges to rise in flight], some keep guard and some go with the falconers to see the hawks released in pursuit of the prey."

14   **3–4**: "the third falconer goes with his hawk near the master of the hounds, and wants a good release towards the flock of birds"; **coppia**: "spancel" (a rope that ties the hounds in pairs). The hunt now starts in earnest.

15   **1–2**: The reference here is to races of Barbary horses in Florence, like the one held annually on the feast of St John, patron saint of the city. The hounds depart as speedily as do horses when they hear the trumpet peal to start the race; **a chi scuote il pesco**: "to some he gives a hiding" with the rod (**pertica**).The image comes from the vigorous beating of a peach tree to gather its ripe fruits.

16–17   General exhortations to the hounds to incite them to make the partridges rise.

16   **4**: "keep an eye on Sacco [a hound], who has stopped"; **guata brigata adorna!**: "look what a fine flock of birds!"; **che volta fu quella!**: "what a fine way you have turned [towards the scent]!"; **vella!** = *vedila!*

17   **frulla!**: The partridge is the subject.

18   **1–2**: "I see that [**Buontempo** the hound] is on their tracks; I see he's chasing them and will make them take off"; **ancor non ti dispiaccia**: "do not be surprised."

19   **sentille** = *sentirle*; **5–8**: "Giovan Francesco had released his hawk in pursuit of the flock of birds, and he filled the countryside (**ville**) with shouts [of joy] and words of encouragement: 'Ah! what a great bird you are!'; but in his haste he had released it hooded."

20   **non istar piú**: "do not delay"; **6**: Martelli, ad loc.: "sottile nota ironica, nella sua giocosamente epica magniloquenza, contro lo sparvier di

Guglielmo e, indirettamente, anche contro questo ultimo"; **braccia**: a *braccio* was a linear measure of 58 cm in Florence, but slightly different in other Italian cities.

21   **Garri a**: "shout at", meaning "recall"; Guglielmo does not want the bitch (**Guercina**) to destroy his hawk, so he throws a stone to save (**riscampar**) his bird because the rods are too short. The hawk could give himself away through the sound of bells in his collar (**sonagliare**), hence Guglielmo remains as quiet (**cheto**) as possible, so as to be able to hear.

22   **gliel venne veduto** : "he was able to see it"; **5–7**: "he took it [the hawk] by the jess [leather strap fastened round the legs of a hawk] and held it; he gave it the head and brains [of the partridge], as he did not much care for these; he freed the bird from the claws and beak of the hawk that were clutching it."

23   **a lui ne venga teso/uno starnone**: "a young male partridge is coming towards him, with its wings fully and tautly splayed out"; **7–8**: "the mother partridge, wily with the years (**vecchia**), manages to get free of the hawk and plucks him well"; this comment is figurative, meaning "lo fa restare scornato e sconfitto" (Martelli, ad loc.).

24   "It was, indeed, not much of a hawk, young and resembling a kestrel, and I do not think it would have managed to catch even a small goldfinch (**calderugio**), well and firmly held with a noose in a snare (**calappio**); any delay, and all hope of success was lost as it would then go and play like a gentle bird (**fatappio**); the reason it caught nothing was because it did not put its mind to it and did not pay attention." *Fatappio* was also used of a frivolous, inconstant man.

25   **fegli un gentil getto**: "[Foglia] released his hawk with a fine gesture"; **presegnene *to* becco**: "[the hawk] caught [the young partridge] front on. Foglia runs down and feels sure of his prey, as his hawk does its job perfectly: it took it out in a clearing, where there were no bushes, and on the ground [the hawk] got blood on its claws and beak [instead of delivering the bird neatly to Foglia]." Note the change to the present tense in 5–6, which highlights Foglia's joy in his (presumed) success and his pride in his bird.

26   **soro**: "inexperienced"; **5–6**: "spancel the hounds, for Rocca will suffice; she is so able that she can drive the game from their holes"; **le mettete in mezzo**: "surround them."

27   **3–4**: (said to Rocca, the bitch) "It fell here, see. Ah! if you get it first, you can keep it; come back, hold on, hold it in your mouth."

28   **1–2**: "The hawk let the partridge go and takes care to flee from [Guglielmo's] hawk that is pursuing him." Guglielmo is pretending to rejoice with Foglia because his hawk has caught the partridge, but in fact he has seen the real situation and is secretly hoping that his hawk will overcome Foglia's.

29   **ta'** = *tali*; **1-3**: Foglia also realizes that the two hawks are struggling with each other, and because he thinks that his is coming off worse in the fray, he seems to speak angrily to Guglielmo; **'l tuo sparvier** *to* **certo**: "your hawk, so full of its own self (**massiccio**), spots able hawks [rather than partridges]"; **7-8**: "you do take to villainous and strange games, and I'm the fool to get involved with children!"—i.e. "to hunt with people who are inept". This sarcastic remark by Foglia is quite justified given Guglielmo's inflated opinion of his hawk's ability.

30   **fanno alla franciosa**: Martelli (ad loc.) suggests as a possible meaning *si buggerano a vicenda*; **5**: "thereby revealing the mirth that he had tried to keep hidden".

31   **logoro**: "lure", gadget made of leather and feathers to simulate a wing for the purpose of luring back the hawk to the falconer; **egli** is Guglielmo himself; he was confident that it was his hawk that had damaged Foglia's; **8**: "he all but hit him."

32   **si leva**: "[Foglia] gets out of the way" so as not to be struck by Guglielmo's fury; **3-5**: "his expression and words were like those of a man who expected a judgement in his favour [at a trial], but found himself condemned." Martelli (ad loc.) suggests a possible reference here to the episode of Brunoro in *Morgante*, III. 57ff. **7-8**: "we shall perhaps agree to meet somewhere, sometime, and I shall make you sane if your are mad"— a veiled challenge to a duel.

33   **1-4**: "The sun about noon is lowering and exhausting (**stremando**) the shadows, thereby reducing them; they get out of perspective like a figure foreshortened in a painting." **5**: The cicada is heard only in the intense heat of summer; **ogni fronde salda**: "every bough [stays] firm", as there is no breeze.

34   **Io son** *to* **rincresco**: "I feel the urge to go, as it will become very disagreeable for me if I stay"; **per pascer poi di presa**: "just for the sake of eating what I catch".

35   **infrescatoio**: container for keeping items (generally drink) cool in water; **3-4**: Majority opinion was in favour of departure; **8**: "it seemed as if the stubble were on fire."

36   **8**: "because he hunts to please the others, not because he is drawn to it himself".

37   **Corona**: falconer of the Medici. **Giovan Simone** was one of the Tornabuoni family, as was Lorenzo's mother Lucrezia. It is to him that the **gran naso** belongs (it was a family trait from which Lorenzo himself was not exempt) and not to Luigi Pulci, as stated in editions prior to Martelli's; **sia rimaso**: "stayed away, did not come with us"; they obviously did not excel in fowling; **7-8**: "he has killed more unfortunate hawks than Saracens were killed by Orlando." There is no doubt about this reference to Pulci's chivalric epic *Morgante* (1478 and 1483) with its rumbustious narrations of

the exploits of Charlemagne's paladin Orlando and his extraordinary albeit incredible fights against the Saracens. Pulci himself will be mentioned in 40.

38   **1**: "He has probably gone off in a sulk (or whim)"; **3–4**: "it would be better (**me'**) to lose him for good than have him missing temporarily: to have him along with me [in the group] was an insult to me." Corona having been dismissed as not much good, Giovan Simone also comes in for short shrift. **5–8**: "When a certain humour comes over Gioan Simone, he saddles his horse or a mule, whatever is to hand, and furiously grabs his baggage, and this is just typical of him: in my opinion he ought not to come to Fucecchio." A fishing expedition to the lake of Fucecchio is obviously being planned.

39   **1**: The **ciambellotto** was a cloth that when creased, retained the crease permanently; the saying therefore refers to being obstinate in one's decision. Virtually the same line is used in *Rappresentazione*, 131. 8. **1–4**: "[Giovan Simone], obstinate in his decision, has gone off without saying goodbye to the group; he has gone back to his work (**bottega**), the silly chap (**cappelluccio**), to an overall that has become his darling and love." There is jovial mockery of the absent friend, whom we know to have been a very active businessman, "il quale, mentre gli amici stanno serenamente insieme a divertirsi, se ne va sempre a far la persona seria, che lavora ed ha impegni importanti" (Martelli, ad loc.). **6–8**: "hounds and horses shy away and are put off their stride; nor can he smell a rose properly without shoving the tip [of his nose] into the flower."

40   **guarti**: *guardati*, "take care"; **8**: Pulci, following some whim of his poetic imagination, is likely to make Corona a character in a *frottola* (a popular song generally of a humorous, quasi-nonsensical nature, something like a limerick) or a *ballata* (**canzona** here is probably *canzone a ballo*).

41   **cuoio**: various items made of hide that have been used for the sport; **4–8**: "they all find themselves together [having attended to the various chores] floating their glasses [to fill them]. Here there is another bird hunt [in their conversation] and every butterfly is called a crane [i.e. there is gross exaggeration]; and though the wine is off (**cercone**) it seems **trebbiano** [a fruity white wine of good quality]; and everyone eats his fill of good food." Compare *Morgante*, XXIV. 44. 8: "e ch'ogni mosca sia per l'aria un grue".

42   **1–2**: "the first onslaught [on the food] was in perfect silence, so busy are they all exercising their jaws."

43   **e' non si tiene a mente**: "one does not carry grudges"; **7**: "be as sensible (**discreto**) as I was"; Dionigi, of course, killed his hawk (Octave 9) and is advocating a philosophical attitude to the whole business.

44   **2**: "La ripetizione del nome [...] non può non avere un valore allusivo e ammiccante" (Martelli, ad loc.); **a desco**: "at the dinner table"; **comparito** = *comparso*; **per arte di maiolica**: "delicately", but here "without

being noticed"; **cicalato**: *cicalare* is a figurative word for idle chatter, associated with the pointless noise of the cicadas, whose nuisance value has been mentioned in 35; **7–8**: "a last sip [of wine] before going to bed, as wine carries [away] the burden from everything".

45   **3–4**: "I know that they will all wish to make up time (**dotte** = hours) [lost from sleep, because of the previous day's early rise] and they will want to sleep until 9 am (**terza**)." **Sieve**: a tributary of the Arno; it flows through the Mugello area and close to the Medici villa at Cafaggiolo; it had plenty of fish, mainly **lasca** (*leuciscus rutilus*), a humble member of the carp family; **compar**: here "friend", not godfather or witness; Orvieto has argued convincingly in favour of identifying him with Poliziano. **8**: Part of the joy of this light-hearted life is the composition of popular verse to an appropriate rhythm. There is, however some doubt: **a zucchero** may mean lines with *rima sdrucciola* typical of popular poetry, but Martelli, ad loc., suggests "peregrine e perciò belle" and composed when the time is ripe.

CANZONIERE

See Introduction pp. 37–41.

The text of these sonnets is taken (with one tiny change) from Zanato's critical edition of the *Canzoniere*, where they are numbered, in Roman figures, 29, 52, 59, 65, 69, 136, 148 and 162. Exhaustive notes are provided by Orvieto in his edition of the *Canzoniere*, referred to as "Orvieto" in the following explanations, which are much indebted to some of his suggestions.

Metrically Lorenzo follows the canonical Petrarchan sonnet form; only one sonnet in the entire *Canzoniere* (*Rime* and *Comento*) departs in its octave from the ABBA ABBA pattern, but the tercets show greater variation. In the eight sonnets selected for this edition four have the common CDE CDE pattern, while the first one selected follows the CDC DCD pattern, which is almost as frequent in Petrarch. The sixth sonnet rhymes CDE DCE, quite frequent in Petrarch but not in Lorenzo. The last has a form used only once by Petrarch, CDE EDC, but very frequently by Cavalcanti; it is also the rhyme-pattern of Dante's "Tanto gentile e tanto onesta pare".

1   "Sonetto fatto per uno certo caso, che ogni dí si mostrava in mille modi"
1   **dileggia**: "mocks". The same verb appears twice in the *canzone a ballo* "Crudel Fortuna, a che condotto m'hai?", with which this sonnet has strong similarities.

2   **m'ingombra**: "fills me"; "la rima in *-ombra*, di origine dantesca e petrarchesca, è nel Quattrocento una delle rime piú popolari" (Orvieto, p. 55).

4   **pe' mortal'**: "by mortals". The use of this noun rather than, say, "human beings" is a reminder that death is man's fate.

5   **aspreggia**: "she exasperates, embitters."

6   **mi sgombra**: "she drives [them] away."

7   "she causes the frightened soul to shy". The underlying metaphor is that of the horse.

8   **s'aveggia**: "she becomes aware."

9–12   These antitheses are typically Petrarchan.

14   It was a feature of popular poetry to end with a proverbial saying or maxim; this is also found in Petrarch.

2   "Sonetto fatto per uno sogno"

This sonnet should be compared with "Datemi pace omai, sospiri ardenti" (*Comento*, XIX) because of the similarity of theme; there are also some half-dozen other sonnets on sleep and dreams, as well as *Stanze*, I. 8, 133 (Castagnola's numbering) and *Ambra*, 5–6. Lorenzo ably blends the various sources: Virgil and Ovid filtered through Dante, Petrarch and Boccaccio. The poet's experience rather lacks originality as he tells of the dream in which his beloved appears more beautiful and kinder than she has ever been; he is daunted by this apparition, and when his desire overcomes his fear and he addresses his lady she vanishes and he awakens to the anguish of loss. The sonnet ends with a harsh line made forceful by effective alliteration.

1–2   Quite a Petrarchan start, with "Piú che mai bella" to be found in CCLXVIII. 45 and the oxymoron "la mia cara nemica" in CCCXV. 6; but the sonnet is not really an imitation of CCCII, as Bigi states, ad loc.

3–4   Virgil, via Dante (*Inferno*, II. 1–3), probably suggested these two lines and the similar ones in *Comento*, XIX (5-6) and *Corinto* (4-6).

9   **pauroso e lento**: used by Petrarch in XII. 8, in the second hemistich of a hendecasyllable, as here.

10   **come solea**: "as was my wont".

11   **disio** is the subject of **vinse**.

13   **súbita**: "unexpectedly".

14   **mia merzé**: "my reward"; the vision of the lady in the dream was a reward for the suffering of love which the poet endures.

3   This sonnet, together with the neighbouring poems in the *Canzoniere*, is a reflection on transience and on death, arising from

the awareness of the fleeting nature of time; the theme, dear to classical authors and popular in Renaissance literature, was to become the most Laurentian of all themes. The idea of the pointlessness of human concern and care is dominant in Lorenzo's philosophical and quasi-religious poem *De summo bono*, in which he explores the view that nothing on this earth will give lasting happiness, which is to be found only in God, the supreme good.

5   **Altri**: "some"; **giostra**: "jousting" or "tournament".
6   "others put their minds to achieving noble things."
11   "[are] always to be seen in this erring world". Dante calls the world **errante** in *Paradiso*, xx. 67, and so does Petrarch in cccxlvi. 7 and cccl. 11.
13   **mal constante**: "fickle".
14   **dura** is a verb that reiterates and adds emphasis to the preceding **sta ferma**, as death is constant and everlasting. This is one of Lorenzo's strongest and most successful lines, though it conveys what may be seen as the most banal statement on human existence. Each word is incredibly simple—bisyllabic—, and the phonic effects make the line easily memorable with its alliteration and use of only eight consonants. The otherwise perfectly regular iambic hendecasyllable with its arsis on the sixth syllable has a trochaic opening foot which isolates the word **sola** and gives emphasis to the only constant in man's life, in the word that ends the poem, **Morte**.

4   "Sonetto fatto in sul Rimaggio"

Orvieto (p. 125) suggests an early date for this poem, possibly no later than 1473–74, when the association between Lorenzo and Poliziano was at its strongest. This sonnet has a virginal quality initially conveyed, paradoxically, by the realm of Venus and then transposed to the Tuscan countryside in the first emerging of spring, as the diminutives indicate. But the darts of love are to be released into this chaste and rarefied atmosphere—an experience presented by the poet not as destructive but as enriching, as *prezzando* suggests. Lorenzo proposes in idyllic terms the conflict between chastity and love (Diana versus Venus) which is a commonplace in literature, and is generally resolved in favour of love. The story seen as the prototype of this conflict is that of Daphne and Apollo as told by Ovid in *Metamorphoses* i.
Rimaggio: a brook and a place near Florence.
1   **l'isola**: Cyprus, where the worship of Venus became prevalent, hence **ciprigna dea** in line 3. See also *Ambra*, 2 and 11, and the *Canzona de' sette pianeti*, line 23.

10   **figlio**: This is Cupid, the god of love, generally portrayed as a young winged boy, darting arrows of love into unsuspecting hearts.

12–14   The implication of the poet's plea is that young maidens dedicated to chastity (here represented by the goddess **Diana**) should no longer go about free (**sciolte**) and fearless but be seized by the power of love.

5   "Sonetto fatto al duca di Calavria in nome di una donna"

There are two sonnets with inscriptions naming the Duke of Calabria, Alfonso of Aragon, son of King Ferdinand of Naples, who spent a year in Florence, from August 1467 to August 1468, negotiating for the resolution of the war with Venice. It is reasonable to date these sonnets to that time. As in "Lascia l'isola tua", Lorenzo is here using a literary commonplace—the lament of the woman "sedotta e abbandonata". The arresting first lines with their detached tone are followed by an image of violation in harsh contrast with the virginal *casta*. The rhyme words *libertate/etate/pietate/beltate* punctuate the tragedy of the woman, quintessentially young, beautiful and free, but now destroyed; *pianti/amanti, bene/pene* juxtapose the two extremes of the love experience. The third line is particularly effective with its *er* and *or* repetitions in the stressed syllables, and the apocopation at the caesura of more than half the lines is in effective counterpoint with the staccato quality of each of the four units (see in part Zanato, *Saggio sul "Comento"*, p. 149). Rochon (p. 157) finds here "such profound sympathy and such a perfectly judged tone that without exaggeration this little piece deserves to be called a masterpiece". As the other sonnet for the Duke, "Tu eri poco inanzi sí felice", can be read *in chiave politica*, it is not unreasonable, as Orvieto (p. 133) suggests, to give an allegorical meaning to this powerful poem, as well as to the sonnet "Una ninfa gentil, leggiadra e bella", which has a similar theme. The lamenting woman may be either Florence or the surrounding countryside.

2   **disiunta e torta**: "[to have] torn and drawn [me away]".

6   **smorta**: past participle of *smorire* ("to go deathly pale"); here it may be an intensification of **pallida**, but the word's connotation and the fact that it rhymes with **morta** rather suggest the meaning "half-dead".

9–14   The turmoil of the woman's feelings is expressed through a set of oxymorons; death would have given her release from her pain were it not for the memory of the joy of yore.

6 In this sonnet Lorenzo uses the myth of the rose, a flower sacred to Venus, which was originally white but turned red with the blood shed by Venus when her foot was pricked by a thorn as she was running to help the dying Adonis. Poliziano rightly praises this sonnet in his *Miscellanea* (*Centuria*, I. 11), where he also tells this story, the source of which is Claudian, *De raptu Proserpinæ*, II. 122–23; but there is more here than a delicate, quasi-precious variation on the myth. Orvieto (pp. 200–01) sees an underlying theological meaning that permeates with Christian symbolism the myth of the divine goddess who fertilizes the earth, and he suggests that Dante, *Paradiso*, XXXI. 1–3 ("In forma dunque di candida rosa / mi si mostrava la milizia santa / che nel suo sangue Cristo fece sposa") may be a possible source of this feature of Lorenzo's sonnet. The white candour of purity receives the blood of Christ and the red fire of the Holy Spirit (symbolized by Venus and Love); not only are the roses white but so too is the lady's hand, and she becomes a receptacle for the blood of the Redemption, through which a new life is generated. Both the roses and the hand can be read in terms of the legend of the Holy Grail, the platter used at the Last Supper and then by Joseph of Arimathea to receive the Saviour's blood at the Cross. The earth itself undergoes regeneration through a ritual of fertility, with water ("lacrime") as the primary factor, but the water comes from tears caused by Death in Love, symbolic of the Crucifixion.

The roses speak throughout, addressing the lady, "madonna", to whom they have been given.

1, 4 **colti** is here a *rima equivoca*, cognate with the verb *coltivare* in the first line and a part of *cogliere* in the fourth.

2 **pestano**: of Pæstum, near Salerno, renowned in ancient times for its roses, as is also stated in "De rosis nascentibus", the poem that may have suggested to Lorenzo the end of *Corinto*.

6 **Adon**: Adonis was a beautiful youth with whom Venus fell in love. He was attacked by a wild boar, upon which the goddess rushed to his aid, but she was unable to save his life. Where the blood of Adonis stained the earth, myth has it that anemones sprouted. He was associated with fertility rites in the Near East. The tale is beautifully told by Ovid, *Metamorphoses*, X. 708–39.

7 **villano**: It is the sharp thorn that is "discourteous" to the foot of the goddess.

9–11 "We then placed our white petals [under her foot], so that the divine blood did not reach the ground: hence originated our deep red colour."

12   **rivi tolti a lunge**: "streams that came from distant springs". In the second tercet the roses explain that neither summer breezes nor brooks have nourished them, but rather the sighs and the tears of the love-stricken goddess.

7   A real or imaginary gift of flowers from the lady to the poet gave rise to a cycle of sonnets (which includes "Belle, fresche e purpuree viole" on p. 123) that Orvieto dates to 1473–75. This one, however, he considers (pp. 229–30) to have been written later because it shows a greater independence of its sources. The Petrarchan images and ideas that feature here are to be found in a number of sonnets in both the *Canzoniere* and the *Comento*, but it is clear that this and the accompanying poems are written in a neo-Platonist vein. The flight of the lover's heart into the beloved is a first phase of a process described by Ficino (*El libro dell'Amore*, II. 8) and called by Lorenzo "commutazione di cuori" in his commentary to sonnet xxx of the *Comento*: "Amore non è altro che una trasformazione dello amante nella cosa amata, e, quando è reciproco, di necessità ne nasce la medesima trasformazione in quello che prima ama, che diventa poi amato, per modo che maravigliosamente vivono gli amanti l'uno nell'altro: ché altro non vuole inferire questa commutazione di cuori." Words like *beata* have religious overtones, and the nurturing water/tears are associated with divine redemption, as seen in the preceding sonnet. Despite this, the repetition of various words in the poem and its phonic effects create an atmosphere of languor to which the repeated *nudo* gives a touch of sensuality. While the last line is somewhat unsuccessful, its return to the opening line gives the poem a gratifying compactness.

1   **violetta**: The *viola* and its diminutive were, for Tuscans, carnations, but some critics suggest that here the *viola del pensiero* or pansy is intended. Poliziano also wrote an elegy "In violas a Venere mea in dono acceptas", in which the flowers are nurtured by the poet's tears.

2   **il primo mio bel disio**: the woman loved by the poet.

3–4   An idea to be found elsewhere in Lorenzo; see for example the preceding sonnet in this selection.

5–6   These lines make most sense if **disio** is taken as the subject, as is often the case in similar constructions; the meaning would then be that the lady's love for the poet nurtured her **Pietate** (kindness, sensitivity to his plight; hence the fact that she shed tears) in that fortunate land where the tuft of pansies grew.

8   The poet's hand and, by extension, the poet himself, through this gift, a symbol of remembrance and kindness, attain a state of bliss.

10   **onde**: "therefore".

11   **nudo petto**: The poet's heart has fled to the lady, and desire and sorrow fill the emptiness it has left—a thought found often in Petrarch and in other sonnets by Lorenzo.

8   A neo-Platonist sonnet in which the love experience is read in transcendental terms according to Ficino's teaching that Love is born of Beauty and finds its fulfilment in union with God. The beauty to be found within our souls is a reflection of the source of all beauty, God, who in turn contemplates his own self within us. To attain this mystical union the physical, and all memory of it, have to be transcended; even sight is ultimately superseded, as the union is within the soul and there is only effulgent radiance. Man is not separate from God because, in the words of St Paul (Acts 17. 28), "in him we live and move and are."

1–4   The throng of thoughts that burden the poet vanishes at a glance from his lady's eyes (**amorose ciglia**), and in his ecstasy even hope and sensibility (**Pietà**) cease.

5–6   Dante describes a similar experience in *Vita nuova*, xv. 2; but, Orvieto notes (p. 270), "Lorenzo va oltre: nell'alienazione totale anche la memoria (e, quindi, le immagini platonicamente 'dipinte' in essa) non ha piú ragione di sopravvivere, anch' essa è 'fuggitiva'."

7–8   Everything is still and suspended in the stupefied happiness of ecstasy; this sensation is similarly described in the *Lauda* in this volume, lines 51–56.

9–14   Here again Lorenzo develops an idea from the *Vita nuova* (xiv. 5–14). The poet's emotions and faculties are hypnotized by a splendour that is divine, which both attracts and destroys. Lorenzo is describing a spiritual experience that has transcended its physical source. He no longer knows the extent to which he is dead unto himself but alive to God; this is the doubt that he wants resolved by a sensitive person (**gentil core**). The rhyme **strugge/fugge** is effectively used in two consecutive lines of a basically non-Petrarchan rhyme-scheme.

COMENTO DE' MIEI SONETTI

See Introduction pp. 41–48.

       The text is from Zanato's critical edition (in this section referred to as "*Comento*"), but to simplify matters for the reader the spelling of certain words has been modified according to Bigi's edition in Lorenzo, *Scritti scelti* ("Bigi" in what follows). "Ficino" here refers to Marsilio Ficino, *El libro dell'amore*, edited by S. Niccoli (Florence, Olschki, 1987).

PROEMIO

Zanato (*Comento*, pp. 62–64) argues for a structural change at the end of the "Proemio" as traditionally printed; he detaches the reflections on death and treats them as a separate, prefatory "Argumento". As this makes most sense, logically and textually, his suggestion has been followed. Only sections 1–16 of the "Argumento" have been included, however, as 17–28 are more narrowly related to the opening sonnets. Section 17 begins, "Morí, come di sopra dicemmo," and opens a passage about the death of the lady who inspired the first sonnets.

1   **occorrevano in contrario:** "were arguments against my writing".
2   **ripreso di poco giudicio:** "accused of not having much sense".
3   **ritrarre:** "keep [me]".
4   **di poco momento:** "of little account".
5   **importanti grandi effetti:** "that involve major matters".
6   **Aggiugnesi ancora a questo:** "let this also be added".
7   **volgare:** "vernacular", rather than its literary alternative, Latin.
8   **non pare declini** *to* **intesa:** "seems in some way inferior, and in those places where this vernacular is unknown, it cannot be understood." The contrast is, implicitly, with Latin, then an internationally understood language among scholars.
9   **a questa parte:** "from this point of view".
10   **sarà bene collocata** *to* **poca grazia:** "[inserting this into my activities] will have been worthwhile and will not have been in vain; were it to be badly received".
11   **notare:** "to accuse". Dante, too, in *Convivio*, I. 2, answers possible accusations of presumption.
12   **di nessuno** *to* **ha scritto:** "the most appropriate interpreter of his writing is the author himself." Probably as many authors believe this as critics disbelieve it.
13   **ministerio:** "occupation" or "activity".
14   **controversia:** "doubt".
15   **satisfaccino a:** "please".
16   **confortato:** "encouraged".
17   **vale assai appresso di me:** "carries much weight with me".
18   **qualche ingegno** *to* **al loro:** "they will find some opinion in keeping with, and similar to, their own."

19   **avendo io**: "that I have".

20   **nelle quali interviene minor male**: "from which results least evil" [or harm].

21   **argumento di gentilezza**: "proof of nobility". This is a concept derived from the poets of the *dolce stil novo*, who linked *gentilezza di core* directly with love. The heart that lacked such refinement, or nobility (both are imperfect translations) could not experience love.

22   **appetito di bellezza**: The view that love is born of man's desire to enjoy beauty comes from Ficino (II. 9. 1–2), who based it on Plato.

23   **quello amore**: Lorenzo is alluding to a distinction between two types of love made by Plato and elaborated by Ficino (II. 7)—heavenly and earthly love, or the two Venuses. Of the first Lorenzo wrote in *De summo bono*.

24   **tiene luogo di bene**: "it is as if it were good". Lorenzo's point is that although such love is not the ideal one it has several positive features.

25   **male possono cadere**: "are unlikely to occur".

26   **ancora che *to* bellezza**: Bigi (ad loc.) cites Ficino, VI. 2. 5: "La figura dello huomo la quale spesse volte, per la interiore bontà felicemente concessa da Dio, è nello aspecto bellissima, per gli occhi di coloro che la riguardano nel loro animo transfonde el razzo del suo splendore." The neo-Platonist concept is that physical beauty is a reflection of an inner goodness; this is blended with the idea of the *stilnovisti*, that those who behold this beauty receive some ray of that inner goodness within their own soul.

27   **che tanto più arguisce l'eccellenzia sua**: "and this [the fact that it is rare] greatly increases its value."

28   **degnificarsi**: "to make himself worthy". Bigi, ad loc., notes that the notion of the reciprocal spiritual advancement of lover and beloved would have come to Lorenzo from Ficino as well as from the *stilnovisti*.

29   **secondo la loro convenienzia**: "as is appropriate".

30   **eccitando**: "stimulating".

31   **obtrettazioni**: "accusations".

32   **Poeta**: This is Petrarch, and the line comes from the opening sonnet of his *Canzoniere*.

33   **Guido *to* medesima**: Guido Guinizelli (1240?–76) of Bologna was regarded as the founder of the *dolce stil novo* group of poets. His doctrinal poem, considered by his followers a manifesto, begins "Al cor gentil rempaira sempre Amore". Lorenzo is obviously merging it here with Dante's sonnet "Amore e 'l cor gentil sono una cosa"; **si convertino**: "converge".

34   **espettibile**: "desirable".

35   **questo appetito *to* spezie**: The concept of earthly love as natural and necessary for the continuation of the human race was outside the range of the poetry of the *stilnovisti*, but not foreign to Ficino, who wrote (II. 7. 18): "L'uno e l'altro Amore è onesto, seguitando l'uno e l'altro divina imagine."

36   occupata: "determined".

37   da una certa conformità e proporzione: "by a certain affinity and aptitude".

38   A me pare to tale obietto: "It seems to me that I have replied very fully to such a point."

39   purgare: "to justify".

40   declinare: "to depart" or "to deviate".

41   che la natura to persuadono: "that nature and the practice of men lead one to do".

42   E dato che fussi vero: "And even if it were true".

43   la fatica to a me: "it is most appropriate that I should be the one to undertake the labour of this commentary."

44   importanti: "containing".

45   In both *Vita nuova* and *Convivio*.

46   Egidio Colonna (1246–1316) was a renowned Roman theologian; Dino del Garbo (d. 1327) was a Florentine physician and philosopher.

47   The Florentine poet Guido Cavalcanti (*c*.1255–1300) was the most famous of the *stilnovisti,* Dante excepted. He is the absent son of *Inferno* X, and also the subject of *Decameron,* VI. 9. Lorenzo's favourable judgement (primo dialettico: "the most famous logician") is similar to the one expressed in the dedicatory epistle of the *Raccolta aragonese,* where Egidio Romano's commentary on "Donna me prega" is also mentioned. This complex and highly philosophical poem is a masterpiece of early Italian literature. Ficino dedicates an entire chapter (VII. 1) to Cavalcanti and this poem.

48   versi vulgari: "poetry in the vernacular".

49   importa: "contains".

50   purgazione mia: "my justification" or "the expiation of my offence".

51   Lorenzo is alluding to the Pazzi conspiracy (1478) and to the serious political unrest of the following years. He returns to these matters with moving words in his commentary on the sonnet mentioned here, X in the *Comento.* His writing was obviously vital to him.

52   per pruova: "through experience".

53   Praise of the vernacular is also to be found in the introductory epistle to the *Raccolta aragonese;* and it is worth comparing Lorenzo's spirited defence with Dante's forceful and emotional one in *Convivio,* I. 5–12.

54   alcuna cosa to comune: "the fact that something is commonly used does not diminish its worth."

55   "sommo bene": God.

56   a me pare to perfetti: "it seems to me that allowing for the diversity of human minds, which are not all well balanced and perfect".

57   **appetito**: "instinct", natural desire for something that appeals to us.

58   **inferire**: "to conclude".

59   **ancora che fussino pochi**: "few though they be".

60   **sottili e gravi**: "ingenious [or subtle] and profound".

61   **accomodati**: "suited".

62   **è necessario *to* mezzo**: "it is necessary to realize that the subject-matter is more praiseworthy than the language, because the subject-matter is the purpose [of writing] and the language only the means."

63   **chi ha scritto *to* materia**: "[if we look at the case of] those who have written on theology, metaphysics, physics and ethics, the subject-matter treated seems to be praiseworthy, and it is this, rather, that has given worth to the language used by the writers."

64   **il successo delle cose del mondo**: "the course of events".

65   **l'essere in prezzo *to* oppinione**: "that a language is held in esteem and highly rated in the world depends on the opinion".

66   **quelle condizioni *to* di quella**: "those conditions could change so that, if the reason for the esteem were no longer present, the dignity and praise [of the language] would easily be lost."

67   **orazioni**: "prose works".

68   **vi troverrà molte cose *to* si truova**: "will find many matters pertaining to theology and natural philosophy discussed with much ability and simplicity; one will also find in his writings, with no difficulty whatever, the three types of style praised by prose writers, the low, the middle and the grand; and indeed Dante accomplished single-handed what is to be found only in a range of authors, both Greek and Latin."

69   Ovid (43 BC–AD 18), famous for his *Metamorphoses* and *Ars amatoria*; Tibullus (*c.* 60–19 BC), Roman elegiac poet; Catullus (*c.* 84–*c.* 54 BC) came from Verona and is best known for a sequence of poems relating to Lesbia; Propertius (*c.* 50–*c.* 16 BC), another Latin elegiac poet, came from Umbria and the object of his infatuation was named Cynthia.

70   **ornato**: "embellishment".

71   **orazione soluta**: "prose".

72   **non solamente la invenzione, ma la copia**: "both the inventiveness and the quantity [of his writings]".

73   **ingegni**: "expedients".

74   **piú tosto essere *to* alla materia**: "there has been a shortage of men who have skilfully used the language, rather than the language having shortcomings for either men or subject-matter."

75   **muovere**: "to persuade" or "to rouse emotion".

76   The most famous fifteenth-century commentator on Dante's *Commedia* was Cristoforo Landino. His interpretation was fundamentally neo-Platonist as he viewed poetry as a source of divine wisdom. Zanato (*Saggio*

sul "Comento", p. 28) comments that here Lorenzo "rende palese riconosci-
mento al lavoro del Landino, quasi un pubblico ringraziamento al vecchio
maestro e una aperta personale ammissione dei propri debiti verso di lui."

77   **allegazioni:** "quotations".

78   **augumento al fiorentino imperio:** Lorenzo establishes a link
between linguistic development and political and economic expansion; he
obviously foresaw and willed such expansion for Florence.

79   **che ne sono in onore e in prezzo:** "who are now held in honour
and esteem".

80   **dimostro** = *dimostrato.*

81   **qualche proprietà:** "the particular".

82   **o al ternario** *to* **difficile:** "to that of [poems in] *terza rima*, to the
canzone or to any other metrical form in the vernacular, basing my argument on its [the sonnet's] difficulty: because the excellence of the achievement, according to philosophical opinion, is related to the complexity of
the task." Bigi (ad loc.) cites Plato's *Republic* (II. 364*a*) and *Laws* (IV. 718*e*),
where Plato cites Hesiod, an early Greek poet. The *canzone* is the most
illustrious Italian metrical form, and has a highly elaborate structure.

83   **sentenzia:** "opinion", but in the remainder of this section it is
better rendered as "concept".

84   **eroico:** "epic".

85   **sanza vizio di chi scrive:** "without some failure on the part of the
writer".

86   **molle e lascive:** "futile and wanton".

87   **è grande differenzia** *to* **sforzi le rime:** "there is a big difference
between composing sonnets where the thoughts are constrained by the
requirements of the rhymes, and sonnets where the rhymes naturally fit
the thoughts expressed."

88   **degno d'essere in prezzo:** "worthy of being held in esteem". The
supreme master of the *canzone* is Dante, and he asserted the superiority of
this form over the sonnet in *De vulgari eloquentia*, II. 3–4. Lorenzo, on the
other hand, wrote very few *canzoni*, and it is obvious from the feelings
strongly expressed here that writing sonnets was headache enough.

89   **Fetonte:** Ovid ends the story of Phæthon, whose father was the
sun, with the burial of his body by Italian nymphs. They wrote on his tomb:
"Here Phæthon lies: his father's car he tried—/Though proved too weak,
he greatly daring died" (*Metamorphoses*, II. 327–28, translated by M. M.
Innes [Harmondsworth, Penguin, 1955]). Applying this to himself, Lorenzo
pleads that he be given credit at least for trying, though he may not reach
perfection.

90   **carro solare:** the chariot of the sun is here, metaphorically, the
writing of sonnets.

91   **assoluta:** "having accomplished".

92   **argumento:** "explanation".

93   *prima facie*: (Latin) "on the face of it", "at first glance".

94   **una donna**: The Genoese Simonetta Cattaneo (*c.* 1453–76), wife of the Florentine Marco di Piero Vespucci, was much celebrated in the poetry of Poliziano and allegedly loved by both Giuliano and Lorenzo de' Medici. Many contemporary Tuscan poets lamented her death, among them Lorenzo, who here states that this sad event "wrung" (**estorse**) from him sonnets in her memory.

95   **corruzione**: "destruction". Lorenzo's main point here is that matter is immortal and constantly undergoes a process of transformation (**si muova sopra la materia**). His authority for this is mainly Ficino (*Theologia platonica*, IV).

96   **un male**: Martelli's suggestion, on the basis of sense, that this should read *uno [corpo] mortale* demands serious attention; it is not out of evil that a new beginning comes. Martelli writes: "Lorenzo accenna qui brevemente all'incessante trasmigrazione della forma della materia, donde ha origine la morte della cosa da cui la forma si allontana e la generazione della cosa in cui la forma si trasferisce e da cui dà vita. Né il male si può ritenere che risulti di materia e forma!" ("Per l'edizione del *Comento*", p. 71).

97   **secondo Aristotile, la privazione è principio delle cose create**: The reference is to *Physics*, I. 9, and the meaning here is that things are created because there is a need for their existence; **privazione**: "lack".

98   *immediate*: (Latin) "immediately".

99   **convenientemente**: "appropriately".

100   **chi vive ad amore** *to* **cose**: Bigi (ad loc.) quotes Ficino, II. 8. 5, who in turn cites Plato's view that the lover, because he is so absorbed in the beloved, is dead to all concerns and feelings for himself. It is in this sense— that love for another begins when love for the self dies—that we are to understand Lorenzo's **troverrà il principio dell'amorosa vita procedere dalla morte**. The quotation from Plato, as given by Ficino (II. 8. 2), is: "quello amatore è uno animo nel proprio corpo morto, nel corpo d'altri vivo."

101   Ulysses's journey to the Underworld is narrated in *Odyssey* XI, and that of Æneas, in *Æneid* VI. Lorenzo is interpreting these journeys as symbols of dying to oneself in order to be reborn to a better life.

102   **perlustra**: "explores".

103   **fussi rivoltosi** = *si fosse rivolto*. Lorenzo interprets the backward glance cast by Orpheus to the Underworld as a sign that he had not totally rejected a life of imperfection and erring; therefore he could not fully reach (**aggiunto**) the perfection of happiness which was the possession of Eurydice. Writing on "Il mito d'Orfeo nell'età laurenziana", *Interpres*, 8 (1988), 7–40 (p. 21), Mario Martelli links Eurydice to the dead Simonetta, who thus becomes, "nella storia dell'*itinerarium mentis in Deum* che impegna Lorenzo, un gradino intermedio—quello della ragione o della vita attiva—tra la concupiscenza sensuale e, almeno nella misura in cui all'uomo è concesso

di sperimentarla in terra, la vita contemplativa; ed è necessario, per arrivare alla perfezione di quest' ultima, morire alla relativa imperfezione di quella che la precede."

The four poems here selected, from a total of forty-one (but Lorenzo intended at least two more to be included), are perfectly regular Petrarchan sonnets rhyming ABBA ABBA CDE CDE. They are numbered 16, 19, 21 and 33 in Bigi and in *Comento*; and CI, CIII, CV, CIX in Zanato's edition of the *Canzoniere*.

1   The theme of the gift of flowers is found in the sonnets "Quella virtú che t'ha prodotto et ale", "Le fronde giovinette gli arbuscelli" and "O bella violetta, tu se' nata" in the *Canzoniere*. Both this last sonnet and the one under discussion show a strong resemblance in theme and images to "Quel beato licor" by Buonaccorso da Montemagno (1391/93–1429), a poem included in the *Raccolta aragonese*. In his prose commentary in the *Comento*, Lorenzo writes of the unbearable grief that overcame him because he could not see his lady for a long period of time; to ease his suffering she sent him three carnations picked from a pot in which she herself grew these flowers. In the sonnet he ponders on the "cagione di tanta eccellenzia" of the flowers, and concludes that it is no natural cause but rather "la virtú e potenzia di quella candidissima mano". This can enhance the flowers beyond measure as it infused nobility into his uncouth heart, by which Lorenzo means that the lady has made his heart capable of the experience of love, an experience essential for the fulfilment of one's natural end. Were the flowers really so exceptionally beautiful?, he wonders; and he adds that perhaps he perceived them to be so in a quasi-ecstatic state, "imperocché gran potenzia ha ne' sensi la immaginazione." Inexplicable wonders happen through the special gifts possessed by some human beings. The concept of the supernatural and healing power of the lady is fundamental to the poetry of the *stilnovisti*, but Lorenzo is moving towards the tenets of neo-Platonist belief when he states that his lady's beauty was the prime mover of his love. In the poem he creates "un sottile equilibrio fra la vaga sensualità e la spiritualizzazione dell'esperienza erotica", which Francesco Tateo finds not just in this sonnet, but in the others inspired by the extraordinary power of the lady's hand (*Lorenzo de' Medici e Angelo Poliziano* [Bari, Laterza, 1972], p. 38). "Candida, bella e delicata mano" (*Comento*, XIII) is another case in point.

It is clear from a rubric in the text, identified by Zanato (*Comento*, p. 124), that this sonnet and the next one were inspired by Lucrezia Donati.

1   **viole**: here, "carnations".

2   **candidissima**: superlative of *candida*, which has strong religious connotations.

3   **volse** = *volle*.

4   "flowers much more beautiful than is their wont".

8   **che *to* vuole**: "which wants to bestow upon you such delight" (namely, the scent).

10   **eri**: *eravate*.

12   The antecedent of **Quella** is the hand of the lady in the previous tercet.

13   **a cui siate consorte**: "whose fate you share", because the flowers, like the poet's heart, have been ennobled by the lady's touch.

2   The prose commentary that follows this sonnet renders forcefully the depth of the poet's anguish during his sleepless nights. From this and other striking descriptions of sleeplessness (compare *Ambra*, 6) one can infer that Lorenzo must have had first-hand knowledge of this condition, in his case caused no doubt by both physical and emotional distress. In his commentary the poet writes that bodily sickness gets worse at night and the same happens to the "infermità dell'animo nostro". Melancholy overcomes us in the depth of the night, generating gloomy thoughts from which we cannot distract ourselves, as we would by day with our other activities. He lay awake and the vexation of his thoughts was due either to jealousy, a feeling that assails the melancholic personality despite there being no ground for it, or to a "grandissima passione" overcoming him as he thought of his lady's beauty. He beseeched "i sospiri che nascevono dallo acceso desiderio", as well as his thoughts, forever fixed on his lady, and his tearful eyes, to give him some respite. To awaken sympathy for his plight he pointed out to them that men and animals rest at night while he was still awake when dawn, Aurora (**la scorta**), drives the sun-god (**febei raggi**) from the east into the heavens on her horse-drawn chariot. The poet realized that "la cagione vera del male mio, quella che moveva le lacrime ed i sospiri ed i pensieri, era Amore", and so he turned to

this god begging for a truce, a lesser demand than peace because peace is everlasting while a truce is only temporary. In order that the request be granted, the poet promised to remain in the bondage of love even while asleep, as his dreams would be filled only by his lady. Such a promise was easy because "ne' sonni si veggono quelle cose che piú s'immaginono e desiderono nella vigilia." But Love is "invidioso", ends the poet, "poiché d'una falsa e brevissima dolcezza non consentiva satisfarmi."

Although the contrast between the poet's plight and the peace enjoyed by the other creatures of the earth is commonplace, this sonnet strikes an original note and has rightly been judged to be "fra i piú misurati ed armoniosi di Lorenzo" (Tateo, *Lorenzo de' Medici e Angelo Poliziano*, p. 43). Certain key words are repeated— *pensier, viso, sonno, Amor, bianco, remissi/missi*—, and "questi vocaboli fanno da trama alla delicata implorazione, e sono infatti i piú pregnanti del componimento, quasi che Lorenzo, nello stendere i versi, fosse stato spinto dalla necessità di liberare (e liberarsi di) un nucleo di parole aggirantisi nella sua mente, insistenti, simili a una manciata di accordi musicali da ripetere, variati, per tutta la testura fonica del sonetto" (Zanato, *Saggio sul "Comento"*, p. 142). The effective combination of nasal and liquid consonants, alliterative sounds and stressed sibilants in the final line leaves it hauntingly in our memories, and this is also the case with several other lines. It should be noted that Lorenzo makes extensive use of the Petrarchan technique of apocopation at the caesura of the hendecasyllable, which adds to the musicality of the line.

1–2   The opening is reminiscent of Petrarch's "Datemi pace, o duri miei pensieri" (CCLXXIV), and these lines also recall his CCCXVIII. 10: "Li alti pensieri e i miei sospiri ardenti".

5   **urgenti:** "pressing", "worrisome".

6   **remissi:** "put aside".

3   While there are verbal links with Poliziano's *Stanze*, I. 17, 37, 53, 55, and while one can accurately point to two of Petrarch's sonnets (x and CCLIX) for a certain similarity of feeling, as well as finding other Petrarchan echoes ("pensier' vaghi e pronti", for example, comes from the opening line of CLXI), Zanato (*Saggio sul "Comento"*, p. 152) draws attention to certain stylistic features in this well-known sonnet that are a mark of Lorenzo's originality: "l'endecasillabo dattilico (v.12), gli accenti ripercossi, di 6ª–7ª (vv.

3–4), il verso uniformemente *a minore* nelle terzine." He also notes "l'iterazione dei termini *pensier* (vv. 4–12), *mille* (v. 4: bis), *bello* (vv. 5–13), *alti* (vv. 1, 9), [...] la percussione timbrica prodotta dalle apocopi in cesura (vv. 1, 3, 4, 5)", the structure with quatrains and tercets as independent units, juxtaposed rather than blended together. All these features make for a musicality quite different from Petrarch's, with "accenti piú cantabili e battenti, andamento piú elementare". Lorenzo's paraphrase of the opening quatrain states that he is referring, with "parole grandi e magnifiche", to the ambitious who seek public honours, and to the pursuers of sensual pleasures or wealth, "perché l'appetito nostro solamente circa queste tre cose si estende, cioè ambizione, voluttà corporale e avarizia, perché l'onore, il piacere e l'utile impedisce ogni altra nostra operazione." Our thoughts of love flourish in very different circumstances, which he describes with "cose piccole e chiamate per vocabuli diminutivi". Solitude induces peace of mind and our thoughts will lose themselves in imagining what they desire and love most; in the poet's case this was "gli occhi della donna mia, come se vedessi lei viva e vera". He concludes in a neo-Platonist vein "che la dolcezza della immaginazione ha qualche similitudine colla vera beatitudine", that is, the state of the immortal soul in its contemplation of divine goodness. Despite the fact that our human state limits our contemplation, its object is "la vera perfezione e bontà, secondo che si può conseguire nella mortale vita". From love, therefore, springs the highest, albeit limited, spiritual experience possible to us.

Both the sonnet and the second half of the explanatory prose passage bear a strong resemblance to the opening *capitolo* of *De summo bono*, and can be directly related to the dispute on true happiness that was fundamental in both Lorenzo and Ficino. The tripartite division of the force that attracts man, quoted above, seems to have derived from Cristoforo Landino. Besides the obvious *Disputationes camaldulenses*, one could give several citations from his writings, but the most concise is his comment on the symbolic representation of this force, Dante's three beasts: "Adonque l'huomo il qual di sua natura ama la virtú [...] sempre procederebbe per diritta via se tre cose non lo impediscono: queste sono piacere utile et honore"—Lorenzo's precise words. The link with Landino is discussed by Zanato (*Saggio sul "Comento"*, pp. 89, 289–90) and remains valid, though this scholar's initial use of it—to date Sonnet xxi and its prose commentary to the latter part of 1473—is inconsistent with his most recent findings on chronology (*Comento*, pp. 123–29).

3   **Quale accompagni**: This is singular like the initial **chi**, but in English one would prefer a plural construction, such as: "let those who care [for such things] pursue [...] and they will be accompanied by [...]."

5–11   **acqueta** is the main verb, but although it is singular its subjects range from **praticel** to **ninfa**. All these features of the rural scene appease the poet's yearning much more; **fugitive**: "wild"; **paurosa**: Nymphs are traditionally so described as they flee from pursuing satyrs.

12–14   **Quivi**: in the country; **qui**: in the city, evoked in the opening lines, though it is not where the poet was in fact writing, according to his own comment: "Bisogna nel presente sonetto presupporre che fussi composto nella città"; **luci**: "eyes" [of his beloved].

4   The identification of the beloved with the rebirth of nature, and the attribution to her of supernatural capacities that create an atmosphere of harmony and peace, have classical antecedents but were also very much hallmarks of the poetry of the *stilnovisti*, which is imbued, too, with a sense of awe that overcomes the poet and prevents his doing justice to the wonder of the vision. Some of this comes to Lorenzo filtered, inevitably, through Petrarch (CXLII, CLXV, CCCXXV, CCCX), but Cavalcanti is probably the primary influence. Lorenzo himself has a similar scene in *Corinto*, lines 67–78. In the prose commentary accompanying this sonnet he acknowledges Ovid when writing of the progression from the lady's glance to her touch: "Sono adunque comprese nel presente sonetto quelle linee, cioè gradi di amore, che pone Ovidio, poeta ingeniosissimo, in quel libro [*Ars amatoria*] ove dà gli amorosi precetti." But he infuses a vitality of his own into this long tradition, as one can see both from this poem and from *Stanze*, I. 19–38. The awakening of the nymphs to the power of love is mentioned by Lorenzo in his commentary as being his lady's "piú maravigliosa operazione [...]. Perché, ancora che sieno grandi effetti far germinare la terra, cantare li uccelli e vestire li arbori di fronde, queste sono tutte cose naturali; ma mettere una impressione contraria in uno subietto è maggiore cosa, come è fare che le ninfe timide e caste, ammettino nella durezza del cuore loro qualche molle e dolce pensiero d'amore: perché l'amore è al tutto contrario alla timidità e castità." About a third of the prose commentary is given over to reflections on harmony, which indicates that Lorenzo himself associated this with the atmosphere

created by the sonnet, one of primordial love that generates life and order in nature; but his discussion of Plato's tripartite division of music into "il parlare, armonia e ritmo" (the latter he takes to mean poetry) is indicative once again of how strong the association between poetry and music was for him. A fine tuning of Lorenzo's techniques went into the making of this successful sonnet: alliteration, apocopation at the caesura and repetition, to which Zanato (*Saggio sul "Comento"*, p. 196) adds "una fitta trama di vocaboli rari (che compaiono infatti solo qui e in nessun altro sonetto del *Comento*): *cantar* [...], *uccelli* [...], *infonde, basti, abonde* (tutti in rima), *secchi, timide, casti, molle.*"

2 **Flora**: Italian goddess of spring and flowers.

9–11 A smile or sigh from the lady's beautiful lips can turn the timid nymphs to thoughts of love. Zanato (*Saggio sul "Comento"*, p. 192) suggests a connection with Ovid, *Heroides*, XIII. 30.

12–14 "At this point neither words nor thoughts are adequate fully to understand the extent and the nature of the grace that is amply infused into all that is touched by her snow-white hand"; both **candida** and obviously **grazia** have religious overtones.

CORINTO

See Introduction pp. 48–52.

In this section "Maier" refers to Maier, *Lettura critica del "Corinto"*. Our text is from Lorenzo, *Scritti scelti*, with modifications from Martelli, "Per la storia redazionale del *Corinto*" ("Martelli").

1 The moonlit scene provides a setting for Corinto's outpourings that is different from the traditional bucolic one of daylight, usually with sunshine (in both Theocritus and Virgil), and is closer to Horace, *Epodes*, XV.

1–2: "Nox erat et cælo fulgebat luna sereno/inter minora sidera"—with which there are obvious verbal similarities.

2 **ciel quieto**: in marked contrast with Corinto, who is denied **quiete alcuna** (11).

4–5 In these two lines there is grammatical inconsistency between singular and plural as Lorenzo uses part of a *terzina* by Dante (*Inferno*, II. 1–2). Both **terreno** and **sciolti** refer to animal.

8 **Galatea**: one of the Sicilian nereids whose story is told by Theocritus in *Idylls* XI and by many poets after him. The story of her love for Acis, who was murdered by the jealous Polyphemus, has also appealed to painters. There is thus no originality in Lorenzo's choice of name.

10–18 **soletto** (11), **dispetto** (13) and **poveretto** (15) belong to the vo-

cabulary of popular poetry, while **luci lacrimose** (10) and **stellato ammanto** (18) belong to a higher stylistic register usually called *aulico*. Corinto
frequently alternates between the two, expressing himself as both the
rustic farmer and the refined poet.

19   **ben pasciuti armenti**: In Corinto's words there is not only a
contrast between the peace of the animals and his anguish but the implication that they, at ease, can eat, which is impossible for him in his state of de-
spondency.

21   **pallenti**: "pale" because the shoots are young and tender.

26   "my pleas and words are planted in the shade" and thus do not
bear fruit (have effect).

28   The subject of **fugge** is Galatea, who flees from her lover's gaze
but never leaves his thoughts. This is a Petrarchan situation, on which
Maier (p. 69) writes: "Anche Lorenzo accetta la sottile distinzione petrarchesca tra il corpo prigioniero della realtà fisico-naturale ed il pensiero che
segue a suo agio, costantemente la donna amata." The rhyme **fugge/
strugge**, dear to Lorenzo, is also to be found in Petrarch.

32–33   **Diana**: perhaps originally a spirit of the woods, this goddess was
worshipped especially by women; she was depicted as a virgin huntress
and was seen as a personification of chastity. She was later associated with
Artemis, hence the characteristic of moon goddess; **impero**: "rule". **Tre
lustri**: "fifteen years"; Lucrezia's commitment to Diana (chastity) was
about to end in marriage.

34   **aita** ("help") and (36) **lasso** ("woe") will be recognized as stock-
in-trade of love poetry.

37–42   There is heavy and unsuccessful borrowing from Virgil, *Eclogues*,
VIII. 69–71 (translated by E. V. Rieu [Penguin, Harmondsworth, 1972], p.
97): "Spells can pull down the Moon herself from heaven. Circe with spells
transformed Odysseus' men. Sing the right spell and you can blast the
clammy snakes that live in the fields." Firstly, there is Lorenzo's mistrans-
lation of *carmina*, which for Virgil are magic formulæ and not poems (poetic
utterances are not likely to move the moon from heaven to earth); secondly,
itaca gente and **fère** are too Latinate for the context, and make even the
well-known story of Circe sound affected and erudite.

46–54   As the wind rustling in the trees carries the name of Galatea to her
lover, he hopes that it will convey to her his lament, which Echo will double
(**gemina**). Ovid, in *Metamorphoses*, III. 369, uses the same verb (*ingeminat*)
for Echo's repetition of the words of Narcissus. Ovid's story (lines 339–510)
of the beautiful youth who fell in love with his own image reflected in water
and pined away in unattainable self-love is drawn on by Lorenzo in 101–10.
There is an unsuccessful mixture of images in 54 regarded by Maier (p. 25)
as a "frutto, probabilmente, di esigenze di rima".

62   **lento**: "pliant". Corinto would make a pipe from the pliant bark
of a willow so that Galatea could then sing to his music.

64   **un tralcio:** "vine leaves". It was the practice of the Bacchantes (female followers of Bacchus, god of wine but originally of fertility) to tie their hair with vine leaves. A lively note, which began in the preceding *terzina* and evokes Vallera's Nencia, is developed in this fantasy of song and dance, though 66 has a weak ending.

69   The rain of flowers on the beloved is quite a Petrarchan scene, but the beloved's smile (71) having the power to bring forth new flowers from the earth takes us back further, to the *dolce stil novo*. Earlier still, in classical poetry, we find the notion of the loved one giving life to nature through her presence, in a rite of spring and fertility. The use of rhyming diminutives in lines 74–78 (**fioretti/ruscelletti/augelletti**) creates a spring scene with an awakening of nature and its creatures. Lorenzo comments on his use of diminutives in his *paraphrasis* to *Comento*, xxi, where he says that the small things of nature "debbono inducere piú tranquilli e queti pensieri".

87   **di sotto:** "below", that is, where Galatea is hidden, and at the point where he will encounter the wild boar.

91   **fère venenose o il balzo:** "poisonous beasts [snakes] or a crag", meaning generally rough and rocky terrain.

93   "Imagining myself in your situation (**per te**), I pointlessly move my feet and raise them to avoid certain hazards."

94–96   "Like someone who has released a swift arrow towards a target and twists his head as soon as he has done so in an effort to straighten the course of the arrow; but it is now far away from the bow [**curvo legno**]"; a cumbersome simile that diminishes the exquisite delicacy of the concern Corinto expressed in the preceding lines.

98–99   Galatea is so light and swift that she could run across waves without wetting her feet. This anticipates *Ambra* (32), where the nymph could run over ears of corn without bending them under her weight. Both nymphs recall Virgil's warrior-maiden Camilla: "She might have skimmed over the tops of uncut corn-stalks without ever harming their delicate ears as she ran, or upheld her way through the midst of the sea supported on heaving waves without once wetting her swift foot-soles in its surface" (*Æneid*, vii. 806–11, translated by W. F. Jackson Knight [Penguin, Harmondsworth, 1956], p. 200).

104   "when the water's movement (**tempesta**) that you caused [when washing your face] was stilled (**queta**)".

107–08   Corinto rushes to the water in the expectation of finding Galatea's reflection still there. Martelli (p. 236) links this "singolare fantasia" to lines 432–36 of the Narcissus story (see note to 46–54, above).

111   "not be rebuked [for self-importance] in asking for you", meaning "for your love". Corinto, up to 135, prides himself on his strength, physique and rugged outdoor complexion. For this there are many literary antecedents, the closest to Lorenzo's text being Theocritus, *Idylls* vi and xi (the self-appraisal of Polyphemus for the benefit of Galatea); in Ovid's

Metamorphoses, XIII. 840–52 Polyphemus begins: "Recently I saw my reflection in clear water, and I liked the look of myself. See how big I am." There is a lively, almost comic, dimension to Corinto with his tendency to hyperbole that dissociates him from literary models; indeed he is at his weakest when he echoes their language and uses their images. Maier (p. 37) describes him as a "rozzo e focoso amatore, tratteggiato da Lorenzo in maniera realistica, con una sugosa, plastica e corpulenta evidenza di segni".

123   **appiccando con le man:** "gropingly".

125   **sentími:** [the she-bear] "heard me".

130   **Alle braccia:** "in wrestling".

131   **Pana:** Pan, Greek god of flocks and shepherds.

132   **la reda:** "her heir", the young calf.

133–35   **a terra piana:** "right down to the ground". Corinto's words must be taken with the proverbial grain of salt: a ram with *four* horns?

136–37   **se ne scorna** = *si offende.* Neifile loves Corinto but he neglects her because of his love for Galatea. Neifile will be recognized as the name of one of the seven female storytellers of Boccaccio's *Decameron,* though it is more the Boccaccio of the *Ninfale fiesolano* that is evoked here. Corinto uses a psychological ploy in attempting to soften Galatea's resistance by arousing jealousy in her.

139ff   Corinto's pride in his wealth also belongs to the literary tradition; nonetheless he reveals a humorous awareness of his own exaggeration that adds lightness to the lines, drawing them away from too serious a lament for Galatea's rejection of him.

149–50   **ambrosia** was the food of the gods, hence the reference to a Jove (Jupiter) who has a touch of the "goloso, villereccio e rusticano" (Maier, p. 40). The honey is sweeter than sugar-beet, which was grown in Sicily, having been brought there by the Arabs in medieval times.

153   **nove:** "strange".

155   **Filomena:** The gruesome story of Philomela, Procne and Tereus is told in Ovid, *Metamorphoses,* VI. 412–674; they were turned into nightingale, swallow and hoopoe, respectively. Here, presumably, Philomela is lamenting the cruelty of Tereus; but the comparison Tereus/Galatea is unsustainable given the measure of his evil. **Questo** (157) refers to Filomena as nightingale (*usignolo*), hence the masculine.

161   **viva morte:** a Petrarchan oxymoron—see, for example, CXXXII (but the idea is quite pervasive in Petrarch's poetry). Here the contrast adds emphasis to **ridi** and **pianto** of 159.

165   **scorto:** "clearly".

167   **vaghe ciglie:** "wandering eyes".

THE ENDING ACCORDING TO EARLIER EDITIONS

184   **allegano:** "take shape".
188–89   **a pena** *to* **addossano:** [the branches] "have difficulty bearing the
weight of the growing fruits and every now and again have to take on more
weight."

AMBRA

See Introduction pp. 52–56.

In this section "Bessi" refers to her edition of *Ambra*, the text of
which is here reproduced, though with orthographical changes
drawn from Lorenzo, *Scritti scelti* ("Bigi" hereafter). Bessi incorpo-
rates a thorough investigation of literary echoes and possible
sources, but it would burden the present notes unduly were constant reference made to Dante, Petrarch, Ovid and Virgil; Bessi
herself (p. 128) excludes them from her index because "esplici-
tamente o implicitamente, ricorrono in pratica in ogni pagina del
commento." Suffice it to mention as subtext for the first 18 octaves
Dante's *rima petrosa* "Io son venuto al punto de la rota", which in
turn has links with a medieval Latin poem, "De ramis cadunt folia",
and with Arnaut Daniel's "Quan chai la fuelha". Dante contrasts
iciness in nature with the intensity of his love, and describes winter
in terms of five sciences: astronomy, meteorology, zoology, botany
and geology (see *Dante's Lyric Poetry*, edited by K. Foster and P.
Boyde, 2 vols [Oxford, Clarendon Press, 1967], II, 258–68). As well
as the winter setting, *Ambra* shares with "Io son venuto" the theme
of the intensity of passion, frustrated and unappeased.

1   **1–2:** The season that has fled is autumn. For linguistic and
thematic links with the end of *Corinto* see the Introduction; **i pochi paion
molti:** "the few [hunters] seem many" because they make a lot of noise
walking in the woods, and the leaves rustle underfoot. This also applies to
the wild beasts mentioned in the next two lines; **vaghe:** "roaming"—
qualifies **orme** but the sense relates it to the animals. (This is an example of
hypallage, a figure of speech in which the natural relationship between
words is reversed.)

2   With the laurel (**lieto:** "luxuriant") begins the list of evergreens
that is in marked contrast with the opening stanza and its emphasis on the
shedding of leaves. **Ciprigna:** "of Cyprus", where the worship of Venus
became prevalent—hence, Venus herself. The tree sacred to her was the

myrtle. Coherence is given to this poem by the strong mythological element that runs through both the description of winter and the story of Ombrone's love and Ambra's metamorphosis; **umil**: "low-growing". It is often obvious from Lorenzo's details of outdoor life that he had first-hand experience of what he describes. The sharp leaves of the juniper will not prick one's hand if carefully plucked.

3   **1–2: uliva** is common in early Italian for the olive-tree. The olive groves, depending on the direction of the wind, seem dark green or silvery white; this detail adds a vivid note to what could otherwise be considered a canonical list; **nereidi, tritoni**: Nereids were beautiful sea-maidens and daughters of Nereus; tritons were sea-deities or imaginary sea-monsters. Infelicitous here, because it is too precious and obscure, is the rhyme **mostri** (verbal adjective of *mostrare*) used in *rima equivoca*—the same spelling with different meanings—with the noun meaning "monsters". Dante uses this type of rhyme to great effect in his *canzone* "Io son venuto". Lorenzo's use of it in Octave 27 is more successful.

4   **1–2:** "Night has fought for supremacy and prevailed over the short day, which it holds prisoner." Here the meaning extends beyond the usual one of night taking over at the end of the day, to the fact that in winter the days are considerably shorter than the nights. Night remains the subject of the next two lines. See also *Stanze*, I. 97; **eterne fiamme**: the sphere of fire according to the Ptolemaic system. This system, named after Ptolemy, a geographer and astronomer who died in 168 AD, was the system of Plato and Aristotle, and dominated science until the century after Lorenzo. It took the earth's position as the centre of the universe, with heavenly bodies revolving round it. **5–6:** "[the starry chariot of the night] does not arise until the beautiful golden one of the sun is immersed in the ocean"; **7–8:** There is conflict between Orion, the mythical hunter, transformed into a large constellation to be seen in winter, and Phœbus, identified with the sun.

5   **vigilie, escubie**: virtual synonyms, "night watches and shifts"; **7–8:** "the one who wakens ill and poor enjoys [in his dreams] good health and wealth."

6   **3–4:** "if he is smitten by a strong and sweet desire which the next day promises him [as a real possibility]"; **8:** All centuries have one hundred years, but the expression is effective if tautological. See *Comento*, XIX ("Datemi pace omai, sospiri ardenti", on p. 124) for the theme of restless sleep contained in this octave.

7   The octave opens with an example of anaphora, the repetition of the start of the preceding octave, in which the poet has sympathized with the insomniac, whereas here he sympathizes with the seafarer, whose winter journeys are full of hazards. The yearning for dawn is expressed as a call to its goddess, Aurora, sleeping in the arms of her old husband

Tithonus; **7–8**: "[The seafarer] sadly counts the slow steps of sluggish night, yearning for [daybreak]."

8   **6**: The moulting season precedes winter, hence the birds have renewed their plumage; **deposto**: "ceased"; **alquanto**: In fifteenth-century Florentine this adverb may mean *un po'* or *assai*. It is difficult to establish which is meant here, as also at 22. 3 and 34. 8.

9   **1–4**: The migration of cranes is often used in poetry to typify the onset of winter, going back as far as Homer and Hesiod. There is a shift in the gender of **gru**, which in line 1 is masculine; this feature reappears in 10. **4–5**. The sense is that as the birds move forward the last one rests its head on the tail of the preceding bird, following on an ever-moving track (but for textual problems in these lines see Bessi, p. 118); **leggier**: here, and at 35. 8, "swift".

10   **6–8**: The eagle is sacred to Jupiter (Jove); Ganymede was borne to heaven by Jupiter's eagle to become his cupbearer, but according to some writers he was seized by Jupiter himself in the shape of an eagle. It is this version of the myth that Poliziano uses in *Stanze*, I. 107 (Bessi, p. 79). The crane caught by the rapacious bird will have no such happy fate.

11   **Zeffiro** (Zephyr) is the personification of the west wind of spring-time, and **Flora** is the Roman goddess of flowers. The two are associated with an eternal spring of love, hence the reference to Cyprus; **gialla**: "golden [with sunlight]"; **Borea**: Boreas was the cold sharp north wind in Greek mythology, called Aquilo in Latin, so in effect the two are one, as is implied by the two singular verbs that follow; **ghiaccio** is the subject of **incristalla**: "the ice congeals the running querulous water"; **ambra aurea**: Amber is a golden yellow fossil resin that is transparent, hence the appropriateness of the simile. Although the nymph does not yet feature in the poem, this homonym prepares us for her presence; the insect is trapped and frozen in death as will be Ambra's fate. For a link between this octave and Lorenzo's "Dolci pensier', non vi partite ancora!" see A. Schiavo Lena, *La poesia mitologica nei secoli XIV, XV e XVI* (Caltagirone, Scuto, 1907), p. 15.

12   Mount Morello, being NW of Florence (**il gentil fior**), protects the city from the mistral (**Cauro**). The mountain is personified, hence the hoary head (= snow-covered summit) and white hair (= snow-covered trees) falling on the white (**candenti**) shoulders (= slopes); the beard of this old man of the mountain is solid with ice, and a frozen waterfall gives shape to his eyes and nose.

13   **Noto** (Notus, the humid south wind) increases the rain-dense clouds that cover the upper slopes, but these are dispersed by Boreas. Notus persists (appropriately, with wings that are **umide**; they are **maligne** in so far as, by bringing storms, they cause damage), and more mists cover the mountain. Morello, at the mercy of either Notus or Boreas, threatens the plain with rain or snow.

14   **1–3**: "The warm **Austro** [Latin Auster, another name for Notus, better known as *scirocco*] leaves Ethiopia blackened (**tinto**, with grey clouds) and, as he releases rain (**intinto**) into the Tyrrhenian Sea, he satisfies the thirsty sponges"; **stringe poi ambo le pugne**: "he squeezes both fists" thereby releasing heavy rains, friendly (**acque amiche**) to the happy rivers. This is the beginning of the flood.

15   The rivers are the subject of 1–4. The Ocean (Oceanus) was, for the ancient Greeks, a river supposed to encircle the earth, and was personified as parent of the world's rivers. The spirit believed to inhabit a river was often portrayed with a crown of reeds and a hunting horn. Here **ulva** is seaweed or related freshwater plants; mythological depiction aside, the river's waters, as they swell and gather momentum, carry vegetation with them (**fronde fluvial**). The horn, as well as fertility, may symbolize the tortuous course of the river (Bigi, p. 515). While **superbo** carries the meaning of haughty, in *Ambra* it is used of the rivers (see also 19. 2, 23. 2, 24. 7, 36. 4), and always in a context that makes Bessi's gloss "gonfio di acque" appropriate (p. 84). The overflowing of the rivers is depicted as their disdain, nurtured (**conceputo**) for several days, unleashing itself (**s'adempie**) against the frightened (**timide**) banks; **7**: A plural verb is intended—"the frothing [rivers] have broken [the resistance of] the enemy bank."

16   **1–3**: The rivers make haste (**sollecitan**) towards the sea (the **padre antico,** as in the previous octave), but do not follow their usual course, which is tortuous (**oblico**) like many coiling snakes; **i lontan fiumi**: The literary substratum in this section is such that Bessi writes: "dietro ai fiumi toscani par bene [...] di scorgere il Danubio, il Reno, il Rodano [...] e, perché no? il Gange e l'Istro..." (pp. 84–85). The garrulity of the rivers as they fail to find their outlet to the sea (**foce**) is less than successful.

17   The river, though really intended as plural, is the subject of **ristrigne** ("narrows"), **pigne** ("shoves"), **gira** ("lashes") and **freme** ("seethes"); the waters are strident because they are restrained (**frenate**) by the banks; **calle** originally meant tracks made by animals through fields or woods etc.; **sicur,** of the shepherd, means safe, as he is viewing the scene from on high. Because of the dearth of Scriptural echoes in a poem outstanding for its classical ones, it is worth noting the syntagma **pietre sopra pietre**, as in Matthew 24. 2, Mark 13. 2, and Luke 21. 6 (Bessi, p. 85).

18   The octave compares the flooding river forcing its way through mountain gorges to the volcanic phenomenon of fumaroles in the area of Volterra (SW of Florence). The earth, fiery (**adusta**) in its hollow womb, emits steam, flames and water; Volterra fears the muddy, bubbling fumaroles; the steam of the **lagon** rises on damp days, so rains (**piove** = *piogge*) are expected. The simile is a poetic feat with its strong verbal links between the two parts of the comparison: between Octaves 17 and 18 we find **freme/fremito, stridon/gridando, turbide/torbidi, miste/mista, angusto/angusta,**

spumose/spumano, orribil/terribile, alto/alta, teme/teme. Volterra, like the shepherd, is safe because it is on high ground but fearful of what might happen (Bessi, pp. 86–87).

19   As Morello was **irato** (13), so the fierce river is **crucciato** ("vexed") as it shudders, the turbulence of nature being often so described. Bessi (pp. 87–88) notes the effective use and alliteration of *r* in the latter half of the first two lines. **3–4:** The river is almost still after overflowing, not moving forward nor retreating. The sexual element that will emerge clearly later in the poem is to be seen in these stanzas describing the crescendo of the swelling river and its appeasement when spent. The shuddering of the earth can be read in the same key.

20   **1:** "The country woman has managed, just in time".

21   **famiglia:** in the extended sense of household and tenants on the estate. From documents we know that in 1485 "more than 170 workers were employed by Lorenzo [on his estate], that construction of embankments and other work on the Ombrone was under way at this time, and that the estate was producing not only cheese, but butter, cottage cheese and grain" (see P. E. Foster, *A Study of Lorenzo de' Medici's Villa at Poggio a Caiano*, 2 vols [New York, Garland, 1978], I, 63); **per sospetto/di sé stesso:** "uncertain about his own fate".

22   **3:** "the age-old and justified desire [of the fish] is somewhat satisfied"; **5: vaghi,** as in 1, means "roaming", hence "this new pleasure leads them to roam."

23   With this octave begins the story of the metamorphosis of the nymph Ambra into the rock on which Lorenzo (**Lauro**) had his villa built. The River Ombrone rises in the Apennines (24: **d'Appennino/figlio**) near Pistoia and flows into the Arno near Signa, close to Poggio a Caiano the village, which is on a rise, hence its name. Ambra, loved by Lauro, is a dryad (a nymph of the woods) beloved of Delia (= Diana, see *Corinto* note 32–33); she is beautiful and noble, to the point that her beauty will ultimately harm her.

24   **Lauro** is Lorenzo, here self-styled **pastore,** a role he also assumes in *Corinto.* As the word **ambra** (11) has prepared us for the nymph's entry into the poem, so **lauro** (2) has anticipated the presence of the shepherd she loves; Lorenzo himself (Laurentius) is disguised in both the plant and the shepherd's name; **alpino:** Given the story's setting, this is an appropriate adjective, but it may also refer to the origins of the Medici in the Mugello, a hilly area near Florence; **peregrino:** "singular for its virtue". **Fuggendo il caldo** highlights a shift of season and makes certain features of the ensuing story difficult to reconcile with the flood, although the **allor** of the previous stanza seemed to indicate that it is taking place at the same time.

25   **sentío:** "[Ombrone] became aware [that the virginal body etc.]". Lines **4** and **8** of this octave establish a similarity between Ombrone and the rivers in 14 and 15; **torto corno, nudo** and **acceso di disio** make more

explicit the sexual undertones of the earlier part of the poem; **febei** = of the sun-god Phœbus Apollo.

26   It is surprising, in the context of the flood, that of his two natures, fluvial and divine, Ombrone should choose the form of the latter for the pursuit of Ambra; it creates a certain inconsistency with the earlier section.

27   **qual**: has value of *che*, as at 36. 6; **par si scuopra**: "[when Ombrone] reveals [his presence]". Bigi (p. 487) and others, in making Ambra the subject here, reduce the logical sense.

28   **strigne il passo**: "she quickens her pace", repeated at 42. 3; **stral, arco, turcasso**: obligatory accoutrements of Diana's nymphs; 4: details that will reappear at 31. 5–6 and 46. 7–8; see also *Corinto*, 88–92; **tarda**: Ombrone's opening lines in the next octave will explain what he means.

29   5: "So lamenting in vain his initial mistake"; 8: Love poetry is full of oxymorons, and Ombrone draws repeatedly on the apparent contradiction of his "river" nature being overcome by the flames, albeit metaphorical, of love, as he will explain early in the next octave.

30   **ombra**: Twice used, this may be a deliberate echo of Ombrone's name.

31   **timore** is the subject; **ghiaccia e suda**: the paradoxical state of Ombrone, both cool, with his refreshing waters, and perspiring with the intensity of his desire. This may also be read entirely in terms of his nature as a god, rather than as a river, because an intense emotion often gives both cold shudders and perspiration.

32   The frightened (**Timida**) Ambra, fleeing so swiftly that she could skim over ears of corn, which would sustain her without bending, recalls Camilla, the loveless maiden warrior of the *Æneid* (VII. 806–09), as does Galatea (*Corinto*, 97–99). 5: "Ombrone sees himself continually losing ground"; 7: "[Ambra] in the wide plain gains so much ground" because the river loses momentum once it is no longer descending.

33   **repenti**: "steep"; **a lei**: *di lei*; 4: "led him to hope that something would work in his favour"; **pian patenti**: the *piano largo* of 19. 3 and 32. 7 now becomes *patente*, with the same meaning of "wide open"; **morso**: "brake"; when the weary river reaches the plain its flow is slowed down. There is frequent shifting between Ombrone the river (here reducing speed on the plain) and its personification as a god-man (whose feet are slowed down in the pursuit).

34   **accende e pugne**: "[passion] inflames and incites"; **Arno mio**: This is Lorenzo speaking of the river that flows through his city, Florence; **si congiugne**: another instance of a singular for a plural, *si congiungono*.

35   Lorenzo's rhyme **fugge/strugge**, usually applied to time, is not so used here, but the connotation is nonetheless one of loss of what we desire; 8: "interrupt and cut across her swift flight".

36   Ombrone implies that he has a right to the Arno's help because his plentiful waters, added to those of the greater river, enable the Arno to flow

with pride despite men's attempts to control it. That Ambra is Ombrone's prey he makes clear by showing the tufts of golden hair he has snatched; **vola**: Ambra now assumes the movement of the bird to which she was compared in 35. 3.

37   If Ombrone's chase had been part of the river's winter flooding, it would have given coherence to the two parts of the poem; the shift to summer and the treatment of Ombrone more as god-man than river create a discrepancy. Nonetheless, it is clear from this octave that the Arno posed a real threat to the fleeing nymph only through flooding. It held (**ritenne**) its water, became **gonfiato e grosso** (in 17. 1 the flooding river was **gonfiato e largo**) and thereby hinders her (**osta**—note the increase in dramatic tension conveyed by the change of tense). The nymph saw before her **un lago**, because the river spread beyond its normal boundary. While one can always argue that Lorenzo might have written a different story, the change to summer is required for reasons of credibility. The river is roused by the beauty of Ambra when she seeks the coolness of his waters, but the poem ends, as it began, on a very wintry note; **vago**: as earlier in the poem, means "roaming", "wandering"; here her heart, lacking certainty of direction, figuratively wanders; the negative **né sa che farsi** will reappear in both 38 and 39.

38   **già difesa/da' can**: "has already succeeded in escaping the dogs"; **periglio** is the danger represented by Ombrone, but there is of course Arno ahead. Daphne fleeing from Phœbus runs like a hare from a Gallic hound, and this stanza clearly recalls Ovid, *Metamorphoses*, I. 533ff; a comparison of the texts highlights Lorenzo's dramatic power. With the crescendo of Ambra's panic, her terror reduces her to immobility (6) and is finally released in a scream; the change of tense—**grida** in this octave and **gridava** in the next—highlights the difference between Ambra's scream of paralysed terror and her subsequent plea for help that is almost commonplace in literature before a metamorphosis.

39   **casta dea**: as always, Diana; 8: "you alone, give me help in my last labour [death]"; **aiuta** is an imperative.

40   **non basto**: "I am inadequate [to handle two enemies]"; **voce estrema**: "my last words"; 7–8: compare *Corinto*, 43ff and Poliziano, *Orfeo*, 80–81. Interestingly, the rhyme *fugge/strugge*, which Lorenzo has just used (35), is used by Poliziano at lines 72–74 of *Orfeo*, with reference to the fleeting quality of beauty and the destruction caused by time.

41   **novel rigore**: "stiffness not previously experienced"; 7–8: "her limbs have the appearance [of female features], like a stone statue that is outlined and unfinished"; the reverse process, the changing of stones into human beings, is described in similar manner by Ovid, *Metamorphoses*, I. 400ff: "they were like marble images, begun but not yet properly chiselled out, or like unfinished statues" (translated by M. M. Innes, [Harmondsworth, Penguin, 1955]).

42   The various stages of Ombrone's pursuit and the ensuing bewilderment and anguish recall Poliziano, *Stanze*, I. 35–37.

43   **parco**: "game reserve"; qualified by **chiuso**; **materia**: "wooden fence"; an analogous simile occurs in *Stanze*, I. 69, where Lorenzo uses the rhyme *fugge/strugge*. For both, the likely source is *Æneid*, XII. 749–55, but Lorenzo's octave is a superb rendering with a precision of detail not found in Virgil. The beast at bay, swiftly and nimbly jumping the wall, gives a most successful line (5); the dog that has just missed its prey is left looking in blank disappointment. The rhythm of the octave changes to render the contrast between the movement towards freedom in the nimble jump and the static, shocked powerlessness.

44   **qualche poco sente**: Ambra has not yet totally become stone and is therefore still capable of a little feeling; **informa**: "move" (the subject is plural); **pianto/acque**: this association is frequent in Lorenzo, and is also to be found in Petrarch and Boccaccio (we still speak figuratively of bursting into a flood of tears). Here the two natures of Ombrone are united.

45   **propria**: "my own". Ombrone's sorrow at the loss of Ambra is great, but greater still is the sorrow he feels for her fate, and it is for this latter reason that he weeps; nonetheless, the fact that as a god he is immortal and can feel implies a fate worse than Ambra's, because being of stone she is without feeling (**non aver senso**). 6 recalls two *canzoni a ballo*, Lorenzo's "Amor, poi ch'io lasciai tuo gentil regno", 17–18, cited by Bigi (p. 492), and Poliziano's "Dolorosa e meschinella" (Bessi, p. 109); both poems express sorrow at the loss of love.

46   **ne' monti** *to* **eccelsi**: "in my high Apennines"; Ombrone (24, 30) is the son of Appennino, hence **paterni**. The **sacro sangue** shed by Ambra, while recalling 28 and 31, also recalls Lorenzo's sonnet "Non de' verdi giardini" (p. 109), another story of unfulfilled love ending in tragedy.

48   1–3 are obviously ironic as Ombrone's tactics have resulted in a failure beyond what he could imagine; **stagni**: the north wind slows down the flow of rivers by freezing their waters; 5: singular verb with plural subject, as is not infrequent in Lorenzo; **pietra fatto**: Ombrone wants to freeze until he too has become stone; it was commonly held that rock-crystal, in conditions of severe cold, resulted from the freezing of water. Editions prior to Bessi's have "fatta", referring to Ambra, which makes little sense.

CANZONI A BALLO

See Introduction pp. 56–64 for both *canzoni a ballo* and *canti carnascialeschi/trionfi*.

The text of 1–3 is from Lorenzo, *Scritti scelti*, with slight modifications from Lorenzo, *Canzoniere*, edited by Zanato. The source of 4 is Lorenzo, *Opere*, edited by Simioni, with an adjustment suggested by L. de' Medici, *Tutte le opere*, edited by G. Cavalli, 3 vols (Milan, Rizzoli, 1958), ɪ, 125.

1 Martelli hopes to show in a forthcoming publication that this poem is in fact a *madrigale*, arguing that it has a tripartite structure and that it lacks the *volte* and *mutazione* required by the *ballata*. Nonetheless, it is here being retained in the section to which it has traditionally belonged. Whether *madrigale* or *ballata*, it is metrically and phonetically one of Lorenzo's greatest achievements; it skilfully combines *settenari* and hendecasyllables, rhyming ABbC dEED AFfC, in a compact, sophisticated poem which has, however, remarkable linguistic simplicity.

4   **in una tempre**: "unchanged".

7   **gentil**: here and later, "noble", as in the usage of the *stilnovisti*.

11   In the *canzone a ballo* "Crudel Fortuna, a che condotto m'hai?" Lorenzo rails against Fortune and her deception ("Io non credevo al tuo falso sembiante"). Using much the same phrase as here, "dunque folle è chi spera", he accuses those who place their trust in her of foolishness.

2 This thoughtful and moving reflection on the fleeting nature of time, and exhortation to us to value our youth, is entirely in hendecasyllables; it opens with a couplet that rhymes *fugge/strugge*, and these words are then used alternately at the end of each stanza. The rhyme-scheme of the stanza is, as often in these songs, ABABBX.

1   "He who bides his time will long regret it."

5   **'l bel tempo**, following **La bella gioventú** (3), leads to an equating of the two nouns, so the line means: "but anyone who is young and yet bides his time".

7   **discreto**: "intelligent", in opposition to *folle* as used in the preceding poem.

8   **dispensa il tempo**: "uses his time judiciously".

15–16   A reader of Dante will associate **maggior dolore** with Francesca. Her greatest sorrow is different, but the fact that there is here an echo of *Inferno*, v. 121 (strengthened by the presence of **tempo** in both texts) is appropriate, as the poet is stressing the guilt of those who fail to make the best use of their time (**a sua cagione** = "through our own fault").

25–26   This is the fire of love.

3   The *ripresa* rhymes xyX; the seven lines of the stanza rhyme AbAbbcX. In the last line of the *ripresa* and of the stanza the fourth and fifth syllables rhyme internally with the preceding line (*ballo/fallo, accenda/intenda* etc.).

6–7   "one who does not feel that fire [of love] could never be a noble heart"; **gentil** is coupled with **alto** at 27, and the adjectives are virtual synonyms, as **alto** could be translated "of a superior nature" hence, noble.

4   It would be unrepresentative wholly to exclude the coarse songs, in most of which the text is open to two levels of meaning, one generally sexual or obscene. This is one of the simpler ones, both linguistically and in terms of its metaphor: the **giuoco** is sexual practice and the **modo** is sodomitic though heterosexual, hence the wife's complaint. Metrically we have a variant (in *ottonari*) on the *ballata*; the *ripresa* rhymes the words **sodo** and **modo**, and this rhyme is used to end each stanza, which has the pattern ababbccx.

1   **di sodo**: "seriously".

3   **Stu** = *se tu*.

8   **muta loco**: "change place"; the wife is requesting that the husband change from a deviant to a more normal sexual practice.

18   **stessi**: *stessa*.

19   **se miglior viso avessi**: "were your face more attractive".

25   The wife asks her neighbours if their husbands act like hers.

29–36 The husband exhorts her to endure his practice (**Porta in sofferenza**), as once she has become accustomed to it she will far from scorn it; she will consider herself to be charmingly treated and realize that his is the right way.

CANTO CARNASCIALESCO; TRIONFI

The text of these three poems comes from Lorenzo, *Opere*, edited by Simioni, with modifications derived from Lorenzo, *Canti carnascialeschi* ("Orvieto" in this section), which includes extensive explanatory notes; "Bruscagli" in these pages is *Trionfi e canti carnascialeschi toscani del Rinascimento*, edited by R. Bruscagli, 2 vols (Rome, Salerno, 1986).

"Canzona de' confortini"

    METRE: The *canti carnascialeschi* and *trionfi* have metres similar to those of the *canzoni a ballo*, but although Lorenzo's preference is to use the hendecasyllable in more serious compositions, he also uses it in this and five other carnival songs. The rhyming couplet with which the song begins provides the rhyme for the last line of each of the ensuing quatrains. The pattern is AA BBBA etc.

It will assist the reader to bear in mind that in the repertory of metaphors used in the *canti carnascialeschi* "predomina in modo quasi assoluto una caratterizzazione in senso fallico: dato che l'attività erotica e gli stessi movimenti del lavoro umano sono concepiti da un punto di vista maschile, e dato che il canto si finge quasi sempre rivolto alle 'donne' come principali destinatarie, la maggior parte degli oggetti metaforici vengono presentati in una posizione 'maschile'; basta a qualificarli tali la loro capacità di occupare spazio e di creare movimento" (G. Ferroni, "Il doppio senso erotico nei canti carnascialeschi", *Sigma*, 11, ii–iii [1978], 233–50 [p. 243]). There is much linguistic ingenuity in the erotic exploitation of seemingly neutral images and in the recommendation of sodomitic practice for copulation during menstrual periods; this results in a highly sophisticated verbal display which leads Paola Ventrone to suggest that Lorenzo intended this type of composition for the "cerchia ristretta degli intellettuali raccolti intorno a lui come raffinato *divertissement*" ("Note sul carnevale fiorentino", p. 354).

1   **Berricuocoli** and **confortini** are pastries of dough and honey, the latter possibly round in shape. They are offered as prizes to the winners of the games suggested; **confortini** suggests *conforti*, the delights on offer.

4–6   **tempo**: In erotic terms this indicates the menstrual cycle; **pentolini**: a popular game of the period, but here it stands for the buttocks. "Lorenzo sembra avvertire che la donna attempata rimane appetibile soltanto per rapporti sodomitici" (Bruscagli, p. 3). The word also suggests *pentimenti*.

8   **imbratti**: "disgusting mess".

9–10   The co-operation of the two good neighbours (orifices) signifies natural and unnatural intercourse.

11   **garzoni** = *ragazzi*; it is therefore "an easy matter".

15–18   The erotic metaphor here is that of a card game, **bassetta**.

19–22   The sexual game can be played in various positions leading to orgasm (*venire* is used figuratively to indicate this); **mugolar come mucini**: "to purr like kittens".

23–28   **Chi si truova al di sotto** is the loser in the game; **Chi vince** is the winner. Interpreting the card game in sexual terms, the two are partners in sodomitic intercourse. **24**: "he/she writhes and grimaces [literally, makes a face like an ape]"; **succia**: "soffia forte per il dolore" (Bruscagli, p. 4); **si diguazza**: "he thrashes about with delight".

29–30   **Fortuna** is a phallic symbol and the winner is warned not to be too cocksure.

31   **spacciativo**: swift.

32   "it can be played standing up and in both positions."

34   Those with a narrow orifice are advised to practice the game often.

35–36   **flusso** is another card game, but it stands here for diarrhoea; **netto**: "without loss" with reference to the game, but "clean" in the second context.

38   "Il motivo dell'invadenza campagnola nell'ambito dei costumi sodomitici, ritenuti appannaggio dei piú 'civilizzati' cittadini, o comunque di classi sociali superiori, era assai comune" (Bruscagli, p. 5).

40   **a mal partito**: "in a fix".

42   **Sforzo Bettini** was occasionally employed by the Medici, even as a spy (see Rochon, *La Jeunesse de Laurent*, passim, and Orvieto, p. 91). His name here lends itself to two puns: "sforza-bettini, ovvero stupra-fanciulli" (Bruscagli, p. 42), and "lo sforzo della defecazione" (Orvieto). The mention of Bettini helps us to date the song to the years 1474–78.

43–46   **trai**, **pizzico** and **dritta** are other games that acquire a sexual double meaning in keeping with the rest of this poem; **carte** are figurative for "buttocks" and the Florentine coins **grossi e fiorini** stand for male attributes.

47–50   The men promise the women that they will not spare themselves, contrary to advice at line 37, and are willing to stake not just the **confortini** but the very containers (**casse**) provided they find a way in (**per mezzo il vostro**); **metter tutto il nostro/in una posta**: "to stake our all".

"Canzona di Bacco"

METRE: This poem is a *barzelletta* (also known as *frottola*), a metrical form that was very popular in the second half of the Quattrocento for poems intended to be sung. As is generally the case in these light-hearted compositions, the line is the *ottonario* with the *ripresa* rhyming xyyx; each stanza introduces two new rhymes, one of which is used three times (ababb); the next line picks up the final word of the second line of the *ripresa*, and the stanza is rounded off by lines 3 and 4 of the *ripresa*.

While the central motif of the poem is the classical *carpe diem*, which enjoyed extensive popularity in both the Trecento and the Quattrocento, Orvieto argues that the poem is also a "parafrasi pressoché letterale dell'*Ecclesiaste*. Libro scritturale ch'è tutto un invito a godere l'attimo fuggente 'nei pochi giorni di vita che Dio dà' all'uomo, ad evitare le vane fatiche e preoccupazioni; a vivere insomma intensamente il presente perché nessuno sa cosa accadrà nel futuro" (Orvieto, p. 107). This Biblical message was very dear to Ficino, who chose as a motto for his Platonic academy: "Fuge excessum, fuge negotia, lætus in præsens"; this we may translate literally as "shun excess, be not burdened with cares, take pleasure in the present moment", or "Live today: he who lives tomorrow never lives."

5   **Bacco**: one of the names of the god Dionysus. Popularly a god of wine whose rites often involved orgies, he was usually surrounded by satyrs (see 13) and often represented as an effeminate youth, with grapes and vines or ivy. Caravaggio's famous portrait of Bacchus in the Uffizi typifies the god in the art and literature of the Renaissance. In Ficinian terms, however, he can represent a supernatural *furor*, "l'apogeo mistico della poesia e della divinazione" (Orvieto, p. 109). **Arianna**: Ariadne helped Theseus to escape from the labyrinth, after which he abandoned her on the island of Naxos. Bacchus rescued her and married her. This marriage between the god and the earthly woman had a mystical meaning for the neo-Platonists, who saw it as a paradigm of the union between the human soul and the divinity whence it derived (Orvieto p. 106). The triumph of Bacchus and Ariadne is a popular theme in poetry and art. Bacchus, Theseus, Ariadne and Silenus (see 29–30) feature in Poliziano's *Stanze*, I. 110–12, and the story's popularity owes much to Ovid's fine telling of it in his *Ars amatoria*, I. 525–62.

9   **ninfe**: beautiful, young female spirits, personifications of rivers, trees and mountains, fond of music and dancing.

13   **satiretti**: young woodland gods or demons, partly human and partly bestial, lustful and fond of revelry.

17   The satyrs are roused by the wine.

21–22   "These nymphs are quite pleased to be caught out by them [the satyrs]."

23–24   "Only those who are uncouth and ungrateful can protect themselves from Love". The reference here is to the tenets of the *stilnovisti*, who believed that Love took refuge only in the hearts of those of gentle and noble disposition.

29–30   Silenus, leader of the satyrs and a follower of Bacchus, is generally represented as a jolly and drunk old man, having difficulty in remaining seated on his ass. He symbolizes supernatural wisdom and prophetic inspiration. The ass was a sacred animal in eastern religions, and Silenus on the ass may be seen as a *figura Christi* recalling the triumphant entry of Christ into Jerusalem, or the flight of the Holy Family into Egypt (Orvieto, pp. 107–09).

37   Midas, a semi-legendary king of Phrygia, in return for a kind deed done to Silenus was granted his wish that all he should touch turn to gold, without realizing the dire consequences that would ensue.

40   **s'altri**: *se uno*.

46   "Let none nourish (**paschi**) himself on the thought of [living] tomorrow."

58   A version of that well-known Renaissance saying: "Che sarà, sarà."

"Canzona de' sette pianeti"

METRE: The poem opens with a rhyming couplet, with which the final line of each stanza rhymes. The other lines rhyme ABABB, as in the previous song.

Although seven planets address mankind, there is a panegyric only of Venus; it is quite likely that other stanzas have been lost, as there is evidence to suggest that there were seven floats (see Ventrone, "Note sul carnevale fiorentino", pp. 355–66).

1–2   "We are seven planets, who leave our lofty dwelling to bear witness on earth to what is [known] in heaven."

3   **son**: "proceed".

7–8   "We put pressure on those who try to oppose us, but we give gentle help to those who believe in our power."

9   "[Whether men be] melancholic, stingy and subtle"; **miseri** here differs in meaning from 4. Bruscagli (p. 20) notes on 9–13 that "le tipologie che seguono sembrano rimandare ai 'caratteri' propiziati dai vari pianeti: nell'ordine, da Saturno (v. 9), dal Sole (v. 10), da Marte (v. 11), Giove (v. 12) Mercurio (v. 13)."

14   **vil**: "earthly".

15   **chiara**: an adjective appropriate to Venus depicted as a star. This entire section on Venus may be read in the tradition of the two Venuses, one of earthly love and one of divine love.

17–18   "anyone who is touched by the fire of the sweet star [of love], will burn for ever [with passion] for the beauty of the beloved."

20   As human life is renewed through love (Venus), similarly Venus, who is associated with fertility and spring, brings about the rebirth of nature.

23   **Ciprigna**: "Cyprian" is often applied to Venus, with reference to Cyprus, one of the most important places of her worship.

LAUDA

See Introduction pp. 64–67.

Toscani's text is here reprinted with orthographical modifications from Lorenzo, *Scritti scelti*. According to the manuscripts, this *lauda* (number III in Toscani's edition but VI in earlier ones) "cantasi come la canzona del *Fagiano*", for which see *Canti carnascialeschi del Rinascimento*, edited by C. S. Singleton (Bari, Laterza, 1936), pp. 130–31. The "Canzona del *Fagiano*" is an anonymous and obscene song that uses the pheasant as a metaphor for the male organ. Like the present *lauda* it is in hendecasyllables and rhymes XX ABABBX, but it is shorter, having only seven stanzas. The first ten of Lorenzo's eleven stanzas end with *mai* or derivatives, while the last, like the first line of the poem, ends with *fai*.

Because of the strong similarity between part of this hymn and *De summo bono* VI, the reader will find it useful to have access to lines 49–69 of the latter: "Fonte d'ogni letizia, gaudio intero,/io so che tu se' solo, ed in te giace/quel che appetisce il nostro desidèro./ Perché, se questo ovver quel ben ne piace,/non cerca il disio nostro o quello o questo,/ma il Bene in essi, dov' è la sua pace./La qualità del Bene il cuore ha chiesto/in ogni cosa, e il salutar licore/che vive in sé, e spargesi pel resto./Al fonte di quest' acqua corre il core;/ questo perenne fonte cerca e cole/sparto in qualunque cosa inferiore./E come quel che l'occhio vede è sole,/che in quella e questa cosa chiar si mostra,/così è un solo ben, che il mondo vuole./Però non manca mai la sete nostra/per questo o quello, o questo e quello insieme,/fin ch'altro maggior ben se gli dimostra./Il fonte sol, che 'l santo liquor geme,/spegne la sete nostra: o liquor santo,/spegni la sete mia che troppo prieme."

5   **per te**: "because of You".

9–11   **strugge/fugge**: The rhyme is here not associated with the flight of time, but rather with the flight of that peace which only God can give; in pursuit of it, the soul is "melting away".

15–16   **Se a cercar di te**: the *di* is pleonastic. "If I look for Your presence in pursuit of wealth, honour or carnal pleasure". This triad is not casual, as M. Martelli shows in "Nota a Lorenzo de' Medici, *Laudi*, VI. 16", *Interpres*, 9 (1989), 275–83. One can find it in the first epistle of St John and in St Bernard's "the world, the flesh and the devil", where the world means the inordinate pursuit of wealth, and the devil stands for pride and pursuit of worldly honours. Several writers before Lorenzo use this triple combination of the deceptive distractions from inner peace and true happiness. See Lorenzo's own commentary to "Cerchi chi vuol le pompe e gli alti onori" (*Comento*, XXI).

18   **vano**: a strong adjective for Lorenzo, meaning "worthless", in an existential context. More than elsewhere, it may be suggested by Dante's "ben vani" (*Inferno*, VII. 79), where the poet emphasizes that whatever Fortune takes or gives in this life is irrelevant in terms of our final end, union with God; **affetto**: desire.

22   **e [sei lucente]:** "and yet", *eppure*; also at 24.

25–26   The subject is **senso:** "every sense is seeking that sweetness that all desire."

29–50   One may sense in the use of paradox in this section an over-intellectualizing that contrasts negatively with the emotional spirituality of the rest of the poem (see Lorenzo, *Opere*, edited by Martelli, p. xxiii).

29–32   **Cerca quel cerchi pur:** "By all means continue your search." Toscani cites Augustine, *Confessions*, IV. 12. 18: "There is no rest where you are searching for it. By all means, continue your search but it is not where you are looking. You are looking for a happy life in the very region of death, and you will not find it there. How can there be a happy life there, where there is no life at all?" (p. 81).

33–34   See *Comento*: "E però il principio della vera vita è la morte della vita non vera" (p. 123 of this book).

35–36   "death comes to all men (**in moltitudine**) but in You alone is there life eternal, for You are life."

38   **converso:** *rivolto*.

39   **vani:** here *vuoti*, "empty".

43–44   A direct rendering of Matthew 11. 28: "Come to me, all you that labour and are burdened, and I will refresh you."

53–54   "Detaching my experience of good [from earthly and unsatisfactory enjoyment], I find an everlasting good, and it is my sweet God."

57–59   No water of any earthly river ever quenches our thirst, but rather, literally, "it adds logs to the evil fire." This means that the pursuit of those passions and activities that we believe will quell our desires merely serves to increase them. The concept that our thirst is insatiable when satisfied with the earth's liquor also occurs in the *Canzona di Bacco*, 41–42.

61–62   Compare John 4. 13: "He that shall drink of the water that I will give him shall not thirst for ever."

67–68   "As You have pierced my heart most sweetly, heal that wound which is Your doing." The subject of **fai**, both here and in the first line of the hymn, is God, who is here personified in the second person of the Trinity.

RAPPRESENTAZIONE DI SAN GIOVANNI E PAOLO

See Introduction pp. 67–73.

The text printed here is from Lorenzo, *Scritti scelti* (hereunder "Bigi"), with a couple of slight modifications, of which *vita* instead of *vista* in 18.1 comes from the early printed editions.

In this section "Martelli" refers to Martelli, "Politica e religione". Occasional quotations from the Vulgate will highlight the closeness of linguistic similarities; but references to the Bible have been extensively reduced so as not to burden these notes.

1   **San Giovanni e Paolo**: SS John and Paul, martyred in Rome in 362, were beheaded by order of Julian the Apostate. The Christian Church commemorates their deaths on 26 June. It is believed that their bodies were interred under the present basilica of SS John and Paul. In Jacopo da Varagine's *Golden Legend* and in Lorenzo's play John and Paul are two officers (*primicerii et præpositi*) in the household of Constance. They are not sons of Constantine, as is stated by some commentators (for example, Bigi, p. 566).

2   **Costanza**: daughter of Emperor Constantine. Historically she was an intriguer, twice married, who between the years 337 and 350 had a basilica erected in Rome and dedicated to St Agnes.

3   **Sant' Agnesa**: a Roman Christian martyred at the age of thirteen; generally portrayed with a lamb, symbolizing Christ. Her feast-day is 21 January.

4   **Costantino**: This is Emperor Constantine the Great (*c.* 274–337). Through a series of victories he became sole ruler of the Roman world; he gave the name Constantinople to Byzantium, which he made his capital. Earlier, with the Edict of Milan (313), he gave rights to Christians in the Empire, and Christianity became a state religion in 324, though without concomitant persecution of paganism. It is possible that he received baptism shortly before his death.

5   **Gallicano**: History makes no mention of Gallican among Constantine's generals, but according to medieval martyrologies he did hold this position and was converted to Christianity during the war against the Scythians. Banished from Italy by Julian the Apostate, he was finally killed in Egypt.

6   **Imperadore, il nuovo**: This is Julian the Apostate (*c.* 331–63), who became Roman Emperor in 361. Born at Constantinople, youngest son of Julius Constantius, half-brother of Constantine the Great, he shed his Christian belief as a result of the murder of several close relatives in his youth. His policy towards Christians and Jews was one of toleration, despite his commitment to restoring the ancient religion. A man of learning, he was neither necromancer nor monk, as is claimed in Octave 115 and in the *Golden Legend*.

7   **San Basilio**: St Basil (*c.* 329–79), known as The Great because he was one of the greatest of the Greek Fathers, was born at Cæsarea in Cappadocia. His feast-day is 14 June.

8   **non forni' l'intero**: "I did not say all that I wished to say."

9   **ègli suta accetta**: "he has found it acceptable." In this octave alone, Martelli has found echoes of Psalms 30, 33, 36 and 96, and one could continue *di questo passo*; see Martelli.

10   **gli umani eccessi:** "the sins of men". The noun is retained even in the English translation of Psalm 115. 11: "I said in my excess".

11   **la letizia intera [...] vien per tuo rispetto:** "my joy is increased and fulfilled by yours."

12   **Augusto:** synonymous with "Emperor" after Augustus (63 BC–AD 14), the first and most renowned of Roman emperors.

13   **Persia:** It is doubtful whether Constantine ever waged war against the Persians.

14   **1–2:** The pursuit of glory in worthy service and as an end in itself is very much a Roman concept, whereas that of the *cor gentil* we associate with the poets of the *dolce stil nuovo*, for whom true *gentilezza* was nobility.

15   **Non c'è boccon del netto:** Lorenzo is quick to use common sayings that are figuratively rich. The literal sense here is that whatever morsel of food we eat, we shall stain our lips, which means that we pay a price for whatever we enjoy.

16   **Dacia:** modern Romania. Historically, Constantine's army undertook no such campaign.

17   Costanza has two markedly contrasting sides to her nature: the filial loving daughter, full of concern for the father who is troubled by her illness, regrets that she cannot bear him grandchildren; but this speech reveals that she also has an astute and steely side. What she recommends is what Machiavelli will call "godere el benefizio del tempo" (*Principe* III), a tactic that he maintains was much practised in his times—in all times, one might add. It should be noted that the advice is given by the born-again Constance, physically and spiritually healed, and that her father (in 39) attributes it to God speaking through her.

18   **Alessandro** and **Antonio** are clearly two of Gallican's officers.

19   **spaccia:** here with the sense of *sbriga*, "make all my people hasten"; but the implication may also be to pay the soldiers once they are gathered. The same applies in Octave 139.

20   **7–8:** The play portrays a conflict between those who uphold the Roman gods and those who are willing to die for Christ; on both sides there is strong religious sentiment and a recognition of dependence on greater powers than we can contradict. Both Gallican and Julian show strong belief in God, which for them is Mars (**Marte**), the god of war. Julian will dismiss what the astrologers say and place his trust in his god (144).

21   **forza o arte:** Bigi (p. 571) notes this "coppia petrarchesca", as in L. 67. But in Lorenzo's play the influence of Dante and Petrarch is virtually absent, so interwoven is it with Biblical language. Conspicuous also through their almost total absence are allusions to classical poetry.

22   Giuliano, too, will call life "fallace" (146), and Constantine says much the same in 96: "brieve e traditora è questa vita." That life is brief and deceives us, hiding the uncertainty of tomorrow and the fact that we are

made for another existence elsewhere, is a recurrent theme in Lorenzo's work.

23   Compare the *lauda* "O maligno e duro core", 13–14: "Liquefatti come cera,/o cor mio tristo e maligno".

24   **parlando, apristi l'intelletto:** This may mean "as you spoke, you opened your mind [to me]" or "as you spoke you opened my mind." In Italian the possessive adjective is used much less than in English, occasionally giving rise to ambiguity.

25   **getta:** "generates" or "causes". After this prayer the three women exit and have no further function in the play. The focus in the next forty octaves or so will be on Gallican's conversion, in which John and Paul are instrumental.

26   **5:** "because you were too full of conceit and arrogance". In its figurative sense **fumo** is virtually synonymous with **boria**.

27   **ferma il pensier:** "be firm in your decision."

28   See Matthew 20. 1–16. This is a reference to the parable of the householder who hired labourers for his vineyard. All, whether they started late or early, received the same remuneration, meaning that God rewards us with His grace no matter how late we turn to Him.

29   Compare the *lauda* "O peccator, io sono Dio eterno", 8: "tu non uom, anzi un vil vermin che muore"; and Psalm 21. 7: "Ego autem sum vermis, et non homo [But I am a worm and no man]."

30   The Biblical incidents are mentioned as evidence that God will fight on the side of His faithful against the infidels; it is on this basis that John and Paul pray that He will now aid Gallican, who has given proof of his humility. **Giosuè** (Joshua), fighting the league of five kings as part of the campaign to establish the Israelites in the Promised Land, asked the Lord to make the sun stand still and to hold back the moon so as to give him extra time for battle (Joshua 10. 12–14). **3–4** may refer to Deuteronomy 32. 30 ("Quo modo persequatur unus mille, et duo fugent decem millia [How should one pursue after a thousand, and two chase ten thousand]?"), as Martelli suggests (p. 204), or to Samson, who slew one thousand Philistines with the jaw-bone of an ass (Judges 15. 14–16), and to Jonathan son of Saul, who, with his armour-bearer, smote the Philistine garrison. For these two lines Bigi (p. 576) suggests I Kings 18. 7 ("Percussit Saul mille, et David decem millia [Saul slew his thousands, and David his ten thousands]") and Psalm 90. 7 ("Cadent a latere tuo mille, et decem millia a dextris tuis [A thousand shall fall at thy side, and ten thousand at thy right hand]"), showing that there is no shortage of sources. Well known is the hero of the final reference, the young David who killed Goliath, the Philistine champion, with a stone (I Kings 17). Michelangelo's statue of David represents the hero just before combat.

31   These rumbustious octaves of military exhortation (71–72) are of

course entirely anachronistic for a play whose action is alleged to take place in the fourth century: the arquebus came into use in the 1470s. The message of the play is timeless, and this is conveyed all the better through Lorenzo's insertion of features redolent of his own society. 8: "and that our bombards be not spiked", and so rendered useless.

32   **1–2:** The appeal is to the Aristotelian quality of magnanimity or greatness of spirit, and to nobility.

33   **da vita esser rimossi:** "to be killed".

34   **San Piero:** The building of a church of St Peter was initiated by Constantine in 324, so Gallican's words have some historical warrant. Lorenzo's audience would readily have thought of this as the basilica in Rome in its own day, without much concern for historical accuracy.

35   **labirinto:** Bigi (p. 583) suggests Petrarch, CCXI. 14 and CCXXIV. 4.

36   **della cristiana scuola:** "a follower of Christianity"; "school" is intended in the philosophical sense.

37   **5:** Compare John 15. 5 ("I am the vine; you the branches") and Romans 11. 16 ("si radix sancta, et rami [if the root be holy, so are the branches]").

38   **6:** similar to *Comento*, III ("che è or del ciel la piú lucente stella"), as noted by Zanato (*Saggio sul "Comento"*, p. 204, n. 16).

39   **8:** If the assertion that one is saved by grace and not by ones's merits had come some three decades later, it would have exposed Lorenzo to accusations of heresy.

40   **7–8:** Gallican here echoes the words of Christ to His disciples: "In mundo pressuram habebitis, [...] ego vici mundum [In the world you shall have distress. (...) I have overcome the world]" (John 16. 33).

41   **starmi:** *starmene.* It is commonplace to read Constantine's abdication speech as the heartfelt utterance of Lorenzo himself; but Gallican's final octave may also express closely how Lorenzo felt about the service he had given to Florence and how strong his desire was to find peace in God. The play moves naturally from this to Constantine's reflection on the treachery of life and his abdication speech.

42   **2:** Some elision is required to make this line a hendecasyllable.

43   **7–8:** quoted by Machiavelli in *Discorsi*, III. 29—in a chapter appropriately entitled "Che gli peccati de' popoli nascono dai principi"; he also cites a similar statement from Livy. Martelli (p. 210) suggests that the image may have come to Lorenzo via Ficino's compendium of Plato's *Politicus*, written in 1468 and printed in 1482.

44   **4:** "others sleep as his eyes are watching on behalf of theirs."

45   **avarizia:** This is a very strong term, as is well known to readers of Dante. It is the *cupiditas*, or inordinate greed, that St Paul defines as the root of all evil. Bigi (p. 586) here suggests Machiavelli's definition (*Principe* XV): "*avaro* in nostra lingua è ancora colui che per rapina desidera di avere."

46   **servo de' servi**: a designation of the Roman pontiff (*servus servorum Dei*); but the concept of the ruler as a public servant is to be found in the political writings of many humanists.

47   There is another structural break in the play with the definitive departure of Constantine, and virtually a new play begins with the speedy rise and fall of Constantine's three sons and Julian the Apostate. The link between the two parts lies in John and Paul, whose martyrdom provides a focus for the play; but in the average religious play their position would have been central and their "nascita, morte e miracoli" would have furnished virtually the entire plot.

48   **onde mancar poi suole**: "and [the empire] would be lost."

49   As Emperor, Julian is the heir of Augustus, but less gloriously of Julius Cæsar, who, though given the title of *imperator*, was murdered in 44 BC, allegedly suspected of wanting a hereditary monarchy.

50   **Giove** (Jove or Jupiter) was the chief of the Roman gods; the chief goddess, who was both sister and wife to him, was Juno (**Giunone**). **Febo** (Phœbus Apollo) came to the Romans from Greek sources primarily as a god of prophecy and oracles. **Minerva** was originally Etruscan but joined Jupiter and Juno as one of the major deities of Roman religion, later to be identified with Pallas Athene; she is often a symbol of wisdom. **Vittoria**: adored by the Romans as a goddess, the *Victoria Augusti* became the protective deity of the emperors, and her statue was erected in the *curia Julia* (or senate house) by Augustus in 29 BC. Flavius Julius Constantius, third son of Constantine the Great, was responsible for the removal of the statue of Victory and, although evidence is not specific, it is assumed that Julian replaced it.

51   Rather than Matthew 19. 21, Mark 10. 21 and Luke 18. 22 (Bigi, p. 592), the source here is more likely the one suggested by Martelli (p. 204), Luke 14. 33: "qui non renuntiat omnibus quæ possidet [that doth not renounce all that he possesseth]". The linguistic similarities between the Latin version and Lorenzo's text are strong.

52   **Ostia**, now a suburb of Rome and its seaside resort, was a Roman city founded at the mouth of the Tiber, hence its name (the Latin word *ostium* means "mouth of a river"); it was an important commercial port for imperial Rome.

53   **5**: Compare Matthew 7. 15: "Attendite a falsis prophetis, qui veniunt ad vos in vestimentis ovium; intrinsecus autem sunt lupi rapaces [Beware of false prophets, who come to you in the clothing of sheep, but inwardly they are ravening wolves]."

54   **3–4**: A **podesteria** was the jurisdiction of a *podestà*, the chief magistrate in a medieval Italian town. The meaning here is that a ruler of a state establishes his authority within the first four days of his taking up office.

55   **signoria**: This term could not have been used by Julian, as it designated the governing body of a medieval Italian republic.

56   **eri**: *eravate*, as the subject (**voi**) is plural.

57   **5**: "But time oft disposes man [to reflect further on his decision]."

58   **Terenziano** is one of Julian's officers.

59   **Cristo si dimetta**: "Christ be abandoned"; *dimettere* = "to remove" or "to discharge".

60   **5**: In the *lauda* "Peccator', su tutti quanti" Lorenzo uses the same metaphor to express the Christian belief that in death there is a renewal of life: "Oggi al ciel la spiga arriva/di quel gran che in terra è morto;/questo gran, se non moriva,/frutto alcun non aria pòrto." Martelli (p. 205) suggests I Corinthians 15. 36: "quod seminas non vivificatur, nisi prius moriatur [that which thou sowest is not quickened, except it die first]"; and Toscani (p. 91) adds John 12. 24–25: "nisi granum frumenti cadens in terram, mortuum fuerit, Ipsum solum manet; si autem mortuum fuerit, multum fructum affert [unless the grain of wheat falling into the ground die, Itself remaineth alone. But if it die, it bringeth forth much fruit]."

61   Compare the *lauda* "Ben arà duro core", 21–22: "Chi sanza te t'ha fatto/sanza te stesso non ti vuol salvare."

62   **giovinetti**: The play is full of miracles, not least the perennial youth of John and Paul. To call them *giovinetti* conflicts with the passage of time in the play as well as with the "molti anni" of Octave 120.

63   **Agnello**: The Lamb is Christ, which makes line 2 all the more an echo of Isaiah 53. 7: "Sicut ovis ad occisionem ducetur [He shall be led as a sheep to the slaughter]."

64   **7–8: Giove** (Jupiter) is one of the planets in the Ptolemaic system (see *Ambra*, 4); Christians believed that the divinities to whose care the planets were committed were themselves subject to God as creator of the universe.

65   **8**: Lorenzo uses virtually the same words in the *Uccellagione*, 39, where the meaning is much the same: "they are set on their course." The colloquialism has been rendered into English through the use of a similarly figurative expression: you can take the horse to the trough, but you can't make it drink.

66   **'l cumular**: "the accumulation [of goods for his personal use]"; Zanato (*Saggio sul "Comento"*, p. 271) numbers this word among the "latinismi direttamente attinti alla romanità" recently introduced into the vernacular.

67   **Parti**: The Parthians lived in Mesopotamia and were traditional enemies of the Romans; the Persians had defeated them in the century previous to Julian's, and their empire is deemed to have ended in the year 224. Julian was killed in an expedition against the Persians, so to that extent there is historical accuracy here.

68   **1–2**: the opening words of the Divine Office as designed by St Benedict in *c*. 538: "Domine, labia mea aperies./Et os meum annuntiabit laudem tuam."

69   **Mercurio**: Lorenzo follows the *Golden Legend* quite closely. In the chapter on St Julian we are told that Mercury was a soldier whom Julian the Apostate had killed for his faith. The act of retribution was requested by the Virgin Mary.

70   **3**: Christians believe that after the end of the world the angels will sound the trumpets for the final judgement of mankind and the dead will arise (Matthew 25. 31–32).

71   **4**: "every hour [that they must wait] before they can engage in battle seems as long as one hundred"; Lorenzo uses similar hyperbole in *Ambra*, 6: "gli par la notte un secol di cento anni."

72   **8**: That astrology is only tittle-tattle well reflects Lorenzo's own views, but there was strong belief in the predictions of astrologers in medieval times, and even in Lorenzo's own enlightened society, though philosophers like Ficino and Pico firmly denounced such belief. Lorenzo expresses similar views in *Stanze*, I. 74, where the writings of astrologers are dismissed as "sciocche carte".

73   **1**: Compare Wisdom 7. 29: "et super omnem dispositionem stellarum [and above all the order of the stars]".

74   **4**: "I have been killed before I could fear the oncoming of death."

LETTER TO GIOVANNI

The Giovanni in question (born 1475) is the second of Lorenzo's three sons, who was officially proclaimed a cardinal on 9 March 1492, left for Rome three days later, and eventually became the first Medici pope as Leo X (1513–21). This letter was written in 1492, between Giovanni's proclamation as cardinal and Lorenzo's death on 8 April.

The text is taken from Lorenzo, *Scritti scelti*.

1   **tutti noi per rispetto vostro**: "and we [to God] on your behalf".

2   **M. Domenedio**: "the Lord our God" (**M.** = "Messer").

3   **comprobando questa condizione**: "giving proof of your gratitude".

4   **il vostro buono instituto**: "your good upbringing".

5   **gli esempi muovono**: "the example [of others] influences us."

6   **impedire la perfezione di questa vostra dignità**: "to prevent your rising to such dignified office".

7   **confidandosi *to* età vostra**: "confident that they will be quite successful because of your [young] age".

8   **Collegio**: The college of cardinals is here intended.

9   **Scilla e Cariddi**: Scylla and Charybdis are the mythological names given to two perils associated with the Straits of Messina; "to avoid like the plague" renders the saying equally figuratively.

10   **mediocrità**: This is the Latin *aurea mediocritas*, or golden mean, the balanced middle way.

11   **farebbono sempre un buon papa**: Since the pope is elected from their midst, if the cardinals are all worthy men, so will he be.

12   **riposo**: here means "peace"; no doubt a yearning on Lorenzo's part for less warlike popes than had been seen, periodically, for some centuries.

13   **quando la passione** *to* **facilmente**: The point here is that if one loses a friend through an offence in the heat of passion, one may regain that friend (whereas one will not do so if the offence has been coldly calculated).

14   **adoperare piú gli orecchi che la lingua**: Lorenzo regularly slips into a colloquial register. Here he is bidding Giovanni to listen and learn.

15   **S. Chiesa** = "Santa Chiesa".

16   **facciate ben capace ciascuno**: "ensure that all are given reason to believe".

17   **né vi mancherà** *to end of paragraph*: The Church first, but Florence and the Medici immediately after, is Lorenzo's exhortation; that the two are intertwined in his mind is revealed by "la casa ne va colla città." Again he has recourse to a popular saying, **salvare la capra e i cavoli**: "to have something both ways".

18   **concistoro**: a formal meeting of cardinals summoned by the pope.

19   **l'opinione**: "public opinion".

20   **a largo conversare con ciascheduno**: The phrase depends on **si vuol**, so it means "[one should] in a general manner, converse with all."

21   **pompe**: "public occasions".

22   **bella stalla e famiglia ordinata e polita**: "a good stable and a well-organized, clean household".

23   **riducendo a poco a poco le cose al termine**: "reducing your expenses gradually in the future".

24   **Piú presto**: "sooner", but a verb is needed for clarity: "[you should] sooner [have]".

25   **cibi grossi**: "plain food".

26   **in cotesti panni**: "in your habit", meaning "in the life of a senior prelate".

27   **l'ufficio**: This is the Divine Office, or daily public prayer of the Roman breviary, recited by priests, religious, and some clerics.

28   **cosa alcuna immeditata**: "anything unexpected".

29   **Santità di N. S., causando che**: "His Holiness our Lord [the Pope], alleging that"; **N. S.** = "Nostro Signore".

30   **officio:** here "duty".

31   **S. S.** = "Sua Santità", "His Holiness" (the Pope).

32   **per molte specialità:** "on several issues".

33   **Ingegnatevi *to* molestia:** "Strive at the start to ask him for as little as possible, and do not bother him."

34   **gli spezza gli orecchi:** A figurative expression which may be rendered as "buzzes in his ears" and means "deafens him with pleas".

35   Had he lived long enough, Lorenzo might have been disappointed by Giovanni's response to his election as pope. He is reported to have remarked, "Let us enjoy the papacy since God has given it to us"; and John Hale comments, "Leo's enjoyment of the papacy was obvious" (*A Concise Encyclopaedia of the Italian Renaissance*, edited by J. R. Hale [London, Thames and Hudson, 1981], p. 183). He was a great ruler of Rome, and created there an artistic and literary golden age, as his father had done in Florence. As a pope, he is remembered for licensing the sale of indulgences rather than for initiating much-needed ecclesiastical reforms.

VOCABULARY

Unless otherwise indicated, nouns ending in -*o* are masculine and those ending in -*a* are feminine. Where the tonic stress does not fall on the penultimate syllable of a word, or is otherwise open to doubt, the stressed syllable is indicated by an accent, though this does not appear in the text except where required by Italian usage. Accents are similarly employed to distinguish between open and close *e* and *o* in tonic position, an acute accent (*é*, *ó*) marking a close vowel and a grave (*è*, *ò*), an open vowel. Words explained in the Notes are not necessarily repeated in the Vocabulary. The English equivalents given are those appropriate to the text.

The following abbreviations are used:

adj	adjective	*p part*	past participle
dim	diminutive	*pl*	plural
f	feminine	*pres*	present
fig	figurative	*subj*	subjunctive
m	masculine	*v*	verbal

abbondare, to abound
abéte (*m*), fir (tree)
àbito, habit, custom
accètto, pleasing; agreeable
acciò che, in order that
acconciare, to settle
accòrto, shrewd; judicious
accostumato, well-bred, morally proper
accozzare, to throw together
acume (*m*), sharpness (of insight)
adórno, fair; graceful
adunque: = *dunque*, so; therefore
adusto, scorched, burnt
àere (*f*): = *aria*, air

affannato, grieving; troubled
affanno, worry; trouble; anxiety; anguish
affrontarsi, to confront
aggirarsi, to hang about
aggiúgnesi: = *si aggiunga*
aggradare, to please
agguato, snare; trap; ambush
agognare, to yearn
aita, help
algènte, icy cold
allegrézza, joy
allettare, to entice; to allure
allòro, laurel
almanco: = *almeno*, at least

alpino, of the mountain
altèro, proud; haughty
àmbito, range
ammanto, mantle
ammiccante, with a wink
ammonire, to warn; to admonish
ancilla: = *ancella*, handmaid
anco: = *ancora, anche*
ancoraché: = *benché*, although
àngue (*m*), serpent
angusto, narrow
ansare, to pant
antefatto, previous history
antro, cave; den
aoprare: = *adoprare*, to use
apogèo, height
appannàggio, prerogative
apparato: = *imparato*
appariscènte, good-looking
appetíbile, desirable
appetire, to crave for, to desire intensely
appunto, exactly, just so
aprico, sunny, bright (of an open space); bright, welcoming (of a person)
arbítrio, will
àrbore: = *albero*, tree
arbuscèllo, shrub
arbusto, shrub
archibúsio: = *archibugio*, arquebus
àrdere, to burn
ardire (*m*), courage, boldness
ardito, bold
arèbbe: = *avrebbe*
àrgine (*m*), bank, barrier
arieggiare, to resemble
arménto, herd
arnése (*m*), equipment, tools; (*pl*) arms
arò: = *avrò*
arrecare, to bring
arso: *p part* of **ardere**
ascési (*f*), ascent, rise

ascóndere:= *nascondere*, to hide
ascóso: *p part* of **ascondere**
aspro, harsh, rough
assediato, beseiged
assèdio, siege
assimiliare: = *assomigliare*, to resemble
assordare, to deafen
assuefatto (*p part*), accustomed; **essersi assuefatto**, to have become accustomed
attaménte, aptly
atto, suited, capable, apt
attristare, to sadden
augèo, augellétto: = *uccello, uccelletto*
àura, air, gentle pleasant breeze; **aurétta**, *dim*
aurato, àuro, golden
àvolo: = *avo*, forefather
avveduto, astute, wary
avventurato, blest with good fortune, happy, fortunate
avvèrso, adverse, hostile; **gente avversa**, enemy
avvertènza, warning
avvézzo, accustomed
avviare, to set going, to steer
avvocato, someone who will plead on our behalf
baldanza, boldness; confidence in one's own strength; pride
baloccare, to play games, to dally
balza, crag
bando, proclamation, ban
begghi: = *begli, m pl* of *bello*
belato, bleating
beveràggio, drink
biacca, face powder
biasimare, to blame, to reprove
biato: = *beato*, blessed
bòccia: = *bocciolo*, bud
boccóne (*m*), mouthful (of food)
bòia (*m*), executioner, hangman

bombarda, bombard
borbottare, to mumble
bòria, self-conceit
botare: = *votare*, to vow, to promise
bòtto, blow; **di bòtto**, suddenly
bozzato: = *abbozzato*, outlined, unfinished
bracco, hound
bramare, to yearn, to long (for)
bramòso, desirous
bravo (of an animal), fine, strong
bravura, cleverness
briève (*adj*): = *breve*
brigata, group, people; flock of birds
bríglia, bridle
bruma, mist; cold wet weather
bruno, dark-skinned; brown, dark
cacciarsi, to plunge forward
cadére, to fall
càggio: = *cado*
cagióne (*f*), cause, motive, reason
calle (*m*), way, path
campare, to live
campato: = *lasciato in vita*
càndido, snow-white
canuto, white-haired
càppio, slip-knot, loop
carestía, scarcity, serious lack
caritativo, charitable
carnaiuòlo: now *carniere*, game-bag
cartòccio, parcel; **cartoccino**, *dim*
castèlla (*pl*), castles, small towns surrounded by walls
casto, chaste
castróne (*m*), lamb castrated for slaughter
cavare, to draw out
cavo, hollow; deep
cèdere, to yield
centellino, sip
certare, to compete, to vie
cèrulo, sky-blue (more commonly *ceruleo*)

cèrvia: = *cerva*, doe
césto, tuft
chéto, quiet, silent
chiòma, foliage; thick hair, lock
ciància, tittle-tattle
ciarlare, to chat, to gossip
ciascheduno, every
cicalare, to chatter idly
cignale (*m*): = *cinghiale*, wild boar
ciòttolo, pebble, cobble
cognizióne (*f*), knowledge, understanding
colezióne (*f*), dinner
cólmare, to fill
coltèlla, large knife with broad blade
combàttere, to fight
compiacére, to gratify, to please
comportare, to allow, to tolerate
concèdere, to allow
còncio, *v adj* of *conciare*, to ill-treat
concióne (*f*), exhortation
conciosiaché, in so much as
concórrere, to contribute, to lead to, to come together, to occur, to concur, to co-operate
condótta, soldier's wage
confidare, to trust
confortare, to encourage
congiunto, a follower of Christ (*p part* of *congiungere*, to connect, to join)
coniunzióne (*f*) **di sàngue** (*m*): = *parentela*, kinship
conseguire, to attain, to achieve
consuèto, usual, customary
consuetúdine (*f*), custom, habit; familiarity
contèmpo: **nel contempo**, meanwhile
cónto: **far conto**, to suppose, to imagine
contraggènio, against one's inclination, unwillingly

contristare, to grieve, to be afflicted

conveniènte, suitable, proper

convenιènza, suitability

convenire, to be necessary; to be appropriate; me convènne, I had to

convèrso, transformed, changed

convièmme: = *mi conviene,* I must; I want

convitare, to entertain, to invite to a feast

convito, banquet

córso, course; race; flow; track

cospètto, presence; al cospetto di, in the presence of, in front of

costante (f), constant feature

costellare, to strew (like stars in the sky)

costumatamente, in a proper manner

costumatézza, propriety, decency, decorum

crèdesi: = *si crede,* it is believed

crine (m), hair, locks

crucciarsi, to fret, to be distressed

crucciato, vexed

crudo, cruel, harsh

cucciòtto, simpleton

dallato: = *dal lato,* beside

danàio: = *danaro,* money

dannare, to condemn, to accuse

dardo, dart, arrow

degnificare, to render worthy

desiare: = *desiderare*

desira: = *desidera*

destare (*v adj* désto), to wake

destrézza, adroitness, skill

dèstro, having skill, skilful

dí (*sing* and *pl*), day, days

diacére: = *giacere*; porsi a diacere, to lie down

difficíllimo = *difficilissimo,* most difficult

dileggiare, to scoff

dilètto, beloved

dilezióne (f), affection, love; avere in dilezione, to love

dilucidaménte, lucidly

dimésso, plain, unassuming

disgràzia, accident; per disgrazia, accidentally

disiato, yearned for

disío: = *desiderio,* desire, yearning

disióso, desirous

disire (m), desire

dislegarsi, to free oneself

dispètto, vexation, contempt; scorn, disdain

dispettóso, haughty, vexed

disútile, useless

diurno, daytime

diuturnaménte, for a long time

divéglia: = *divella, strappa*; from *divellere* = svèllere

divo: = *divino*

dòglia, sorrow, pain

dògliersi, to lament, to regret

domare, to crush, to subdue

Domenedío, God

dòndolo, pendant

dònna, wife

dòtto, learned, erudite; skilled

drappèllo, host, crowd

drappo, cloth

drièto: = *dietro,* behind, at back of

duòlo: = *dolore,* sorrow, pain

èbbro, drunk

eccèlso, high

elèggere, to choose, to select, to deem the best

elezióne (f), discernment, insight, choice

elígere: = elèggere

énto: = *entro,* in

errante, wandering; flowing (of locks of hair)

èrta, steep slope

esàngue, bloodless; utterly drained

esaudire, to grant
escusazióne (*f*), excuse, defence
esemplo, example
espedire, to expedite
espedizióne (*f*), execution
estimazióne (*f*), esteem, value; good opinion
etate (*f*): = *età*
faccènda, business; work to be done, chore
facundo, eloquent; **facundíssimo**, *superlative*
fàggio, beech
fallace, deceitful, false, perfidious
fallo, offence, transgression
famíglia, household; throng
fanciullétti (*dim* of *fanciulli*), young boys
fante (*m*), foot-soldier; servant
fascina, faggot
fasto, pomp, display
fava, broad bean; **prèndere due piccióni con una fava**, to kill two birds with one stone
favellare, to speak, to talk, to utter
fé: = *fede* (*f*), faith; promise, word given
febèo, of the sun; of Apollo
fèra: = *fiera*
fèr(o): = *feroce*, fierce
fervènte, blazing (of the sun)
fiàccola, torch, flame
fiata: = *volta*, time
fièra, wild beast
filare (*m*), row (of teeth)
fiorito, splendid
fiso, fixedly; **mirare fiso**, to stare
fluviale, of the river
fóce (*f*), outlet, mouth of a river
fólto, dense, thick
fòra, fòre: = *fuori*, out
fortézza, strength
fossato, fòsso, ditch
fracassato, shattered, broken

frappare, to talk idly
frate, brother; **fratèi, frati**, *pl*
frèmito, shudder
frèndere, to shudder
frómba: = *fionda*, sling
frónda, frónde (*sing*), branch, foliage
fruitóre (*m*), user
fúlgere, to shine
furare, to steal
furibóndo, furious
gagliardo, vigorous; bold
gastigare: = *castigare*, to punish
gàudio, joy
gavazzarsi, to rejoice, to make merry
gèmere, to lament
gentile, noble, worthy
gètto, the releasing of the hawk in a hunt
ghignare, to sneer
giacére, to lie
ginépro, juniper tree
ginocchióni, on one's knees
giocóndo, joyous
giógo, yoke
giovare, to be of use
giovènco, steer; year-old ox
giovenile: = *giovanile*, youthful
gire: = *andare*, to go
gittare (*m*), the releasing of the hawk in a hunt
gnuno (= **ignuno**), any, none
gonfiato, inflated
gonnèlla: *dim* of *gonna*, long dress, worn by males or females
gòra, ditch
gòrga: = *gorgia*, throat
gòta, cheek
governare, to tend animals; to treat
gratíccio, faggot; rush matting; hurdle
grato, pleasing, agreeable; acceptable

grave, weighty
gravità, seriousness, intensity
gràvido, laden (with), heavy (with)
grégge (f), flock
grèmbo, lap
grillo, cricket
gròsso, big, large; thick-headed
gru (f, but also m), crane
guastare, to spoil, to upset; to damage
guastatóre (m), sapper
guatare: = *guardare*, to scrutinize; guatalla, to look at her
guisa, guise, manner
iddío: = *dio*
ignaro, unaware; ignorant
ignuno, no one, anyone
immantenènte, immediately; suddenly
impetrare, to implore, beseech
imprésa, enterprise, undertaking
incèdere, to advance, to move forward
incèndere: = *accendere*
inchinarsi, to bow
incitatóre (m), tempter
incréscere: = *rincrescere*
incristallare: = *gelare*, to freeze (of water), to reduce to ice
inculto, wild, dishevelled
indi, from that place, thence
inèzia, trifle, ineptitude
infastidire, to annoy
ínferi (m pl), the underworld, Hell
inferire, to signify
infiorare, to strew with flowers or petals
infóndere, to instil
informare, to inspire; to rouse
infrascritto, undermentioned
ingegnarsi, to strive
inghiottire, to swallow
insigne, distinguished, outstanding

into: = *dentro*
intra, among
intraversare, to cut across; to pierce through
intrínseco, intimate
invitto, unconquered, undefeated
involare, to steal; to catch
ire: = *andare*; ito, p part
irsuto, hairy, shaggy
iscacciare (p part iscacciato), to send away
istòria: = *storia*, story, tale; history
lagnarsi, to complain; to grieve
lància, spear
languènte, languishing, lifeless
lascivo, wanton, unchaste
lasso, tired, weary; lasso! (as exclamation), alas!
lato, place
laudare: = *lodare*, to praise
làude (f): = *lode*, praise
làuro, laurel; bay tree
lèbbra, leprosy
leggiadro, fair; graceful
legnàggio: = *discendenza*, lineage
lèpido, subtle, witty
letízia, joy, happiness
licenziare, to discharge, to dismiss
licóre: = *liquore*
lièva: si lieva: third person singular *pres* of *levarsi*, to remove oneself, to flee
linfe (f pl), waters
liquefare, to melt
líscio, make-up
lito: = *lido*, shore, beach
livi, there
lòco: = *luogo*, place
luci (f pl): = *occhi*, eyes
lunge, lungi, far
lussúria, lust, lasciviousness
lustro, five-year period
màcchia, bush
macèllo, slaughterhouse

maculare: = *macchiare*, to stain, to blemish

màglia, mesh (of a net)

magno, great

mancaménto, imperfection, shortcoming, fault

manco (*adv*), less; (*adj*), left (opposite of right)

maneggiare, to wield

mano: **a mano a mano**, at once; subsequently; while

marróne, hoe, mattock

martíre: = *martirio*, martyrdom (also *fig*)

martirizzare, to put to a martyr's death

mascèlla, jaw

masserízia, chattels

màssime: = *massimamente*, mainly

matrigna, stepmother

mèl: = *miele*, honey

mèrto: = *merito*, merit; prize, reward; **merti**, deserts

merzé, **merzéde**, reward, prize; grace, mercy

meschino, meschinèllo, wretched, poor

mésso, messenger

micidiale, lethal, deadly

midóllo, marrow (of the bone)

miètere, to reap, to harvest

minacciare, to threaten

miràbile, extraordinary, wonderful

molèsto, troublesome, harmful

mòlle, gentle, tender; weak

móndo, cleansed, healed, purified; chaste

montatóre (*m*), erector, fitter (military)

montóne (*m*), ram

móstro (*v adj* of *mostrare*), shown

mòtto, word; witticism; **non fare motto**, not to utter a word

muggito, roar, bellow

multitúdine (*f*): = *moltitudine*, abundance, large number

mutuare, to borrow

nétto, healed, clean; clear-cut; sharp, fresh

niuno: = *nessuno*, none; any

nól: = *non lo*

novélla, news

novéllo, new

núgolo, cloud

nuòcere, to harm

nuòva, nuòve, news

nutricare: = *nutrire*, to feed, to nourish

oblío, oblivion, forgetfulness

offício: = *ufficio*, duty

ognindí, every single day; continuously

omai: = *ormai*, now, at last

òmero, shoulder

ónde, whence

onusto, laden

operare, to do

òpra, achievement, action

orare, to pray

orazióne (*f*), prayer; discourse

órma, track made by animal, footprint, step

orsatto (*dim* of *orso*), bear-cub

orsú!, come now!

osservare, to watch

ostare, to hinder

òtta: = *ora*, time

padiglióne (*m*), large tent, pavilion

palése, clear, evident; **in palese**, openly

pare (*m*), equal, peer

partita: = *partenza*, departure

partito, decision, resolution; **prendere partito**, to decide, to resolve

pàscere, to feed on, to eat (also *fig*)

passavolante, long-range culverin

pàssera, female sparrow

passíbile, liable to, subject to
pàvido, fearful
pégno, pledge
pelare, to pluck (fowl)
pèndere, to be inclined
pennuto, feathered, plumed
percòsso: *p part* of *percuotere*, to strike
períglio: = *pericolo*, peril, danger
persecuzióne (*f*), series of misfortunes
pèrtica, rod
perturbazióni (*f pl*), vicissitudes; events
piàggia, gentle slope
pianta, sole (of the foot)
piccino (*dim* of **picciolo**), very small, tiny
pícciolo: = *piccolo*
piè: = *piede, piedi*
pigne: = *spinge*, pushes
pio, kind, merciful
pómo, apple
pómpa, pomp, splendour, magnificence; (*pl*) public occasions
posare: = *riposare*, to rest
potènzia, power, strength; **in potenzia**, potentially
pravo, wicked, perverse
prèda, prey, booty; **in prèda**, plundered, sacked
prègio, esteem, value, worth
prégno, saturated, full
presàgio, omen
prèsto, prepared, ready; nimble, quick
presúmere (*p part* **presunto**), to assume as a right
pretèrito, past, previous
prezzare, to value, to prize
prèzzo, esteem; **èssere/avére in prezzo**, to hold in esteem
priègo (*pl* **-ghi**): = *preghiera*, plea, prayer

prigióne (*f*), prison, gaol; (*m*): = *prigioniero*
procacciare, to obtain
procèsso, course of events
pròda, bank, edge
pròra, ship
pruòva: = *impresa*, exploit, enterprise, effort
pudóre (*m*), shame
punto, point; **a punto**, precisely
pupilla, ward
purpúreo, deep red, purple
quèrulo, querulous, complaining
quinamónte: = *qui su*, up here
quinéntro: = *qui dentro*, right here
ràbido, rabid, furious
rado, occasional
ragunare: = *radunare*, to assemble, to bring together, to gather
rassettare, to tidy, to settle
ravviluppare, to entangle, to confuse
reame (*m*), kingdom
recare, to bring
refrigèrio, solace, relief
règgere, to rule, to govern
réne (*f pl*), loins
rèo, rio, wicked, evil, bad
reprensíbile, reprehensible, blameworthy
reprensióne (*f*), negative criticism, censure, reproof
reputare, to think, to deem
retícolo, web, network
rézzo, cool air, shade
ricòrdo, precept, warning, reminder
ricorrai: = *raccoglierai*
ridúcere: = *ridurre*, to turn (into)
rième: = *ritorna*
rilevare: = *allevare*, to rear
rimpugnare, to grasp again
rinnovellare: = *rinnovare*, to renew, to revive

rio: = *rivo*, brook, stream

rio (*adj*): see reo

ripa, steep bank

riprèndere, to censure, to find fault (with)

riscattare, to redeem

ritòrtola, withy

ritróso: andare a ritroso, to go against, to go backwards

ritto, upright, erect

riverènza, curtsey

rívolo, brook

rizzare, to lift up, to raise

ròco: = *rauco*, hoarse, harsh-sounding

ròdere, to erode

rorante, dewy, damp; weeping

rótta, rout, utter defeat; mettere in rotta, to rout

rótto (*p part*), defeated, routed

ròvere (*m*), oak tree

rovinare, to fall crashing, to collapse

rózzo, rough, uncouth

rubacuòri, bewitching; that would steal one's heart

rugghiare, to roar

rugiada, dew

ruina: = *rovina*, ruin

saccomanno, sack, plunder

sàglia: = *salga* (*pres subj* of *salire*)

sàlcio: = *salice* (*m*), willow tree

saldo, steady, firm

salsa: = *salata*, salty, briny

satisfazióne (*f*): = *soddisfazione*, satisfaction

saviaménte, wisely, sensibly

sàvio, wise man; (*adj*) wise, prudent

sazietà: alla sazietà, to overflowing, more than enough

sàzio, satisfied

sbilènco, lopsided

scadiménto, falling off

scàglia, scale (of a fish)

scagliarsi, to hurl oneself

scalco, steward, person in charge of victuals, carver

scalzo, bare(foot)

scellerato, wicked, atrocious

scèttro, sceptre

schiamazzare, noise that combines the chirping and fluttering of sparrows

schièra, flock

scinto (*p part* of *scingere*), with one's clothes loosened

sciòcco, silly, foolish

scoccare, to dart off

scòrno, disgrace

scòrta, escort, convoy

scompigliare, to over-bloom (of roses)

scorticaménto, peeling

scòrza, bark (of a tree)

sdrucciolare, to slip

sèndo: = *essendo*

sentènza, sentènzia, thought, opinion, saying

sentina, sink, den (of iniquity)

sepoltura, burial, grave

serbare, to keep, to set aside, to maintain

serrare, to surround, to press hard

sèzzo, last; (d)a sezzo, in the end

sfogarsi, to relieve one's feelings

sicurtà: = *sicurezza*, security, guaranty

signoreggiare, to rule, to be master of

signoría, lordship, dominion, rule

simigliare: = *somigliare*, to resemble

soggiogare, to conquer

soggiornare, to bide one's time

soggiórno, delay

solére, to be in the habit of

solétto: = *tutto solo*

sollecitare, to hasten, to quicken

sòma, burden

sómmo, most high (superlative)

sopraffatto (*p part*), overpowered, overcome

sòrte (*f*), fate, lot, outcome

sotterrato (*p part*), buried

sottométtere, to conquer, to overcome

sparvière (*m*), hawk

spasimante (*m*), suitor, wooer (facetious)

spèco, cave, cavern

spelónca, cave, cavern

spème (*f*): = *speranza*, hope

spennecchiare, to pluck (fowl)

spièdo, hunting-spear; spit

spiga, ear of corn

spingarda, springal(d); musket

spróne (*m*), spur, stimulus

stagnare, to make stagnant, still

stàio, bushel

stanza, waiting, delay

starna, grey partridge; starnóne, young male partridge

stàtico, hostage

stendardo, standard, banner

stíen: = *stiano*

stima: fare stima, to reckon

stólto, foolish, silly

stóppia, stubble

straccare, to wear out, to exhaust

stracco (*v adj* of straccare), worn out, exhausted

stracciare, to tear, to rend

strale (*m*), dart (also *fig*)

strame (*m*), hay, fodder

strano: = *straniero*, foreign, barbarian

stravolgiménto, contortion

stràzio, torture, torment; fare strazio, to tear to pieces

strídere, to screech, to shriek

strúggersi, to melt; struggersi il cervello, to cudgel one's brain

suave: = *soave*, gentle, soft

subiètto: = *soggetto*, subject-matter, theme; subietto amato, loved one, the object of one's love

súbito, hasty, impulsive

subiugato (*p part*), subjected, defeated

succhièllo, gimlet

sugnàccio, inferior quality of lard (from *sugna*, lard)

sugóso, pithy, full of substance

supèrbia, pride

supèrbo, proud

supplire a, to meet the needs of

supplízio, torture, torment

suso: = *sopra*

suto: = *stato* (*p part* of *essere*)

suvvenire: = *sovvenire*, to afford assistance

svèllere (*p part* svèlto), to uproot, to pull out (of hair etc.)

tale (*m*), man

tana, den

tardo, slow

tèdio, distress, boredom

tèmpli (*pl*), temples

testura, texture

tíngere, to immerse

tinto (*p part* of tingere), very dark, blackened

tirocínio, apprenticeship

tócco (*v adj*): = *toccato*

tòrbido, túrbido, cloudy (of water)

tòrre: = *togliere*, to remove, to take away

tosare, to shear

tósco: = *toscano*, Tuscan

tòsto, at once, soon, quickly

traboccare, to overflow

tràlcio, spray (of a shrub)

tralucénte, transparent

trastullarsi, to dally

trastullo, game, amusement

tratto: ad un tratto, suddenly

travaglióso, troubled
tréccia, plait
tríboli (*m pl*), tribulations
triègua: = *tregua*, truce, respite
tristo, wicked, evil; sad
trombétto: = *trombettiere*, trumpeter
truòva: = *trova*
túmido, swollen
turba, multitude
túrbido: see tòrbido
turcasso, quiver
tuttavía, unceasingly; nonetheless
uccèi: = *uccelli*
uccellagióne, fowling
uccellare, to fowl, to go fowling
uccellatóio, fowling-ground
uccellatóre (*m*), fowler
úggia, shadow, shade
ulcerato, ulcerated, covered with ulcers
ulva, seaweed
úscio, door
usufrutto, use and enjoyment of goods or property
vacca, cow
vaghézza, beauty, charm
vago, pretty, lovely, charming; roaming
valicare, to pass, to cross by means of a ford
vanaglòria, boastfulness
vano, empty, futile, useless; deceptive
vecchiézza, old age
vègga, vèggio, vèggo, vèggonsi, etc.: all parts of *vedere*

vèllo, fleece
venustà, beauty
vèrbo, word
vèrmine (*m*): = *verme*, worm
véscovo, bishop
vettovàglia, victuals, provisions
vézzo, habit; fare vezzo, to fondle
vie, beyond
vigna, vineyard
vile, base; poor; mean; humble; cowardly
villa, countryside
villana, countrywoman
villano, boor; (*adj*) rude, uncouth
villanía, rudeness, uncivil behaviour
villeréccio, rustic
virata, change of direction or position
virtú (*f*), virtue; strength, power
vituperare, to revile
vituperóso, disgraceful, reprehensible
vivanda, food, dish
voglióso, desirous
volato: = *volo*, flight
volgare, vernacular
vólgo, common people
vólto, face, countenance
voluttà, pleasure, sensual pleasure
vóto, vow
vulgo, common people
zampógna, pipe
zana, cradle
zanzara, gnat, mosquito